Migrations of Gesture

Migrations of Gesture

Carrie Noland and
Sally Ann Ness, Editors

University of Minnesota Press
Minneapolis • London

MIN
NE
SO
TA

Portions of chapter 4 have been previously published in Deidre Sklar, "Qualities of Memory: Two Dances of the Tortugas Fiesta," in *Dancing from Past to Present: Nation, Culture, Identities*, ed. Theresa Jill Buckland (Madison: University of Wisconsin Press, 2006), 115–47; reprinted with permission. "Mimique," by Mark Franko (the second section of chapter 9), originally appeared in *Bodies of the Text: Dance as Theory, Literature as Dance*, ed. Ellen W. Goellner and Jacqueline Shea Murphy (New Brunswick, N.J.: Rutgers University Press, 1995); reprinted with grateful acknowledgment to Rutgers University Press.

Excerpts from Henri Michaux's poetry in chapter 6 were originally published in *Oeuvres complètes*, volume 2 (2001), and *Mouvements* (1957); copyright Editions Gallimard; reprinted courtesy of Editions Gallimard.

Published by the University of Minnesota Press
111 Third Avenue South, Suite 290
Minneapolis, MN 55401-2520
http://www.upress.umn.edu

Library of Congress Cataloging-in-Publication Data

Migrations of gesture / Carrie Noland and Sally Ann Ness, editors.
p. cm.
Includes bibliographical references and index.
ISBN-13: 978-0-8166-4864-1 (hc : alk. paper)
ISBN-10: 0-8166-4864-6 (hc : alk. paper)
ISBN-13: 978-0-8166-4865-8 (pb : alk. paper)
ISBN-10: 0-8166-4865-4 (pb : alk. paper)
1. Gesture. I. Noland, Carrie, 1958- II. Ness, Sally Ann.
PN2071.G4M45 2008
792.8—dc22 2007041674

Printed in the United States of America on acid-free paper

The University of Minnesota is an equal-opportunity educator and employer.

15 14 13 12 11 10 09 08 10 9 8 7 6 5 4 3 2 1

Contents

Acknowledgments

The editors express their sincere gratitude to the University of California Humanities Research Institute, to Rosemarie Neumann for her administrative support and good cheer, and most especially to the director of the Institute, David Theo Goldberg, who helped in every way possible to facilitate the continuing work of the Research Residency Group on "Gesture and Inscription" during fall 2002, without which this book could never have been produced.

We also thank the contributors for their willingness to share ideas, bibliographies, insights, and good times.

Introduction

Carrie Noland

> What characterizes gesture is that in it nothing is being produced *[facere]* or acted *[agere]*, but rather something is being endured and supported *[gerere]*.
>
> —Giorgio Agamben, "Notes on Gesture"

In one of those brief but intensely evocative fragments from *Minima Moralia*, Theodor Adorno asks pointedly, "What does it mean for the subject that there are no more casement windows to open, but only sliding frames to shove," no portals to close "discreetly," but only doors to be "slammed"?[1] If modern subjects learn to slam and shove, rather than latch and release, how will their general experience of movement be transformed? "What does it mean for the subject" if, under the sway of advanced technology, only gestures "precise" and "brutal" may be executed within the modernist regime?

Adorno is worried that the loss of even the smallest gestures, involving the wrist or forearm, reveals a "withering of experience," a change in the "most secret innervations" of human beings as they navigate an intersubjective and object world. Similar to many thinkers of the gestural before him, Adorno recognizes the extent to which both instrumental and communicative gestures encode, express, and perpetuate the values of specific historical and cultural formations. Adorno thus provides a useful starting point for a volume on gestures and their migration because he understands gesturing to be more than simply a conduit of socialization, a *technē* that constitutes subjects in a thoroughly mechanical and predictable way. He also knows that gestures offer opportunities for kinesthetic experience; they "innervate," or stimulate, the nerves of a bodily part, and thus allow the body to achieve a certain awareness and knowledge of itself through movement. A further but unexplored implication of Adorno's observation, then, is that by retrieving gestures from the past, or by borrowing gestures from another culture, subjects can actually produce new innervations, discover new sensations to feel. The essays collected in this volume follow Adorno's cue insofar as they demonstrate, in a rich variety of ways, that gestures *migrate* (as well as disappear) and that in migrating they create unexpected combinations, new valences, and alternative cultural meanings and experiences. In a world of inescapable global circulation, gestures, too, undergo appropriations and enjoy afterlives that change their initial function.

It is arguable, then, that the "withering of experience" Adorno feared to have been brought on by the industrial rationalization of gestural routines—the expelling "from movements [of] all hesitation"—has not resulted in a reduction of gestural possibilities (although the specific innervations they afford may indeed have suffered alteration). Instead, as the essays included here propose, gesturing may very well remain a resource for resistance to homogenization, a way to place pressure on the routines demanded by technical and technological standardization. Consequently, it is incumbent upon us to undertake a contemporary theorization of gesture that sees gesture as supporting the survival of the past while potentially engendering meanings that bear that past toward an unpredictable future. By following the migration of gestures across many fields (geographical, disciplinary, and medium-specific), this volume aims to provide a convincing narrative both of the ways in which bodies become socialized, submitted to historical forces, and, alternatively, of the ways in which bodies exert agency by drawing on the kinetic energies of a moving self.

Migrations of Gesture represents an attempt to think through the various ways in which gestures shape and are shaped by sociohistorical imperatives and transnational displacements. Sally Ann Ness, an anthropologist and dance ethnographer, and myself, a critical theorist and scholar of the European avant-garde, join forces here to offer readers a heterogeneous set of disciplinary and interdisciplinary perspectives on gesture. The impetus for our collaboration is the recognition that *gesture*, as a mobile term, has accrued considerable critical currency in a variety of scholarly domains and yet has remained dramatically undertheorized as a cross-disciplinary vehicle. Derived from the Latin verb *gerere*, to carry, act, or do, gesture may be conceived in multiple and sometimes conflicting ways: as movement intimately and exclusively related to the body and its expressiveness (phenomenology); as conventionalized movement belonging to a system of signification imposed by culture upon the body (semiotics, linguistics, and rhetoric); as movement situated within operating chains responsible for producing knowledge, culture, and even types of consciousness (anthropology, paleontology, and Marxism); and as movement that is not exclusively related to the body but generated instead by any apparatus—including the body understood *as* apparatus—capable of being displaced in space (deconstruction and new media studies). In this volume, we juxtapose a variety of approaches to gesture, each one associated with a different disciplinary or theoretical perspective, in order to draw out the value of the term as a hermeneutic and interdisciplinary tool. We believe that thinking about cultural production and subject construction through the category of gesture allows scholars from different domains to move back and forth between an organic, phenomenal understanding of human sign production (as expression or experience based) and a historicist, semiotic understanding of how the "human" is itself constructed through gestural routines.

As a corporeal practice engaging the fleshly human being, gestures have often been seized as the least conventionalized of signs, the most natural and performative in the sense that they are permeable to physiological idiosyncracies of execution. Gestures, as conceived by Condillac and Husserl (to take the most well-known examples), are closest to natural expression and therefore indexical of the presence and intentionality of an individual human subject.[2] For Merleau-Ponty, to cite another seminal figure, gestures are not only productive of communication between agents, they also provide the individual agent with a private somatic experience of his or her own moving body.[3] And yet, as poststructuralists have persuasively argued, gestures are a *technē*, a language, even a semiotic regime; within any given culture, gestures inevitably become—or, to put it more strongly, already are—conventional and arbitrary rather than spontaneous and motivated; they are iterable and easily detached from the specific contexts of their performance. The event of gesture can in fact furnish a semiotic material to be appropriated, manipulated, and reinvested with meanings that potentially have very little to do with the somatic experience of the subjectivities executing them.

The tension between the two positions—gestures as indexical of subjectivity and presence versus gestures as signifiers for meanings generated by the mechanics and conditions of signification itself—can be sensed in many of the most important treatments of gesture published over the last forty years. Jacques Derrida's seminal essays on Antonin Artaud, "La parole soufflée" and "The Theory of Cruelty and the Closure of Representation," examine the epistemological problems that arise when gesture is accorded the privilege of the inaugural, the singular, the authentic, and the unmediated.[4] Likewise, art historians Mary Kelly, Richard Schiff, and Amelia Jones have considered the ways in which the artistic gesture—materialized in the brushstroke, drip, or other "painterly signifier"—can come to signify not a specific motor action or somatic experience but instead "authenticity" itself, the nonreproducibility and thus the marketability of the work of art. "The [art] object's investment with artistic subjectivity," writes Kelly, "is secured by gesture . . . *his* person, *his* image, *his* gestures."[5] In a similar vein, dance theorist Mark Franko has emphasized the tension between presentation and representation in his groundbreaking essay, "Mimique," included in this volume.[6] Building on Derrida's treatment of dance as writing, gesture as inscription, Franko argues that while gesture can be read as a trace functioning within a trace structure, it nonetheless differs from other types of traces in that it requires physical embodiment, the support of a human body. Franko suggests that deconstruction's understanding of gestures as signs caught in and generated by a system of signification neglects the ways in which the body's singularity—its gender, race, size, scope of movement, and so on—necessarily inflects the generalizing momentum of the signifying process, bringing into play embodied, performance-specific, and therefore noniterable instantiations of meaning-making forms of movement.[7]

In recent years, the notion that gesture is a form of personal experience as well as a conveyer of abstract and predetermined meaning has been rigorously explored by theorists of acting, performance, and ritual. Dance ethnographers in particular have been attentive to the affective content of kinesthetic sensations produced by the act of gesturing, seeking to extend Merleau-Ponty's mid-twentieth-century work on embodiment to claim the status of knowledge for the somatic experience of motility.[8] In her contribution to this volume, dance ethnographer Deidre Sklar relates the experiential content of gesturing to the memory of *previous* instantiations of the gesture and thus to a type of knowledge, both cultural and personal, encoded in communicative or ritualized physical acts. For Sklar, the lived experience of executing a gesture is as important an object of study as the symbolic dimension of the gesture, if only because the one—the subject's experience of gesturing—potentially inflects the other—the transmission of meaning the gesture enables.[9] Understanding how these two dimensions are interrelated is a primary goal of other essays in this volume as well. Ketu H. Katrak, Sally Ann Ness, and Carrie Noland all seek to determine how symbolizing (making culturally meaningful marks) *feels* as well as how feeling informs the shapes meaning takes. Whereas it is rare for a semiotician to consider the ways in which the experience of producing a sign (orally, scripturally, or corporeally) contributes to a sign's contour, dynamics, duration, or communicative force, in contrast, several of the theorists included here focus explicitly on the experiential and thus contingent dimension of sign-making itself.

Further, as contributions by Lesley Stern and Blake Stimson demonstrate, the emotional experience of the gesturing subject/sign can generate affective and even mimetic responses on the part of the viewer. Performed gestures have the capacity to *move* us—in all senses.[10] As types of "modeled energy" (Eugenio Barba's term), gestures give shape to affects that might not have precise, codified, or translatable meanings. The gap between the "maintained" gestural routine (produced through training, redundancy, acquisition of impersonal skills) and the "modulated" gestural routine (emerging as a result of the more particularized energies of the performer) suggests that there resides within the performance of gesture a moment of negativity, an unpredictable force of nonidentity in mimesis countering the signifying potential of the conventional sign. If

Catherine Cyssau is correct and "there is a manifest presence of the negative that a gesture brings into being . . . [which causes] a suspension of the interpretive regime,"[11] then gesture cannot be reduced to a purely semiotic (meaning-making) activity but realizes instead—both temporally and spatially—a cathexis deprived of semantic content. That is, gesture can indeed transmit a predetermined, codified meaning, but it can also—and simultaneously—convey an energetic charge or "vitality affect" that overflows the meaning transmitted.[12] To some extent, all iterable signs possessing material (graphemic, phonic, phenomenal) supports "overflow" their conventional meanings. However, gestures dramatize this extra-semantic dimension of signs, dependent as they are upon actual living bodies charged with eros, affect, and corporeal materiality. It is while gesturing—and thus while signing—that a body displays most clearly the extent to which it remains "at war with itself *as a sign*."[13]

A variety of approaches—from film studies to dance ethnography—have thus emerged to contest the tendency of Foucauldian and deconstructive analyses to reduce bodily experience to purely semiotic (or, more narrowly, in Foucault's case, discursive) mediations.[14] When poststructuralist treatments of gesture threaten to dissociate entirely corporeal signs from the subjects performing these signs, scholars of culture oriented toward phenomenological (or, in some cases, materialist) approaches remind us that the body is a source of experience—and therefore of knowledge—as well as a support for the transmission of knowledges already congealed.[15] As Thomas Csordas states unequivocally in "Somatic Modes of Attention," "meaning cannot be reduced to a sign." He then adds, however, that the necessary "critique [of a purely semiotic perspective] should not be construed as negating the study of signs with respect to the body, but as making a place for a complementary appreciation of embodiment and being-in-the-world alongside textuality and representation. [Semiotics and phenomenology] are complementary and not mutually exclusive standpoints. . . ."[16]

This volume is dedicated to engaging semiotic, phenomenological, *and* historicist perspectives in an attempt to realize the project Csordas envisages. In concert with Csordas, the contributors seek to theorize the meaning of gestural signs from a large number of interdisciplinary points of view, challenging the linguistic model conventionally used to explain corporeal sign languages by attending to the somatic, experiential, aesthetic, cultural, and contextual dimensions of gesturing. The contributors understand gesturing to be an activity that relies both on the singular and the iterative, the improvised and the convention-bound. It is clear—and must always be kept in mind—that gesturing is not a purely spontaneous, autogenerated mode of self-expression, for while employing an individual body (and motivated by the anatomical specificities of that body), gestures also depend on an arbitrary signifying system as well as a specific cultural and geographical location of performance and reception from which they draw, in large part, their meaning. Without the constraints of convention, gestures could not be recognized *as gestures;* they would lose their affinity with other types of intentional marks and appear instead to be isolated instances of uninflected movement or inexpressive motor response.[17]

The editors of this volume thus propose the study of gesture as a bridge between discourses privileging the biological body, subjectivity, and somatic experience on the one hand and, on the other, discourses indebted to a deconstructive critique of embodiment as a staging of the body through structures of signification that are not necessarily the body's own.[18] A crucial category for the study of meaning-making as a whole, gesture is at once evidence of the body's implication in systems of signification and a reminder of the body's fragility and resistance to infinite deferral. The goal of this volume is to articulate a multifaceted theory of gesture that takes into account both the complex corporeality of gesturing *and* the mediations that corporeality undergoes as it seeks to address the Other—that is, culture and its signs.

A central consideration that has been left out of many studies of gesture is the extent to which location—understood both as the place where the gesture is executed and the support upon which the gesture is inscribed—contributes to determining the way in which the gesture signifies. Location is one of those messy contingencies, such as gender and ethnicity, that a deconstructive model sometimes fails to integrate fully into its account of how corporeal signs acquire and transmit meaning. The specific contribution of postcolonial and diaspora studies in this regard is to suggest that when gestures change location, when they migrate from one site of performance to another, they in fact confront a different reception and may even be experienced in a new way. As Lesley Stern advances in her essay "Ghosting," every instantiated gesture is, in a sense, its own undoing in that its displacement—from body to body, from temporality to temporality, from one medium to another, or from one cultural location to another—unfixes the gesture from its inscription in a trace structure and releases it into potentially new networks of expressiveness based not on the differences among (gestural) signs but on *the differences among the bodies executing them.* It clearly matters where, when, and by whom the gesture is executed. The energy of the gestural can be harnessed to represent but also to construct ethnicity, sexuality, or class status. Psychological or emotional states are expressed as well as brought into being through gestures, and such states can come to define a culture's structures of feeling, transmitted from one generation to the next but also modified and in some cases utterly transformed by a generation that has been displaced. It is because gesture is such a potent means of cultural self-definition (and identification) that it merits attention from theorists of the diasporic condition.[19] As embodied signifiers, gestures are more vulnerable to dehiscence (less fixed by convention to their signifieds) than are scriptural signs; for that very reason, however, gestures invite reinvestment and thus play a large but hitherto unexamined role in (the performance of) diasporic experience.

As can be seen, the title of this volume closely associates the phenomenon of migration with the act of gesturing. The contributors intend the word *migration* to be taken literally, as referencing the voluntary and involuntary historical displacements of human, gesturing populations from one geographic location to another. However, many of the essays in the volume also evoke the more figurative connotations of the word. As film scholars Akira Lippit and Lesley Stern suggest, gestures can "migrate" from one support to another: a certain way of waving the arm finds its way from a profilmic body to a purely celluloid body invented by an editor; a gesture executed by a falling body is imitated by—and displaced onto—

the boom of a camera as it continues the swooping motion a profilmic body initiated. In the realm of painting, drawing, or molding, gestures are in a sense always being displaced. The marks left on a support evidence gesture's migrations from hand and instrument to fiber or stone. Finally, while it is clear that gestures migrate from one physical location to another, it can also be shown that gesture, as a semiotic structure, migrates from one *disciplinary* location to another. The particular relation gestures establish between a body and a sign is understood in different ways by discrete disciplines. Gesture in the domain of dance theory means something quite different from gesture in the domain of art history. Generally, when dance theorists talk about gesture, they are referring to a body movement that occurs in the limbs (the head being considered a limb), as opposed to posture, which is static, or ambulation, which involves traversing a space.[20] Art historians rarely make this same distinction, since all painted, sculpted, or photographed gestures are necessarily static, suggesting movement but frozen in place. Further, dance theorists often conceive of gesture as a nonverbal form of communication that expresses specifically that which words cannot. In contrast, linguistic anthropologists speak of gesture as a *pre*verbal rather than a nonverbal language; gestures foreshadow what words will eventually be able to do in their place.[21] In literary theory, gesture often signifies the act of evocation as opposed to indication; an argument might "gesture toward" a corollary point without, however, formulating it in words. Finally, in film and performance studies, gesture is often related to "styles" of acting; histrionic gestures are differentiated from everyday gestures, melodrama from naturalism. Here, gestures are understood as belonging to "gestural regimes," codes of expressive movement that neatly associate a particular movement with a particular meaning in a consistent and readable way.[22]

Several of these discrete definitions of gesture appear in the following essays, and no effort has been made to smooth over the friction that arises among them. Each essay pursues in a different direction the itinerary of the term *gesture* as it migrates from one disciplinary territory to another, creating links and revealing aporias that could not have been envisioned in advance. The tensions created by incompatible understandings of gesture (and by differing accounts of gesture's constitutive role) have been addressed directly at the end of the volume in a conclusion authored by Sally Ann Ness. Responding to the multiplicity of perspectives represented, Ness advances an inclusive agenda for inter- or cross-disciplinary work: to investigate how, both "within and outside the constraints of culture and its conventions," freedom to reinvent the moving body is, or could be, acquired. Ultimately, our hope is that this collection of essays will inspire similar attempts on the part of other scholars trained primarily in one discipline (or in an interdisciplinary field) to share their distinctive methodologies, knowledges, and points of view.

In the first essay of the volume, "The Inscription of Gesture: Inward Migrations in Dance," Ness sets out to discover what it would mean to take the poststructuralist view, that gesture is a form of inscription, as literally as possible. Studying the anatomies of two dancers (belonging to two different dance traditions, the classical ballet and the classical Indian Bharata Natyam), Ness demonstrates how repeated gestural routines can actually leave lasting imprints on the body. She makes the case that bone deformations should be read as inscriptions and that further, such inscriptions are evidence of *thought* as well as movement and discipline. The body becomes a kind of monument, a support that archives the gestures it has performed. Its deepening marks are evidence of self-correction, acquisition of knowledge and skill, testimonials to a methodological and reasoned way of being in the world. Gestural routines, in that sense, can be seen as writings on the body insofar as they simultaneously signify and cause to be embodied a particular manner of being in the world.

In "Physical Graffiti West: African American Gang Walks and Semiotic Practice," Susan A. Phillips studies a cultural form in which gesture and writing coincide in an even more literal manner. Instead of approaching the body as a surface upon which gestural routines are inscribed, Phillips analyzes a practice in which the body itself becomes a stylus, an instrument for tracing out letters in space. She follows the history of African American gang–related dances (Crip Walking, Blood Walking, Pueblo Stroll, Villain Dance) as they evolve from earlier forms, such as the Cake Walk, noting the necessarily covert nature of communicative, inscriptive practices when forced to function in an environment of oppression and erasure. Migration is a fundamental part not only of the history of African American bodies but also of the history of their expressive practices; these practices, as Phillips shows, move from medium to medium (tattoos to graffiti to hand gestures) and from locale to locale (cotton fields to urban neighborhoods to Internet Web sites). By choosing to privilege dance as one of the most powerful—and literate—forms of resistance available, gang members "bind what is supposedly insulated from physicality (writing) to the very epicenter of sensation, feeling, and emotion (the body)." In this way, they cause gesturing—primarily with the feet but also, as in finger dancing, with the hands—to take on an overtly political as well as semiotic resonance.

The political resonance of particular gestures is also the concern of Blake Stimson. In "Gesture and Abstraction," Stimson contrasts the photographic series of Henri Cartier-Bresson and Robert Frank, arguing that they instantiate two opposed understandings of how the gesture of photography creates empathy and community among human subjects. By "the gesture of photography," Stimson refers to the pressure of the finger on the camera's shutter, that tiny, operational gesture that nonetheless produces meaning. In the case of Cartier-Bresson, the shutter-release gesture (and the photograph that results) is intended to capture the "decisive moment" when the photographer seizes the universal quality—"humanity"—embodied in an individual subject's gesture. Conversely, in the case of Frank, the shutter-release gesture does no more than register the encounter missed, the transcendence refused (glances never meet, heads rotate in incongruous directions). Universality is not embodied in the moment seized by a photographer's eye; rather, the particular subject and his or her gesture is abstracted, made into just another instantiation of what it is to have a body. Stimson concludes that the gesture of abstraction, or the gesture that abstracts, is a photograph of something akin to Adorno's "remainder," a cumulable but never sublatable embodiment from which, as distinct remainders ourselves, we must turn away. The failure of intimacy captured in the subjects' isolated, incomplete gestures produces affects in the viewer. Visitors to an exhibition of Frank's photographs must move from one framed shot to another, compelled to turn their heads away from gestures that do not satisfy a need for closure. Empathy, as mimesis, occurs, but only as mutual recognition of the profound alienation and nonidentity that makes us both incomplete and free to move on to new definitions of the human.

Deidre Sklar's essay, "Remembering Kinesthesia: An Inquiry into Embodied Cultural Knowledge," approaches gesturing from quite a different angle. Sklar is less concerned with the way gestures create meanings (or inscriptions) than with the kinesthetic sensations they engender. She insists that the kinesthetic sensations resulting from movements have themselves a kind of meaning, one that cannot be resolved into or mapped onto other systems of signs. Particularly relevant to Sklar are aspects of gestural (not necessarily aestheticized) movements pertaining to the experiencing of a quality, or type of vitality, such as soft and caressing or uneven and agitated. Inspired by the work of child developmental psychologist Daniel Stern, Sklar attempts to clear a ground for a consideration of "the cross-modal apprehension of kinetic dynamics as they are differentially developed in different cultural communities." She wants the *feeling* of gesturing, in other words, to be both body-specific, a communion of the self with the self, and culture-specific, a relationship of the self to kinetic dynamics organized according to the categories generated by a cultural regime. Sklar suggests that cultural organizations of thinking might owe an unacknowledged debt to ways of moving, both as organizations of sensory content and as responses to sensory content experienced by animate bodies.

Sklar's effort to reintroduce the lived experience of the organic body into discussions of gesture is countered by Akira Mizuta Lippit's attempt to detach gesture from any organic anchor whatsoever. In "Digesture: Gesture and Inscription in Experimental Cinema," Lippit focuses not on the organic body but on the filmed or inscribed body, whose gestures become the primary material for the editor's construction of inorganic acts. Lippit is particularly interested in the found footage films of the experimental filmmaker Martin Arnold—*passage à l'acte*, *pièce touchée*, and *Alone. Life Wastes Andy Hardy*—in which the small hand, facial, and head gestures of Judy Garland and Mickey Rooney are freeze-framed and repeated hundreds of times before the action moves forward. Lippet claims that Arnold uses these spliced gestures as mechanisms for disrupting the meaning usually associated with them. Gestures become a purely visual, as opposed to a visual *and* kinesthetic, phenomenon. Operating at once as signifying and a-signifying forms, drained of their culturally recognizable meanings and yet released into new dramas, these filmed and spliced gestural interludes challenge the traditional association of the body's gestures with spontaneous feeling and the organic (anatomical) possibilities of human bodily expressiveness. For Lippit, Arnold's procedures indicate that it is possible to produce filmed gestures by means of a body that is not responsible for those gestures organically. At the same time, however, Lippit's study makes clear that even if Judy Garland is not responsible for performing the gestures the editing accords her, it is still Garland's body—as manipulable representation but also as a morphological limit to manipulation—that executes that gesture.

Carrie Noland is also concerned with the potentially mechanical and repetitive nature of gesturing that Lippit's essay brings to the fore. In "Miming Signing: Henri Michaux and the Writing Body," Noland studies the act of mark-making as a kind of gesturing that allows for a specific kinesthetic experience of rhythm and intensity. Turning her attention to Michaux's invented alphabets, his repeated attempts to create series of sign-like marks, Noland examines the role seriality plays in living the body as a semiotic entity. As Noland documents, Michaux is explicitly concerned with discovering, through marking, what kinds of movements are required to make a mark look like a sign. His imitations of the calligraphic stroke recall and reinforce the modeling of energy required to inscribe signs; but at the same time, these repeated strokes also introduce minute variations into the sign-making gestural routine. These variations in the routine constitute what she calls "gestural performatives," movement sequences that bring into being a writing, gesturing body existing in the moment of performance alone.

Lesley Stern's "Ghosting: The Performance and Migration of Cinematic Gesture, Focusing on Hou Hsiao-Hsien's *Good Men, Good Women*" furthers the notion that bodies take on identities through the performance of gestures. Analyzing specific passages in *Good Men, Good Women* by Taiwanese director Hou Hsiao-Hsien, Stern pursues the manner in which specific gestures migrate from one character to another, one temporality to another, and one medium to another. The central migration in question, however, concerns the transfer of gestures from human bodies to mechanical apparati: Stern asks whether it is possible to speak of the film camera, for instance, as performing in a "gestural" manner. Through a close reading of a scene in a Taipei bar in which a man's body falls to the floor, Stern reveals how the profilmic gestures of the actor are leached of affect as this affect is displaced onto the movements of the camera. Stern suggests that not only does the camera reenact, mechanically, the gestures of a live body by imitating—or "ghosting"—the profilmic sweeping movement of falling, but more, the gestures of the live body *are themselves mechanical reenactments.* That is, the gestures produced by the actors at one point in the film can be shown to be ghostly reenactments of bodily gestures executed at another point in the film. To this extent, then, gestures are not organic or even organically inflected expressions of a body but instead elements in what Stern calls a "histrionic" gestural regime, a kind of language or system of inscription.

While Stern evokes the term *migration* figuratively to refer to the displacement of affect (and action) from body to apparatus, Ketu H. Katrak pursues the implications for gesture of literal migrations—here, the concrete displacements of Indian-born dancers to the shores of Southern California. In "The Gestures of Bharata Natyam: Migrating into Diasporic Contemporary Indian Dance," Katrak researches the changes in meaning and experience that occur when a generation of Bharata Natyam teachers relocate far from the site of Bharata Natyam's origin and then teach a generation of American-born, ethnically Indian dancers how to perform the original gestures of the dance form. Katrak begins by describing the intricate and layered use of gestures in Bharata Natyam: rhythmic feet, arm, and hand movements; codified hand and head gestures that, in specific sequences, convey stories and legends; and finally, the equally codified hand and head gestures that render the emotional states of the characters represented. She studies how expressive, representative, and emblematic gestures all change meaning as they migrate across continents and are mixed with gestures taken from modern American and European dance forms. Of particular interest to Katrak is the Indian concept of *rasa*, which is the aesthetic pleasure experienced both sensually and intellectually by the dancer. Katrak discovers that when the dance is displaced, *rasa* is experienced differently; even if the body models the same gesture, the gesture's meaning, and thus the affect or spiritual quality associated with it, changes in relation to cultural context and spatial location. The gestures of dance are thus conceived in Katrak's piece as capable of transmitting certain forms of cultural knowledge while failing to transmit others. The contingency of location is a crucial component of the semiotic process in this case.

Finally, Mark Franko's "Mimique" places even stronger emphasis on the question of location and its influence on the way gestures signify. He maintains that dance in particular "calls social space into being," providing the body with a potentially political, utopian, or critical environment in which to enact and memorialize performed being. His suggestion that dance relocates a body within an architectonic space through acts of spac*ing*, that is, inscription, confirms—or, I should say, anticipates—the intuitions of the essays in this volume. Published originally in 1994,[23] "Mimique" instantiates a dancer's approach to the "inscriptive *force* of gesture," balancing a firsthand experience of choreography as lived movement with a critical theorist's understanding of the body as a product of inscriptions. The editors have chosen to republish the essay (accompanied by a new introduction by Franko) because it initiates a line of thinking seminal for much of the work collected here. Franko sympathetically but also critically takes up deconstruction's emphasis on "gesturality," proposing that dance and the study of embodied practices in general might benefit from approaching the body's movements as a form of *écriture*. At the same time, however, Franko resists collapsing gestural practices into inscriptive ones. He claims instead that what "disappears in the course of its [the gesture's] own inscription" might very well be fixed meaning, but it is certainly *not* the specificity, the incontrovertible presence, of the body itself: "parity with the trace," writes Franko, "can prove problematic [for gesture], for it removes another sort of presence from dancing: the presence of dancing subjects themselves in their gendered, cultural, and political distinctiveness." Most salient and subtle about Franko's analysis is that it simultaneously sustains and contests deconstruction's rapprochement between the embodied and the disembodied sign.

In conclusion, it could be argued that gestural signs are materially different from other types of signs: they require, after all, a corporeal support. In this sense, gestures have to be considered as *events*, singular performances that draw, to be sure, on culture-specific (as well as gender-, race-, sexuality-, and class-specific) conventional vocabularies but *are never performed twice in exactly the same way*. It is equally possible, however, to advance the opposed argument: that gestures, as iterable, possess a deeper affinity with mechanical apparati than phenomenological approaches allow us to admit. As several contributors acknowledge, not only do humans act like machines when they gesture, but machines can execute gestures too. We should therefore question the "organic," somatic origins of gesture and consider instead the role of mechanical prostheses in the generation, preservation, and transmission of that which is supposedly bodily and expressive. The tension between these two opposed but codependent perspectives is at the heart of the volume you now hold in your hands.

Notes

1. Theodor Adorno, *Minima Moralia* (New York: Verso, 1996), 40. Originally published in German in 1951.

2. Étienne Bonnot de Condillac, *Essai sur l'origine des connaissances humaines* in *Œuvres philosophiques*, I (Paris: Presses Universitaires de France, 1947–52). For a broader treatment of Enlightenment discourses on gesture, see Herbert Josephs, *Diderot's Dialogue of Language and Gesture: "Le Neveu de Rameau"* (Ohio State University Press, 1969). On the continuation of the Enlightenment tradition in phenomenology, see Edmund Husserl, *Logical Investigations*, trans. J. N. Findlay (London: Routledge, 2001), and Jacques Derrida, *La voix et le phénomène: Introduction au problème du signe dans la phénoménologie de Husserl* (Paris: Presses Universitaires de France, 1993). For an invaluable account of theories of gesture from classical antiquity (Aristotle, Cicero, Quintilian) through Giovanni Bonifacio and John Bulwer (who contributed to the eighteenth-century belief that gestures are the first and most

natural human language), Joseph Marie de Gérando, Edward Tylor, and William Wundt, see Adam Kendon, *Gesture: Visible Action as Utterance* (Cambridge: Cambridge University Press, 2004). In the domain of anthropology, Marcel Jousse deserves particular recognition as a theorist of all languages, phonetic, corporeal, and scriptural, as "gestural" in origin. See *L'Anthropologie du geste*, 2 vols. (Paris: Gallimard, 1978).

3. Maurice Merleau-Ponty, "The Body as Expression, and Speech" in *The Phenomenology of Perception*, trans. Colin Smith (London: Routledge, 2002).

4. Both published in *Writing and Difference*, trans. and intro. Alan Bass (Chicago: University of Chicago Press, 1978); originally published as *L'Écriture et la différence* (Paris: Seuil, 1967). Derrida argues that all gestures, in order to signify, are iterable, belonging to the order of representation rather than presentation, repetition rather than pure self-identity.

5. Mary Kelly, "Reviewing Modernist Criticism," in *Art after Modernism: Rethinking Representation*, ed. and intro. Brian Wallis, foreword by Marcia Tucker (New York: New Museum of Contemporary Art, 1984), 90, 95. In the domain of art history, there is also a rich literature on *depicted* gestures (as opposed to the gestures of the artist); see Georges Didi-Huberman, *Devant l'image* (Paris: Minuit, 1990), and his preface to Philippe-Alain Michaud, *Aby Warburg et l'image en mouvement* (Paris: Macula, 1998).

6. Mark Franko, "Mimique" in *Bodies of the Text: Dance as Theory, Literature as Dance*, ed. Ellen W. Goellner and Jacqueline Shea Murphy (New Brunswick, N.J.: Rutgers University Press, 1995).

7. On the analogy between linguistic traces and gestural traces, see also Franko, *Dance as Text: Ideologies of the Baroque Body* (Cambridge: Cambridge University Press, 1993) and Susan Leigh Foster, "Textual Evidences," in Goellner and Murphy, *Bodies of the Text.* More recently, André Lepecki has returned to the analysis of dance as a trace structure in "Inscribing Dance" (*Of the Presence of the Body: Essays on Dance and Performance Theory*, ed. André Lepecki [Middletown, Conn.: Wesleyan University Press, 2004]). Lepecki's most persuasive contribution is to propose that the structure of inscription, or trace, as outlined by Derrida, is predicated on the metaphor of movement: "In Derrida, it is movement—the motion of deferment, the tracing of the trace, the writing under erasure, the slipping of the tracing—that quietly reintroduces presence into grammatology" (138). While Lepecki, Mark Franko, and Peggy Phelan all nuance the equation between writing and inscription implicit in Derrida, they do not explore the possibilities of redefining "presence"

itself (see Peggy Phelan, "Thirteen Ways of Looking at Choreographing History" in *Choreographing History*, ed. Susan Leigh Foster [Bloomington: Indiana University Press, 1995]). This volume can be differentiated from those just cited precisely insofar as its goal is to confront deconstruction's account of "presence" (as already haunted by absence) with alternative phenomenological and anthropological accounts of what the "presence" of the body in/as the sign might mean.

8. As Deidre Sklar has written elsewhere, dance ethnography depends on the postulate "that cultural knowledge is embodied in movement" and that, moreover, the knowledge involved "is not just somatic, but mental and emotional as well, encompassing cultural history, beliefs, values, and feelings" ("On Dance Ethnography" in *Dance Research Journal* 23:1 [Spring 1991]: 6).

9. In a similar vein, Susan Leigh Foster has argued that gestures are not merely movements but also ideas and that they can be analyzed within the context of their performance as elements of a choreographic argument. Foster gives intellectual content to gestures; see, in particular, "Choreographies of Writing" (forthcoming).

10. The relation of gesture to mimesis, or the mimetic impulse (the impulse to imitate an affect or physical attitude), is a complex issue that deserves a more thorough treatment than I can provide here. The essays of Blake Stimson and Carrie Noland both engage the notion of mimesis and relate it to gesturing. See also Walter Benjamin, "On the Mimetic Faculty" in *Reflections: Essays, Aphorisms, and Autobiographical Writings*, trans. Edmund Jephcott, ed. and intro. by Peter Demetz (New York: Schocken Books, 1986, c1978); and Michael Taussig, *Mimesis and Alterity* (New York and London: Routledge, 1993).

11. Catherine Cyssau, *Au lieu du geste* (Paris: Presses Universitaires de France, 1995), 35. My translation. For a suggestive meditation on gesture as exceeding the semiotic, see José Gil, *Metamorphoses of the Body*, trans. Stephen Muecke (Minnesota: University of Minnesota Press, 1998).

12. On "vitality affects" and their relationship to movement, see Daniel Stern, *The Interpersonal World of the Infant* (New York: Basic Books, 2000).

13. Deidre Sklar, in conversation.

14. See especially Terence Turner's essay in *Embodiment and Experience: The Existential Ground of Culture and Self*, edited by Thomas J. Csordas (Cambridge: Cambridge University Press, 1994), and Diana Taylor's *The Archive and the Repertoire: Performing Cultural Memory in the Americas* (Durham, N.C.: Duke University Press, 2003), both of which challenge Foucault's approach to the body as discursively constituted.

15. Maxine Sheets-Johnstone and Thomas J. Csordas both posit gesture as the repository of a tactile-kinesthetic consciousness that does not simply respond to but also, and more importantly, informs the way in which sign systems—and especially gestural sign systems—function. See, in particular, Maxine Sheets-Johnstone, *The Primacy of Movement* (Amsterdam: J. Benjamins, 1999) and *The Roots of Power* (Chicago: Open Court, 1994); Thomas J. Csordas, *Body/Healing/Meaning* (New York: Palgrave, MacMillan, 2002).

16. Thomas J. Csordas, "Somatic Modes of Attention" in Csordas, *Body/Healing/Meaning*, 243.

17. In this light, it would be worthwhile to consider the distinction made by Bertolt Brecht between the reflexive gesture and the social gesture *(gestus):* "Not all gests are social gests. The attitude of chasing away a fly is not yet a social gest, though the attitude of chasing away a dog may be one, for instance if it comes to represent a badly dressed man's continual battle against watchdogs. One's efforts to keep one's balance on a slippery surface result in a social gest as soon as falling down would mean 'losing face'; in other words, losing one's market value. The gest of working is definitely a social gest, because all human activity directed towards the mastery of nature is a social undertaking, an undertaking between men" ("On Gestic Music" in *Brecht on Theatre: The Development of an Aesthetic*, ed. and trans. John Willet [New York: Hill and Wang, 1996], 104). Brecht's distinction is implicitly rejected by Merleau-Ponty when he insists that the psychic and the physiological, or the socially saturated and the reflexive and seemingly biological, thoroughly interpenetrate each other; see "The Body as Object and Mechanistic Physiology" in Merleau-Ponty, *Phenomenology of Perception*, 84–102.

18. Judith Butler's work on the way in which the gendered body is constituted through structures of signification is highly pertinent in this context. Her characterization of gender as "the repeated stylization of the body, a set of repeated acts within a highly rigid regulatory frame that congeal over time to produce the appearance of substance, of a natural sort of being," is one that has profound consequences for any theory of gesture desiring to maintain the anatomical overdetermination, "naturalness," or *expressiveness*, of a gestural routine (*Gender Trouble: Feminism and the Subversion of Identity* [New York and London: Routledge, 1990], 33). In my contribution to this volume, I pursue the implications for a theory of gesture of Butler's approach to "the performative construction" of the gendered body "within the material practices of culture" (25).

19. A fascinating early study on enculturated approaches to gesturing is David

Efron's *Gesture, Race and Culture: A Tentative Study of Some of the Spatio-temporal and "Linguistic" Aspects of the Gestural Behavior of Eastern Jews and Southern Italians in New York City, Living Under Similar as well as Different Environmental Conditions* (The Hague: Mouton, 1941). For a discussion of this work, see Sklar's contribution. For a wide-ranging set of meditations on the cultural specificity of gestural regimes, see *A Cultural History of Gesture: From Antiquity to the Present Day*, ed. Jan Bremmer and Herman Rodenberg, intro. Sir Keith Thomas (Cambridge, U.K.: Polity Press, 1991).

20. On this distinction, see Warren Lamb and Elizabeth Watson, *Body Code: The Meaning in Movement*, drawings by Clare Jarrett (London: Routledge and Kegan Paul, 1979): "Gesture is confined to a small part of the body, a shake of the shoulders, curl of the lips, furrowing of the brow, whereas adopting a posture requires every part of the body to be involved in tension" (3).

21. It should be noted, however, that the conventional view, according to which expression by means of gestures precedes expression by means of verbal signs both historically and developmentally, is currently being contested by archeologists Ian Davidson and William Noble; see their *Human Evolution, Language, and Mind: A Psychological and Archaeological Inquiry* (Cambridge: Cambridge University Press, 1996). Further, scholars in linguistics, physical anthropology, and psychology are becoming increasingly interested in the crucial role gestures play in the development of other languages. See especially Kendon, *Gesture: Visible Action as Utterance;* and *Language and Gesture*, ed. David McNeill (Cambridge: Cambridge University Press, 2000). Kendon and Cornelia Müller have launched a journal devoted entirely to the study of gesture, entitled, appropriately, *Gesture;* the editorial statement explains that the journal "is intended to facilitate the integration of the emerging field of 'gesture studies'" and invites the submission of "reports of original empirical research, historical inventions and theoretical views *on any aspect of gesture and from any perspective*" (*Gesture* 3:1 [November 2003], editorial page; original emphasis).

22. Bertolt Brecht's theory of the *gestus* is again pertinent in this regard. See, for instance, "A Short Organum for the Theatre," "On Gestic Music," "On Experimental Theatre," and "On Rhymeless Verse with Irregular Rhythms" in *Brecht on Theatre: The Development of an Aesthetic;* and Elin Diamond, *Unmaking Mimesis: Essay on Feminism and Theater* (New York: Routledge, 1997).

23. The version of "Mimique" found in this volume was originally published in *Bodies of the Text: Dance as Theory, Literature as Dance*, ed. Ellen W. Goellner and Jacqueline Shea Murphy (Brunswick, N.J.: Rutgers University Press, 1994).

CHAPTER 1

The Inscription of Gesture: Inward Migrations in Dance

Sally Ann Ness

My main question in this chapter can be summed up as the following: What might it mean to take the phrase "gesture as inscription" as literally as possible with regard to dance?—dance being understood here as broadly as possible. I am assuming gesture as inscription would assert that the gesturing of dancing was a kind of *linguistic* or quasi-linguistic mark-making. Gesture as inscription would characterize the gestures of dancing literally as a kind of writing or as something that closely approximates writing. Moreover, it would characterize the gestures of dancing as "scripting," that moved literally *in*ward, or, perhaps better, *in*wise.

The *in-* of "inscription"—a very basic yet complex prefix—is not the *in-* of "inside" but the *in-* of "into." It is a place-seeking, not a place-being, "in." Inscriptive gestures can be thought of as gestures that write something into a place. They *create* "place" or "place-ness" out of something that is both a "no-where" and a "no-thing"—the actions of linguistic mark-making themselves. This is what the literal understanding of gesture as inscription would assume and assert.

Having elaborated this literal understanding of the phrase, I can restate the chapter's main question: When we speak of the gesturing of dancing, how far can we push the phrase "gesture as inscription" *away* from a figurative interpretation before we render it nonsensical? By figurative, I mean an interpretation that might be characterized as relatively loose, playful (in all senses), or poetic.

Needless to say, the work that such figurative interpretations can do discursively in relation to the gestures of dance is not in any general sense unhelpful or insignificant. It tends, in fact, to be quite effective and can be cast pragmatically as the recommended type of usage with regard to the subject of dance. Given the interpretive license granted to the figurative mode of employment, its referential validity is not subject to the narrowly focused scrutiny required of the literal mode. The figurative mode can be used unproblematically, which, however, is also why the figurative use of "gesture as inscription" is unhelpful here. It allows the phrase to do its work too fluently. Its tendency toward more ambiguous forms of aptness does not raise the questions that I seek to raise about how the gestures of dance can and cannot engage in meaning-making. For this reason, I move in the opposite direction, in the direction of the literal.

The strategy here adopted should be understood as semantically *processual.* I am only engaged in "pushing" or "leaning" on the phrase "gesture as inscription" in the direction of its literal sense, not in reaching that ultimate definition. I am only interested in the staging of a gentle sequence of pushes, each as gentle in its individual impact on the phrase as can be managed. It is not a matter of arriving at the expression of an invalid claim. I want to sidle up to the phrase's breaking point with truth—approach it as closely as possible so as to identify where the brink of nonsense is located. In this way, it seems possible to observe exactly when, why, and how the notion of "gesture as inscription" stops making sense in the case of dance.

For, eventually, it does become untrue to claim that the gesturing of dancing is literally the same kind of a thing as is characterized by the more classic examples of inscription. The sort of public writing and symbolism found etched into monuments, tombstones, and coins seems strikingly different in both form and function from danced gestures. Even the more intimate, personal, and private sorts of inscription, those found on infant bracelets, pocket watches, and anniversary lockets, as well as inside the covers of books, seem to have little if anything in common, in either their purposes or their signifying characters, with the movements of a dancer. It is not my intention to attempt to force "gesture as inscription" into some redefinition that would equate it to these more standard forms of inscription. Such a redefinition would undoubtedly torque the phrase's meaning to the point that it would become dissociated from its common sense. Redefining "gesture as inscription" is not my project. I want the phrase to remain connected to its deepest, broadest meanings, even while I lean on it in this unlikely manner.

I lean on it with several purposes in mind. First, it compels a close examination of the full range of semeiotic capabilities evident in dancing. Second, it compels a rethinking of the relationship between the body and the unconscious, and between embodiment and "nonconsciousness." Third, it calls into question established theories of the relationship between corporeal performance and ephemerality. For, while I do believe that eventually it becomes literally untrue to describe dancing in terms of gesture as inscription, I also believe that one can lean on the phrase in that direction, in the case of dance, quite a bit farther than is generally done. Pushed to its extreme, it becomes nonsense. However, it takes a while to reach that point, and the meanings revealed along the way are as significant as they are, for the most part, overlooked.

Gesture as Inscription: A Best-Case Scenario

Dance refers to an extremely diverse array of practices. The boundaries of its referential scope are themselves a matter of controversy. Of the many kinds of performance that might be subsumed beneath this rubric, I ask two questions. At their intersection, the answers delimit a subset of uncontroversial examples of the art form. These examples provide a kind of best-case scenario supporting the attempt to find out just how true it might be to claim that the gestures of dance can be understood as forms of inscription. The forms of dance identified by these questions are among the most "inscriptive" in character of any that might be selected for examination. Where they fall short of the literal meaning of the phrase, then, marks something like the limit for the art form as a whole.

The first question: Which forms of danced gesturing have the greatest capacity to "leave their mark" in a most permanent manner? Permanence is a defining feature of inscription. It endows inscription with a character of "written-ness" that exceeds all other forms of writing. To inscribe is not simply to mark but to mark in a *durable* way. It typically requires a hard surface of some kind, be it stone, brick, or metal, so as to accomplish this task. In order to function as an inscription, the writing or symbolism must occur so as to leave a lasting mark, one that will withstand the accidents and contingencies of everyday life. It must be one that will continue to signify consistently for an indefinite, even infinite, period of time. In so doing, it enables an "unforgettableness" with regard to the symbolic content of the mark made. It preserves its meaning by sinking deeply into an unchanging place.

Yet, inscription does not work by simply placing its symbolism in a fixed location. Instead, it transforms and creates a different kind of place for its writing through its own distinctive actions. Whether they be chiseling, engraving, incising, carving, shaving, etching, or some other form of cutting into, the actions of inscription render an ordinarily unchanging material permanently altered in some fashion. The place of an inscription's writing is *not* the material itself—which serves as a kind of "host" for the writing. The "place" (for we are already edging away from the literal here) of the writing is the hollowed out consequence of the process of inscription.

This I take to be the main meaning of the *in-* of inscription. The prefix is not used in the sense that it most often denotes—the sense of *in-* as inclusion ("sitting in the dark," being "inland"). It is not this *in-* of containment and passive placement. Neither is it used as the *in-* of qualification ("in a stage whisper"), the *in-* of being in a certain way. Rather, the *in-* of inscription is the less frequently used verb-formative *in-*. It is the *in-* that turns a subject into a process of action. Specifically, it indicates a setting into motion with directional intent—a motion of migration ("immigration"). The *in-* of inscription signifies specifically an intention to move toward somewhere but not to *get* to a place. It has the character of a migratory *in-*, but it is caught up completely within the movement process of that migration. It is in this sense that it is perpetually place-seeking but never place-finding.

The *in-* of inscription is closely related to, although less all-engrossing than, the *in-* of into when it is used in phrases like "she is into rock-climbing." There is an important contrast here. Inscriptions must pierce deeply enough into their host materials that they create permanent marks, but they do not submerge themselves completely, they do not lose themselves inside their hosts, and they do not penetrate them so as to alter the material's enduring character. They do not aim for a center let alone pierce through some core or move in any way that would weaken durability. Inscriptions work toward depths but not to or through them.

The *in-* of inscription is also the *in-* of transition, not only the migratory transition from one place to another but also the substantive transition from one condition of existence to another ("to tie in knots," "to inaugurate"). To inscribe is to change the fundamental character of something from that of a brute surface (blank page, platinum cover, granite cornerstone, marble wall) to that of a sign. To move "*in*ward," in this inscriptive regard, is not only to move from surface toward depth and from the outside toward the inside. It is also to change a signifying character from conveying a transient to conveying a permanent meaning. These moves are all *in*ward moves, *non*directional inward moves, that the concept "inscription" denotes as well.

It might be helpful, then, to rephrase the first question once again and ask: Which forms of danced gesturing have the greatest capacity to move inward in these senses of the term? The question now begs some others: Which "way" is "in" for dance? Toward *where?* What would be the "host material" of a dance's inscriptive gesturing?

Generally, the commonsense understanding of danced gesturing is that it expresses itself outward. Dance's gestures are typically seen to move out of the dancer's body onto thin air. They impress themselves onto nothing at all—other than, in some cases, and by no means all, the gaze of a spectator. This view seems to preclude anything but a poetic understanding of dance as gestural inscription. Air is a most inappropriate medium for inscription, entirely insubstantial and immaterial.

The relationship of dance to the airy "host" into which it is typically expressed, a "material" so light that the idea of cutting into its "depths" produces only images of fleeting trace forms or ghostly trajectories, is critical to the discourse that asserts for dance a semiotics that is essentially transient. This is how the vanishing and ephemeral character of dance's gestures is often justified. One has only to focus on the way dancers pour their gestures out into the space in which they occur and then in which they abruptly and utterly cease to exist, to become convinced of the discourse's claims of extreme, absolute impermanence. Understood in this way, dance becomes the antithesis of inscription, although not of writing.

I do not follow this line of thinking, which privileges a visual experience of danced gesturing. Instead, I take my cue from here onward from a well-known quote by the choreographer/theorist of early twentieth-century Europe, Rudolf von Laban:

> Movement not only speaks through an object; a living organism owes its final form to it; movement leads to growth and structure.[1]

That is to say, if we are going to look for the *in*ward moving tendencies of danced gesturing, we might do best to look at the mark they leave not upon the space surrounding their actions or the eyes watching them but *upon the bodies that are their medium.* The dancer's body can be seen to form the "host material," a living tissue, for dance's gestural inscriptions. Its anatomy provides the "sites" or "places" where gesture can leave its mark in the rendering of a "final form"—that is, in a structure that bears an enduring and permanent signifying character.

Following this line of thinking, the literal meaning of gesture as inscription acquires more purchase. The question now appears to seek out dance forms whose gesturing migrates deeply into their dancers' bodies. It searches for gestures that penetrate beneath a dancer's skin to fix enduring marks into their hardest, most durable connective tissues. The question seeks to identify dance gestures that mold, carve, and otherwise impress their way into ligaments, muscles, and even bones, so as to bring about a transformation that is (ideally) not a weakening of the functional structures but a rendering of them as meaningful. This inward direction leads not toward what gesture is expressed onto but who, what, and how gesture is "written" into.

We come now to the second question: Which forms of danced gesturing are closest to linguistic or are most predominantly symbolic in terms of their meaning-making properties? This question centers upon the second defining feature of inscription. While inscriptions may sometimes employ emblems or other types of pictorial signs, the marks they leave are most often linguistic in character. Inscription, literally, is a form of using language.

This question raises a longstanding, still unresolved question in dance studies: whether or not, or in what ways, dancing could be considered a "language." In recent years, the question has been set aside in humanistic dance research. Pioneering comparative projects focusing on dance and language generally failed to foreground, if they addressed at all, issues currently judged to be of central importance for the study of dance semiotics, questions related to the signifying properties of corporeality and performance primary among them. Earlier analyses tended to depend heavily on linguistic theory to define the terms for comparison, and in so doing, they tended to obscure, rather than illuminate, distinctive features of dance's performative capabilities.[2] Dance was often cast in oppositional terms as the "nonverbal" medium of communication. This implicitly positioned dance as an inferior medium, a relatively primitive counterpart to language.

The project at hand, and indeed this volume's originating theme, compels me to resurrect this question. However, I shift from the earlier equation, "Is dance a language?" to search instead for parallels and convergences from within what is currently understood to be the broad and diversely populated field of dance's signifying practices. The interest here is in identifying when and how observable congruencies in meaning-making strategies might appear to be most striking between linguistic symbolism and certain kinds of danced gesturing. Only once these grounds have been established is it possible to move on to identify types of danced gesturing that can be shown to resemble most closely gesture as inscription.

I approach this second question employing the pragmatic semeiotic[3] theory developed by Charles S. Peirce. The Peircean semeiotic architectonic, although laborious in its terminology, carries with it the advantage of not being language-focused or "linguicentric" in orientation. Despite its jargon, it has been employed in anthropological research in a wide array of work that has focused on nonlinguistic forms of symbolism.[4] Peirce's theory of sign types also foregrounds continuity and combination of sign relations. Rather than drawing arbitrary boundaries between various modes of signification, it locates them along continua that are understood to intersect and interweave in practice. In this regard, Peircean semeiotics supports the interest in observing how danced gestures converge on acts of inscription.

The particular semeiotic triad most relevant here is the well-known triad of icon, index, and symbol.[5] These three sign types define the way in which the sign's representamen (the signlike aspect that occupies the mediating position in signification) and its object (that for which a representamen stands) are understood to be connected.[6] While fundamentally different in their signifying characters, the three types of relationships also "nest." The index contains within it iconic aspects, and the symbol, both indexical and iconic aspects.

Linguistic signs, both oral and written, are recognized as belonging to the third sign type, the symbol, a sign whose representamen and object are related by a rule, or a habit, or a continuous *regularity* of some kind. All linguistic signs are symbols. However, not all symbols are linguistic signs.

Dance's gestures have generally been assumed to belong to nonsymbolic sign types. Most often, they have been interpreted as iconic in character, representing their objects by virtue of a relationship of resemblance. The majority of anthropological research on dance, and on performance in general, has opted to interpret the gestures of dance as being engaged primarily in iconic semeiotic processes.[7] Theoretically, icons are characterized as being furthest from symbols in their manner of operating. Their signification is based on relatively transparent forms of recognition.

In addition to iconically oriented approaches, some analysts of dance, and of symbolic action more generally, have also noted that danced gestures can operate indexically as well. Indexes[8] work by processes of signaling, which indicate the coexistence of a gesture with something else also present or evident in the performance context. Referential gestures, those of pointing to someone or something, for example, are indexical signs that appear in many types of narrative dance dramas. In anthropological research on dance, studies of trance have sometimes relied upon an indexical semeiotics to note the entrance into and maintenance of a state of possession.[9] Shivering, shaking, and movements of the eyes are among the most commonly observed indexes of this kind. Indexically oriented research also has gained attention within anthropology with the development of diverse historically oriented, performative, and postmodern approaches to dance practices. These approaches foreground the differences that occur from one performance to the next in a given dance tradition. They identify the contributions of individual performers as well as the aspects of performance that can be shown to be contingent on a particular set of contextual variables.[10]

The index is relatively automatic with regard to the thought required for its operation. Its reliance upon conditions of external fact differentiate its semeiotics from those of symbols.

In contrast to iconically and indexically oriented approaches, relatively little anthropological work has observed or analyzed a specifically symbolic semeiotics of dance. The discourse has not worked to preclude this possibility or reject it outright. However, symbolism in danced gesturing has not received the same consideration that iconic and indexical processes have. While the basic character of cultural dance traditions is often acknowledged to be of an enduring, highly regular, highly habitual type—a type that could not be sustained by either purely iconic or indexical semeiotics—the iconic and indexical properties nested within those patterns of regularity have typically become the focus of attention.

Only in the cases of dance traditions that contain gestural systems similar in character to sign languages, such as some varieties of Polynesian and South Asian ritual dance, have specifically symbolic semeiotics been recognized and studied.[11] This situation, once again, reflects a spectatorial understanding of danced gesturing and its outward expressions. When audience members must understand a semeiotics of gesture that operates via symbolic processes in order to comprehend the meaning of the performance, then, and for the most part only then, has a symbolic semeiotics of danced gesturing been recognized. This outward focus, however, has tended to neglect symbolic processes that are not evident from a spectatorial point of view.

An inward semeiotics of dance symbolism is precisely the semeiotics that I must consider in my effort to push the understanding of dance gestures one step closer to inscription. It is actually an easy step to take, since rule-governed, highly regularized relationships abound in dance training and performance. Wherever codified gestural techniques have evolved, wherever habits of movement practice have stabilized enough to produce a *continuity* of movement style, general principles of conduct are operative in a performance discipline. Even in cases in which iconic and indexical semeiotics are predominant outwardly, they are regulated and given consistency of meaning over time through their incorporation into rule-governed patterns of sign production and processing—into the conventions that constitute a dance "technique."

Technical training, then, forms the context and the content of the inward symbolism of danced gestures. Only symbols enable the kind of continuous growth in understanding that technical mastery requires. Only symbols possess the capability to transform a dancer's "raw behavior" into a recognizable, namable, stylistically coherent, "danced" gesture. Symbolic processes are essential to the learning of a dance form. They provide the consistency necessary for a conventional understanding of whatever movement practices are involved to crystallize.

What the second question asks, then, in Peirce's terms, is this: Which forms of danced gesturing move inward in a most highly rule-governed, habit-forming, principled (i.e., symbolic) manner? However, because Peirce's semeiotic is as elaborate as it is, the question can be understood to ask something much more specific as well. It can be understood to ask something that allows the edge of meaningfulness for gesture as inscription, and the neglected territory being sought here, to come clearly into view. In Peirce's theory, three different classes of symbols are actually defined.[12] To parallel linguistic symbols most closely, the gestures of dance would need to exhibit all three of these nested symbol classes. What the second question specifically asks, then, is this: Which forms of danced gesturing move the furthest along the symbolic spectrum toward the kind of representation that is unique to linguistic symbolism alone?

We must pursue briefly this final classification of signs. The first class of symbol identified by Peirce, called the *term,* defines a sign type that is an individual, stand-alone, general conception. Terms are the most basic form of symbolic representation.[13] In the linguistic symbols of the English language, terms are the equivalent of common nouns. However, not all terms are linguistic. They appear in gestural traditions as well. Wherever a conventional, self-contained meaning can be assigned to a movement, or position, or part of the body, a term is evident. Outwardly expressive terms, such as the "thumbs-up" hand gesture, are frequently observed in many dance forms. Inward terms exist as well. Such terms do not function for the purpose of being interpreted by a viewer but enable instead a means of conventional understanding of the movement processes being enacted to become coherent for performers. In the case of tap dance, for example, there are a wide variety of basic actions of the feet and legs, all of which have been given verbal labels such as "stomp," "flap," "slap," and, of course, "tap." These linguistic labels refer to habits of performance practice that have regularized over time into an "action vocabulary" of movement symbols. They represent patterns of movement that have become regular and that serve as the conventional foundation for the tap dance tradition. Performers embody these symbols as they study and gain expertise in that tradition. In the mastery of the technique, dancers learn to "come to terms" within their bodies so as to perform the form's action vocabulary articulately and consistently.

Let us turn back to the idea of inscription. In the case of the more private and personal forms of inscription, linguistic symbols of this basic term type may often stand alone and constitute an inscription of a relatively simple kind. Such is the case when a pocket watch, for example, is inscribed only with the name of its recipient and dates that mark the beginning and ending of her working life. An equivalent in performance practice, an inward embodiment of movement terms, also can be observed to have a relatively widespread occurrence. For example, in the modern dance tradition developed by Martha Graham, there exists a movement term labeled a "contraction" in English. The movement entails a hollowing out of the abdominal cavity and curving of the spine in the thoracic, lumbar, and sacral areas. The contractions of the abdominal muscles are generally coordinated with an exhalation of the breath. Graham dancers may practice literally hundreds of repetitions of this movement term on a daily basis, which is identified with a broad spectrum of emotional and intentional dramatic expressions. After years of embodying this movement term, their skeletal-musculature gradually comes to bear its "mark." A gesture—or in this case, a postural term—has been inscribed not upon but *into* them. Gesture as inscription, in other words, can now be seen to refer in a literal manner to a process of embodiment paralleling that of linguistic inscription. A danced term or a simple series of terms is embodied habitually and "inscribed" into a dancer's body once the body's connective tissues themselves bear the evidence of that practice.

Beyond the term, in Peirce's theory, a second class of symbols, called *propositions* is defined. A final class, called *arguments*, is identified as well.[14] At these levels, gestural practice is apparently left behind. Propositions and arguments have the capability to define and assert *relationships* between two or more terms.[15] They are described by Peirce as necessarily entailing "subjects" and "predicates" in this work. Their semeiotics depends on parts of speech and grammatical operations. In this regard, they carry a semantic load very different from the more primitive stand-alone terms. The difference between terms and these second- and third-level symbols is the difference between uttering a single word in a language and speaking in full sentences. It is the difference that makes language possible. The gulf between the literal and figurative meanings of gesture as inscription, then, opens up between the semeiotics of terms and those of propositions and arguments.

In the end, what the second question asks most specifically is this: Which forms of dance go beyond cultivating terms and move on to do something more relationship-oriented, more technically sophisticated, with them? Which dance forms, if any, involve rule-governed practices that move via conventions through a nested complex of relationships? These forms of dance would be the performance practices that would show us just how far gesture as inscription can be pushed in the case of dance.

Again, I do not argue that something exactly like Peirce's proposition and argument are operating in the gestures of dancing—even in the best-case scenarios. That would be asserting precisely the kind of ultimate congruence or absolute equation between dance and language that would undermine this exercise. However, the territory between the inward term and *something akin* to a propositional and argumentational semeiotics is, I argue, the neglected territory of meaning-making into which a very broad array of dance practice falls. In the section that follows, I provide examples that begin to map out some general features of this "term-relational" (quasi-propositional and quasi-argumentational) semeiotic terrain.

Classical Dance Forms as Inscriptive Practice

The two questions elaborated point toward kinds of dance that have attracted the label "classical." These are the most tradition-bound, technically developed, and hierarchically institutionalized varieties of dance. Such dance genres typically require a relatively great quantity of practice in order for students to acquire mastery. Training for the most advanced levels also tends to begin at a very early age. These intensive regimes in many cases result in the permanent alteration of deep tissues, even bone structures. I examine a few of the most well known of these cases to explore how the meaning of gesture as inscription comes the closest to acquiring a literal meaning from an inward point of view.

As mentioned previously, relatively little research has been done on symbolism of dance technique. One striking exception in anthropological research stands out and serves as a guide for the exploration at hand. This first example, Balinese classical dance, was explored by Gregory Bateson in his early research on Balinese culture and personality conducted in collaboration with Margaret Mead in the late 1930s.[16] Bateson attempted to develop a means of analyzing Balinese behavior that was language-free, conducted through extensive photographic and film research on a wide array of activities. Classical dance movement performed in traditional ritual contexts figured prominently in his studies.

Bateson's observations of Balinese dance focused specifically on the manner in which postural balance was maintained in ritual performances during highly complex phrases of danced gesturing. Balinese rhythmically syncopated and fast-paced gesturing involved the isolation and orchestration of a large number of limb and torso areas. Bateson was impressed by the extraordinary limb control, endurance, and meticulous precision required for the limb movements to be performed in a manner judged to be aesthetically correct. The performances, in his view, turned the seemingly simple activity of maintaining an upright posture into something akin to a tightrope act. The technique of walking thus required a relatively complex logic of balance, the basic assumptions of which, Bateson argued, went far beyond dance in their cultural significance.

The recognition of the technical challenges inherent in Balinese classical dance, a recognition that was gained as a consequence of Bateson's extensive experimentation in documenting through nonverbal means the whole of Balinese cultural life, inspired a unique interpretation of Balinese dance movement. He noted, "The metaphor of postural balance . . . is demonstrably applicable in many contexts of Balinese culture."[17] He concluded his study with the following finding: "It seems that the Balinese extend to human relationships attitudes based upon bodily balance and that they generalize the idea that motion is essential to balance."[18]

Translated into Peircean semeiotic terminology, Bateson's finding for Balinese classical dance movement identifies the cultivation in movement practice of multiple symbolic terms. He observes these terms in the traditional danced gestures and postures that correspond to his English-language concepts of "motion," "posture," and most significant, "balance." However, Bateson's finding also identifies an ongoing tradition of working through specific *relationships* among these terms via the training, rehearsal, and performance processes of classical dance practice. In the regimes of practice that lead to the development of a mature artist, a mastery of certain truths about the necessarily interdependent character of these terms was acquired. Bateson understood the constantly changing posing performed by Balinese classical dancers to be the ongoing testing of certain hypotheses of what "balance" could be under circumstances that had achieved the status of cultural givens. He recognized the gesturing of Balinese dancing to be a way of demonstrating or asserting a particular way of thinking through the question of how motion could be truly integral to the ongoing practice of balance in a specifically Balinese form of life.

Again, it is important to remember that Bateson's observations were not examples of what I call "outwardly" moving symbolism. They were not attempts to replicate how an informed spectator might interpret what was being expressed to an audience in Balinese dance. Rather, they were observations of what the mastery of Balinese classical technique embodied in Bateson's understanding. In Peircean terms, he interpreted Balinese dancing as presenting a set of term relations that were continuously testing the truth of what balance as a movement experience could be and mean within the specific context of this classical genre. Moreover, in his emphasis on the more general applicability, or "extend-ability," of the movement style, Bateson interpreted Balinese dancing as a quasi-argument for the creative adaptation of the technique's symbolism to a much more general program of principled conduct. Balinese dance was designed to be influential far beyond its immediate performative contexts, possessing the semeiotic capability to persuade or *move through thought.*

Seen in this Batesonian light, the inscriptive effects classical Balinese dance training produces appear to be both less poetic and less purely physical in nature than might otherwise be the case. The permanently hyperextended spines in female performers, the pulled-up shoulders, outturned elbows, and curving fingers of both male and female performers, the lifelong deformations of ligaments connecting dancers' bones—all of this evidence of a career in classical performance acquires a thoughtful, reason-filled character. Seen through Bateson's interpretive lens, training can be understood to inscribe more than a set of terms defining the body parts of the human figure as the distinctly Balinese classical style defines them. Classical training inscribes as well a theory of how these terms interact. In the bodily structures that exist as nothing other than the consequences of habitual patterns of movement, *therein,* in no "thing" other than the traces of performance, is inscribed a record of learning about what core concepts can mean in Balinese cultural practice. The bones, ligaments, and other tissues of the dancers are the host material for the inscription of a living quasi-argument continuously influencing virtually every realm of Balinese life. The body of the classical Balinese dancer serves as an explicit living reminder, both in performance and in daily life, not only of an aesthetic form but also of a reasoned method of understanding and standing "under" the logic of Balinese cultural "balance."

Using Bateson's method as a guide, I turn briefly to two more examples of classical dance. The first is relatively familiar to my own sphere of dance practice, for I have studied versions of its multischooled technique since childhood: classical ballet.[19] I take one specific term of inscription, the arched feet of the classical ballerina, as my focus and identify one quasi-argument inscribed in them.

A living icon of the toe shoe tradition, itself a hallmark index or "summarizing symbol"[20] of all that classical ballet has come to embody, the semeiotics inscribed in the feet of the classical ballerina represent, in a most intensely concentrated manner, principles of conduct that go a long way toward defining the ballet tradition as a whole. The ballerina's arched feet are perhaps *the* predominant symbolic term of ballet. Their structural deformations reflect the most deeply held convictions of this particular classical tradition.

In high contrast to the Balinese quasi-argument for balance, the term-relational semeiotics of classical ballet training do not operate from a set of rules that link the synchronized motion of multiple, isolated bodily terms. A markedly different set of relations is inscribed in the feet of a classical ballerina. Its persuasive powers, however, are no less influential or generally applicable in the western culture that serves as its originating context. The ballet tradition, like the Balinese tradition, develops in its regimes of training a theory of a performative equivalent of the English-language term *balance.* Ballet's performative term, however, is linked most basically not to the idea of mobility but to that of stability, to the maintenance of motionlessness, and to the apparent prolonging of stillness.

In its purest, most archetypal forms, the term of balance in ballet depends necessarily on one key capability: aiming. A balance is not kept in motion so much as it is "struck," or "hit," as a target is struck or hit. Unlike the Balinese case, in ballet, balance "points" are assigned an existential essence. A dancer aims to place herself "dead on" them, so as to be able to sustain a pose for a seemingly infinite period of time. Performing the perfect balance for the ballerina depends on nothing so much as having an aim that is true, an aim that integrates the entire self, mind and body, in its execution. Accuracy in sending a line of force into the ground as well as out the limbs is crucial for the creation of a balanced move, particularly a move performed *en pointe.* The term of balance in ballet is interrelated necessarily with the term of *aim-taking.* To paraphrase Bateson's comment on the Balinese postural metaphor, the ballet tradition, particularly where point work is concerned, seems to generalize the idea that aiming—honing in on a single target—is essential to balance.

The testing of balance, then, in classical ballet, a type of testing that is carried out nowhere more rigorously than by the ballerina *en pointe,* is of an entirely different kind from that of the Balinese dance tradition. However, it is a kind of testing nonetheless. The balancing acts of the classical ballerina are designed to test the dancer's ability to make exceptionally accurate guesses, guesses often asserted by her feet, about where balance points are to be found and how they are to be reached. These hypotheses are locational, as opposed to synchronizing, in character. Mastery of balance evolves in practice as a mastery of directing oneself to places that are extremely difficult to find and extremely easy to miss or lose, places that are literally infinitesimal. They are so tiny that their margins for error are virtually nonexistent. One is either exactly "on" them, or one is obviously "off"—and in disgrace, falling on the floor.

The regimes of practice in ballet devote considerable time to developing an increasingly accurate understanding of the *relationships* between the terms of the body classical ballet defines and to specifying what kinds of moves will guarantee their "placement" on balance "points." Exercises at the ballet bar typically end with a balance of some kind. *Adagio* exercises center floor employ balances as the central subject of their compositions. Even exercises that stress mobility across the floor, involving turns and aerial steps of various types, may also include the finding of balance points. Balance points are conceived in terms of "lines" of balanced energy, lines so narrowly defined as to become nothing other than points that are moving in one, and only one, direction. Thinking through balance, in the logic of classical ballet's practice, becomes a study in thinking through aiming, using the terms of the body, often initiated and maintained by the feet, to develop an understanding of how taking aim could be truly essential to the performance of a certain type of balanced practice.

This inward patterning of ballet's theory of balance seems to have as well an "outward" significance of a nearly identical character, given its explicitly spatial (in the sense of locational) orientation. The "lines" of classical technique pursued by dancers are equally well understood by ballet audiences, as are the balances that ballerinas work to prolong beyond what rhythmic meters require. However, the outward icons of "stillness" and various features of geometrical space manifested by dancers in performance are not typically interpreted as the consequence of an active science of aiming. The imagery of directional realms is not set to work as a means of seeking out a certain knowledge of balance for spectators. Rather, it is understood inwardly by performers alone.

At the same time, the applicability of the term-relating work of ballet's experimental science of balancing also can be seen to extend far beyond the specific confines of the ballet subculture. Such an extension of the theory of balance seems as plausible for ballet as that posited by Bateson for Balinese dance and the various domains of Balinese cultural life. In its principled structure, the applicability of ballet's term-relational semeiotics may extend to any activity in which targeting a goal might be involved or idealized. Such activities are basic to an enormous array of western cultural contexts. Any practice in which direction-finding can be employed strategically potentially would be relevant. Having the "good sense" to find and pursue directions that produce stable, enduring relationships; being direct and "straightforward" in one's dealings with others so as to create a "solid" basis for maintaining an unchanging, "steadfast" connection—such character traits have a basic positive assessment in the domains of western political and economic life as well as in aesthetic and athletic practices. It is difficult to imagine a value more core in western cultures than the value placed on being able to achieve a single, identified goal and hold onto it indefinitely. The technically sophisticated way ballet exemplifies learning how to be more precisely goal-achieving *and* balanced in one's practice resonates broadly, in this regard, with a wide array of western activity domains. As with the Balinese case, the term relationships embodied in ballet's point work are highly generalizable.

Once again, then, in the case of ballet, what is inscribed in a classical ballerina's feet appears inwardly as far more than the natural consequences of a certain kind of physical training process. The rounding of the bones, the stretching of the ligaments, all of the structural changes that will last a lifetime, preserve a way of defining a certain part of the body as ballet would have it defined and of using that bodily term as a thoughtful agent of methodical exploration and informed, cultural conduct. The theory of practice inscribed in the ballerina's feet, in other words, is constantly being put to the test and reassessed each day in regimes of training, rehearsal, and performance. It is constantly being refined, revised, reformed, and *rethought* in an ongoing project of understanding what balance, western-style, can be and mean. It may be understood, as well, as one basis for a wide range of thoughtful practice in other domains of cultural life.

The final example, on which I comment only briefly, although much more can be implied for it from the discussions provided in Ketu Katrak's chapter in this volume, is the Indian classical tradition of Bharata Natyam. In particular, I reflect here on the symbolism inscribed in a Bharata Natyam dancer's hands. Here, movement terms are defined quite differently from those of the traditions just discussed. "Postural balance" is not the only subject of this explicitly gestural technique. Instead, something like "fluency" might take its place as the central technical accomplishment.

This case is markedly different from Balinese dance and classical ballet in that the classical Bharata Natyam tradition does, in fact, include an expressive, interpretive tradition that is explicitly symbolic, and even conceptual, in character. The gestures of Bharata Natyam express discrete, intelligible, linguistically equivalent terms to an understanding audience. Its gestures may express term-relational symbolism to its audiences as well, often in simultaneous combination with narratives being articulated in vocal music.

Because the outward semeiotics of Bharata Natyam possess the capabilities of conventional symbolism, one could posit that these are the sign relationships that are inscribed in a dancer's hands. One could then "read" the handwritten deformations of the carpal bones, phalanges, and wrist ligaments in this way. However, the inscription of this spectatorial semeiotics does not preclude that of a second "discourse" of practice being inscribed as well. In the special case of Bharata Natyam, as well as in those of other classical traditions that have similarly codified outward interpretive traditions, it is possible that a dual semeiotics may occur wherein expression and technique simultaneously work through their respective insights in the gestures of performance. That is, the thought required for signing the outward narrative and that required for dancing the signs may not be one and the same. The inward principles of technical conduct may form a second inscriptive dimension in this case.

The hands of the Bharata Natyam dancer, then, may appear as a material host that serves two inscriptive forms at once. They do so through the development of an anatomical structure that can be "read" in both inwardly and outwardly oriented ways, much as the famous duck-rabbit image employed by Ludwig Wittgenstein can be viewed as both animals simultaneously.[21]

This examination of Balinese, ballet, and Bharata Natyam classical dance forms illustrates how inward forms of symbolism—not only term-like forms but also term-relational symbols—come to be invested in the host bodies of master dance artists. These thought-enabling, technique-enhancing movements are seldom recognized for their full range of semeiotic capabilities. However, in granting them such recognition, one must be careful not to idealize their experience. The training regimes undergone by individuals performing these traditions, those in whose bodies the various kinds of symbols have been most deeply inscribed, tend to be as abusive and unjust, as merciless, as the elaborately hierarchical power structures of the complex societies in which the dance forms themselves are situated. Their politics tend toward the oppressive. This brutal fact of human collective life, however, does nothing to alter the complexity of the technical intelligence such dance traditions continuously advance and inscribe. Within the various technical disciplines of classical dance lies a vast territory of neglected sign production. It is here that "gesture as inscription," taken literally, can perhaps be most illuminating.

Conclusion

I have now pushed the phrase "gesture as inscription" as far as I can in the direction of a literal interpretation. The limits or its meaningfulness now come more clearly into view. They appear most obviously with regard to the manner in which term-relational semeiotics is *itself* made articulate. The limits of similarity between dance and writing are most apparent with regard to something like an explicit codification of the danced equivalent of syntax. In the case of Balinese dance, for example, the relationships between the danced terms of "motion" and "balance" grow implicitly out of practice. They are regularized and come to be rule-governed (i.e., symbolic) through various choreographic traditions of enactment. However, they do not appear to be explicitly encoded via any close equivalent to that necessary for written "parts of speech."

This is not to say that there is nothing akin to a "grammar" of dance technique operating in these traditions, particularly in the Wittgensteinian sense of the term.[22] It is not to say that there is nothing akin to the kind of thought on which grammar relies for its operation occurring in classical traditions of danced gesturing. On the contrary, it seems highly plausible that in a more elaborate technical examination, performative terms that work in a similar manner and with the same kind of thought as such grammatical terms as *and*, *of*, *then*, *not*, and *with* could readily be identified through observations of how the terms of the body alone are defined and coordinated in the technical action vocabulary of the tradition. "If/then" and "both/and" propositional structures would also be relatively easy to identify for the same practices. However, an explicit symbolics of syntax (as opposed to that of performative "re-presentation"), an overtly rule-governed method of setting forth the manner in which the articulation of these term relationships *is itself to be recognized*—this dimension of the inward symbolism of classical dance techniques is what seems to be most strikingly different from the propositions and arguments of writing. While the grammatical *understanding* is evident, its representation is not made explicit in the same way.

It is here that I find the outer limits of inscription as a useful term in any literal sense, where danced gesturing is concerned. A specifically performative (Peirce would have said "energetic" or "dynamical")[23] semeiotics becomes necessary to aptly characterize the distinctive thought processes by which relationships between terms in danced gesturing themselves acquire, convey, produce, and conserve meaning. A performative semeiotics would clarify the different ways in which term-relational regularities are set to work in contexts that are fundamentally and distinctively those of action (versus, perhaps, imagination). It could identify the specific purposes (in contrast to language's predominantly *referential* array of purposes, perhaps) that the term-relational semeiotics of dance are designed to serve. Most important, a performative semeiotics would address the distinctive conditions of corporeal *movement* that integrate the mindful, symbolic aspect of dancing with its other aspects, both regular and unique, aspects not governed by human thought but that work in concert with such givens as gravity, entropy, and a universe of contingent facts that inevitably intervene and affect the actual performance of any gesture. In sum, the profoundly integral relation of dance's symbolics to its actuality[24]—to its grounds of existence and to the array of relatively brute forces, accidental occurrences, unmediated efforts, and other elements characterizing its existential mode—cannot be approached most effectively from a linguistically oriented inscriptive perspective. Neither can the relationship of a performative semeiotics to the human imagination, which forms something like a virtual world for linguistic symbolism and consequently factors into performance in a markedly different way.[25] These subjects require a performative, action-oriented approach to the study of meaning-making in dance.

While there does not seem to be a productive way to push "gesture as inscription" any further, it has been pushed far enough to raise some questions with regard to the received wisdom on the semeiotic character of danced gesturing. Particularly, the claim that dancing has an "ephemeral" communicative nature as a performing art—this spectatorially based assumption of an essential transience for dance's meaning-making capabilities—now can be seen to lose much of its grounding. Understood from an inward perspective, a dancer's body appears as something very much like a living monument to a given technical "discourse," if it is not exactly that. It appears as a durable host, an organism whose "final form" preserves in its very bones the understanding of a certain tradition of intelligent, methodical practice. Moreover, through the institutions of training that insure the reproduction of such bodies, the continuity of the inward semeiotics inscribed by dance traditions, at least in the case of classical dance traditions, can be seen as extending beyond the life span of a single performer and can be measured in terms of generations of dancers. The potential for antiquity for the inward inscription of danced gesturing, in this regard, rivals and even surpasses that of the most durable forms of inscription because the inscription's material host, in this case, can continue to renew and rejuvenate itself and also because inscription becomes an ongoing, perpetually unfinished process even though it has permanent consequences for each individual body entailed to serve its purposes.

The other assumption regarding the dancer's body that is challenged by this inward semeiotic perspective is the universal relevance of the trope of the body as a container accumulating unconscious or nonconscious experience. This was an important trope in Gregory Bateson's work. Bateson argued, somewhat playfully, that consciousness was highly overrated in terms of its contribution to the growth of wisdom in the human species. He tended to conceive of the body as a reservoir for holding vast amounts of experience that had "sunk" beneath conscious awareness. The grace of the classically trained Balinese dancing body in performance evidenced for Bateson the relatively great information-accumulating capability of the body. In Bateson's view, however, this accumulation of knowledge was somehow skill-enhancing by its very existence or presence, even though, and in fact *because*, it remained beyond the grasp of the mover's direct awareness.

Bateson's theories do not preclude or explicitly reject the possibility of a dancer actually remembering and consciously drawing on this "reservoir" of corporeally stored practical knowledge in performance or of being directly aware of and engaging creatively its presence in other contexts. They leave the door open for a very different conceptualization of the body, particularly with respect to the claim that its "ideas" could be "generalized." However, Bateson himself idealized exactly the opposite scenario. The body ideally supported the performance of the conscious mind but *out*performed it in at least two senses of that term, working in a way that was beyond the control of the performer's self-consciousness.[26]

This container-for-nonconsciousness trope is perhaps the hardest to challenge of any regarding the body in western thought, as the convictions that affirm it are among the most deeply held in common sense, or at least in the common sense of those who do not work and think through their bodies in a technically advanced way as a practice of everyday life. Studies of the storage capacity or "muscle 'memory'" of the body, particularly with respect to traumatic experiences repressed from conscious recollection, support this point of view. The body "houses" tensions that are restored to consciousness through therapeutic interventions but that are otherwise locked away "inside" the physical self.

The inward migrations of gestural inscription examined here, however, illuminate a fallacy of the container trope of the body—or at least they expose some limits to its seemingly universal applicability. They challenge the theory of the body as nothing other, semeiotically speaking, than a haven for unconscious processing. As soon as gestures are understood and in fact can be *observed* to be migrating inward, the internality of the body itself, as it *literally* exists, necessarily becomes subject to a very different conceptualization.

What is "inside" the body, as the inscriptions of gesture illuminate, is nothing like "empty space." The internal character of the human being presents nothing that even vaguely resembles a subcutaneous "void," which might serve as a storage tank for repressed, forgotten, or otherwise nonconscious experience. Rather, what is inside the dancer's gesturing body from this perspective is not "sided" *at all.* It is not a "what" at all. It is "inside-*outishly*" structured, perceptually speaking, in consciously developed skeletal-muscular terms. It is a living, historically informed, continuous *movement* of gestural practice. Its tissues are structures that mold and are molded by thinking in action.

The performative monuments into which traditions of dancing render their dancers' bodies, far more so than the materials of inscription's most literal examples, are forms that bring symbols to life. As such, these hosts live to prevent the forgetting, or repressing, or whatever other kind of losing might be posited of what it is that can be actively understood of the gestures that have been inscribed into them. They serve not as a tomb for the dark sides of consciousness but as a constant reminder of the thoughtful practices and principles of conduct that have endowed them with their technical intelligence.

Such a view aligns with a Peircean standpoint on symbols in general and the oft-cited claim Peirce made that "man himself is a sign."[27] Genuinely symbolic signs necessarily entail a presence of mind, a self-analyzing mindfulness that remains aware of the potential for error or misapplication of prior understandings and actions. The authentic symbol, gestural or otherwise, is understood to grow in thoughtfulness as its memory and instances of experimental practice increase its synthesizing faculties.[28] The growth of the symbol produces as a consequence a growth in self-understanding and awareness. It does not lead to "hide-bound habit," as Peirce sometimes characterized the contrasting nonconsciousness-developing case. It leads instead to flexibly adaptive self-control, or "habit-change," as Peirce termed it.[29] The inscription of gestural symbols into a dancer's body, in this regard, would not assume a necessary loss of conscious awareness as a consequence of their inward migration. Rather, it would posit a deepening and expanding of consciousness through the integrative, synthesizing faculty of performance. The feet of a classical ballerina, in this regard, are not understood to be "storing" an inscription *inside* muscle fibers. Rather, their ongoing practice is viewed as intensifying and extending, and continuing to bring *into* or *within* the grasp of consciousness an immense and always changing wealth of recognition gained over the course of a performative history of attempting understanding(s). Such is their commemorative capability as inward moving symbols. Peirce might well have cited them as examples of what he called "ultimate" interpretants[30]—living, purposeful agents of self-controlled, learned conduct. The ultimate interpretant, as Peirce defined it, was "the living definition that grows up in the habit."[31]

These are the challenges, then, that gesture as inscription presents in the case of dance. It calls for a rethinking of the "nature" of the human body and its "parts." It demands a reassessment of the relative significance of the technical/inward and spectatorial/outward dimensions of dance practice in any consideration of the meaning-making capabilities of dance. The phrase calls us to reimagine in a radical way what our gestures are doing in and to ourselves, how they are influencing our conduct both within and beyond the realm of dance, what forms of intelligence they are bringing to our consciousness or molding our consciousness into. Perhaps most important, gesture as inscription reminds us that the body's plastic instrumentality in relation to the human mind and to human thought can never be reduced to any one kind of supporting role. Gesture as inscription challenges us to consider how a gesture can migrate much more deeply into our understanding of ourselves and, more broadly, into the worlds in which we live than we might at first glance, or in our common sense, expect.

Notes

1. Rudolf von Laban quoted in Irmgard Bartenieff, *Body Movement; Coping with the Environment* (New York: Gordon & Breach, 1980), 1.

2. Adrienne Kaeppler's research on Tongan dance, which draws on structural linguistics, is a particularly good example of this pioneering analytical discourse. See, for example, Kaeppler's dissertation, *The Structure of Tongan Dance* (University of Hawaii, 1967).

3. The nonstandard spelling of the term *semeiotic* makes specific reference to Peirce's theory of signs. In this chapter, I draw mainly on three sources for characterizing Peirce's semeiotic: *The Essential Peirce: Selected Philosophical Writings, Volume 2 (1893–1913)*, ed. Peirce Edition Project (Bloomington: Indiana University Press, 1998); *Peirce on Signs*, ed. James Hoopes (Chapel Hill: North Carolina University Press, 1991); and *The Cambridge Companion to Peirce*, ed. Cheryl Misak (Cambridge: Cambridge University Press, 2004). Most of Peirce's work on signs can also be located in the first six volumes of *The Collected Papers of Charles Sanders Peirce*, ed. Charles Hartshorne and Paul Weiss (Cambridge, Mass.: Harvard University Press, 1932).

4. The most well known of the Peircean semeiotic anthropological studies are those by Milton B. Singer (*Man's Glassy Essence: Explorations in Semiotic Anthropology* [Indiana University Press, 1984]; "For a Semiotic Anthropology," in *Sight, Sound, and Sense*, ed. T. A. Sebeok [Bloomington: Indiana University Press, 1978]); Michael Silverstein ("Shifters, Linguistic Categories, and Cultural Description" in *Meaning in Anthropology*, ed. K. Basso and H. Selby [Albuquerque: New Mexico University Press, 1976]); E. V. Daniel (*Fluid Signs; Being a Person the Tamil Way*

[Berkeley: University of California Press, 1984]); and Richard J. Parmentier (*The Sacred Remains: Myth, History, and Polity in Belau* [Chicago: Chicago University Press, 1987]; *Signs in Society: Studies in Semiotic Anthropology* [Bloomington: Indiana University Press, 1994]). With specific regard to Peircean anthropological studies of performance symbolism, see J. Lowell Lewis's study, *Ring of Liberation: Deceptive Discourse in Brazilian Capoeira* (Chicago: Chicago University Press, 1992), and Sally Ann Ness, *Body, Movement, and Culture: Kinesthetic and Visual Symbolism in a Philippine Community* (Philadelphia: Pennsylvania University Press, 1992).

5. For an introductory definition of the icon, index, and symbol as they relate to the triadic character of the Peircean sign, see quotes from Peirce collected in Hoopes, *Peirce on Signs*, 30–31, 183, and 239–40.

6. Hoopes, *Peirce on Signs*, 239, provides one of the more standard of Peirce's many definitions of the triadic sign. It reads, "Anything which determines something else (its *interpretant*) to refer to an object to which itself refers (its *object*) in the same way, the interpretant becoming a sign, and so on *ad infinitum*." For introductory discussions of the Peircean triadic sign, see T. L. Short, "The Development of Peirce's Theory of Signs" (Misak, *The Cambridge Companion to Peirce*, 214–40), and Daniel 's "Introduction" (*Fluid Signs*, 14–40).

7. For a classic example, see A. R. Radcliffe-Brown's graphically detailed analysis of Andaman Islander ritual dance in *The Andaman Islanders* (Glencoe, Ill.: Free Press, 1922). For more recent examples, see the discussion of dance in Edward Schieffelin's study, *The Sorrow of the Lonely and the Burning of the Dancers* (New York: St. Martin's, 1976), and Jerry Leach's film, *Trobriand Cricket an Ingenious Response to Colonialism* (Berkeley: University of California Extension Media Center, 1976). J. Lowell Lewis's study, *Ring of Liberation*, 1992, also emphasizes iconic relationships.

8. I use the nonstandard plural form "indexes" instead of the standard "indices" to mark this term as a technical term in the Peircean framework.

9. Maria Talamantes's dissertation, *The Cultural Politics of Performance: Women, Dance Ritual, and the Transnational Tourism Industry in Bali* (University of California, 2004) provides a discussion of such indexes as evident to Balinese ritual dance performers.

10. Margaret Thompson Drewal's work on Yoruba ritual dance has been seminal in this regard (*Yoruba Ritual: Performers, Play, Agency* [Bloomington: Indiana University Press,1992]). In anthropology, Roy Rappaport (*Ecology, Meaning, and Religion* [Berkeley, Calif.: North Atlantic Books, 1979]) was instrumental in developing this interpretive regard, as was Stanley J. Tambiah ("A Performative Approach

to Ritual," in *Proceedings of the British Academy* 65: 113–69 [1979]). An outstanding example of the historically oriented approach is Jean Commaroff's study of South African ritual performance, *Body of Power, Spirit of Resistance: The Culture and History of a South African People* (Chicago: Chicago University Press, 1985).

11. See Adrienne Kaeppler's "Structured Movement Systems in Tonga" in *Society and the Dance*, ed. Paul Spencer (Cambridge: Cambridge University Press, 1985).

12. The clearest definition of these three symbol types given by Peirce, who defined them in various ways over the course of his work, can be found in Hoopes, *Peirce on Signs*, 30. The definitions used in this chapter paraphrase these definitions. Peirce also invented terms for this triad that are less specifically linked to formal logic: seme, pheme, and delome. While these might have been a better set to use for the purposes of this chapter, I chose not to use them because of their complete lack of familiar reference. For a discussion of these terms in the history of Peirce's semeiotic, see Short (in Misak, *The Cambridge Companion to Peirce*, 225).

13. From "The Normative Sciences" (Harvard Lectures, 1903) in *The Essential Peirce, Vol. 2*, 204.

14. See Short (in Misak, *The Cambridge Companion to Peirce*, 225) on the "force" of propositions/phemes.

15. In some of his discussions of the proposition, Peirce also characterized it as a construction that conjoins a single term with an index so as to assert a real relation holds true between the term and a certain fact. See Hoopes, *Peirce on Signs*, 183.

16. For a more extensive discussion of the research summarized here, see Sally Ann Ness, "Going Back to Bateson: Towards a Semeiotics of (Post-)Ritual Performance," in *Ritual and Event: Interdisciplinary Perspectives*, ed. Mark Franko (London: Routledge, 2007).

17. Gregory Bateson, "Style, Grace and Information in Primitive Art," in *Steps to an Ecology of Mind* (New York: Ballantine Books, 1972), 120.

18. Bateson, "Style, Grace and Information in Primitive Art," 125.

19. While the precise nature of the emergence of "classical" ballet is a matter of debate among dance history scholars, I use the term here to refer generally to the post-Baroque era and specifically to the era defined by the evolution of the toe shoe and point work.

20. Sherry Ortner, in "On Key Symbols" (*American Anthropologist* 75:1338–46 [1973]), coined the phrase "summarizing symbol" to characterize a particular class of key symbols that function to condense an array of meanings for a given domain

of cultural practice into what, from a Peircean standpoint, would be described as a symbolic term.

21. See Wittgenstein's *Philosophical Investigations* (New York: MacMillan, 1968), 194–96. Wittgenstein shows how a single image can be seen as a duck or seen as a rabbit, depending not on how the viewer "sees" it in any phenomenological sense but on how the viewer *thinks through seeing* it. The "aspect" seen, whether it be the duck or the rabbit, appears when the visual experience of the array of shapes, lines, and other features occurs in a certain thoughtful way and with reference to certain objects. Similarly, in the case of the Bharata Natyam dancer's hands, their patterning exhibits two different aspects, one inward and one outward, both a consequence of their practice.

22. Wittgenstein extended the definition of grammar considerably so as to integrate its rules of use with those of practice to as great a degree possible. See discussions throughout *Philosophical Investigations*.

23. Peirce used these term to classify types and aspects of sign-processing that were primarily action-oriented in character. See Short (in Misak, *The Cambridge Companion to Peirce*), 222–37, and selected comments from Peirce in *The Essential Peirce, Vol. 2* (1998), pp. 430, 490–502.

24. "Actuality" is one of three "Modes of Being" Peirce identified for signs. It contrasts with the modes of "Possibility" and "Generality" (or "Necessity"). Symbols have aspects that relate to all three modes but not always with equal significance. See Peirce's comments on signs and the modes of being in *The Essential Peirce, Vol. 2* (1998), 480–81.

25. Peirce drew a very strong distinction between human action—in the sense typified by reflex re-actions—and human imagination. He characterized the former as relatively mindless and automatic, and the latter as the basis of human thought, inner consciousness, and eventually logic and linguistic symbolism. See Vincent M. Colapietro's *Peirce's Approach to the Self: A Semiotic Perspective on Human Subjectivity* (Albany: State University of New York Press, 1989, 114) for a more extensive account of this contrast. The contrast appears to create a pronounced mind–body split in Peirce's general theoretical approach. However, numerous writings by Peirce strongly contradict that interpretation. In this regard, I use the concept of "movement" in my discussion—as did Peirce in many instances—to define an alternative to "action" that has the capability of being both physical (or incarnate or corporeal or bodily) and thoughtful or imaginative. "Movement," in contrast to "action," allows a way of conceptualizing how gestures, as performative

processes (not instantaneous "acts"), can in some cases achieve an integration, and over time an "inscription," of imaginative thought and the actions of active bodily terms. In the cases here examined, the thoughtful aspect is derived from imaginative sources external to individual dancer's selves. Classical dance training, in this perspective, *moves* its own traditions of term-relational semeiotics *in*ward. Such processes could even be seen in some cases as encroaching into a host (a person) who would otherwise be developing a more individual, private, or "internal" imaginative life.

26. In this regard, Bateson's theories aligned closely with those of Pierre Bourdieu, although they left more room for a Peircean perspective on the integrated human Sign to emerge as well. See Ness, "Going Back to Bateson," for a more lengthy discussion of this comparison.

27. See, for example, Milton B. Singer's discussions throughout *Man's Glassy Essence.* See also Colapietro's extensive discussions of this claim as they appear throughout his volume *Peirce's Approach to the Self.*

28. On the relation of cognition, consciousness, and the triadic sign types, see Hoope's presentation of Peirce's Manuscript 901 (*Peirce on Signs,*180–85). The ideas expressed in my discussion relate "consciousness" to Peirce's discussions of the symbol in relation to an active, alert, attentive, thinking mind, which, while it is not the exact equivalent of "consciousness," is how Peirce tended to define consciousness. Colapietro (*Peirce's Approach to the Self,* 41, 54–55, 57, 88, 99, 101) provides more extensive discussions of the concept of consciousness in relation to Peirce's theories of mind, thought, and human subjectivity, and his work serves as my guide here. To summarize Colapietro's arguments, Peirce rejected a "subjectivist" theory of consciousness, arguing against early psychological (Jamesian) views of consciousness that posited it as an isolated, private, and natural condition of an individual interior mental life. Peirce's theory of consciousness characterizes consciousness more as an achievement than a given, more public and shared than private, and most important for the purposes of this chapter, tending to develop as a semeiotic movement inward, from external sources of meaning toward internal, private ones, as the processes of inscription here would exemplify.

29. See Misak's introduction to Peirce's semeiotic and the concept of "habit-change" (*The Cambridge Companion to Peirce,* 10).

30. See Short (in Misak, *The Cambridge Companion to Peirce,* 225–35) for a discussion of the ultimate Interpretant in relation to other types.

31. See Short (in Misak, *The Cambridge Companion to Peirce,* 228).

CHAPTER 2

Physical Graffiti West: African American Gang Walks and Semiotic Practice

Susan A. Phillips

Imagine a kid propelling himself through space. Though he slaps his hands periodically on the soles of his shoes, his feet rarely leave the ground. The root of his motion is nearly invisible as he furthers himself heel-to-toe across the dance floor from left to right, facing first north, then south and east and west. The music pumps, and his right foot gently touches the ground as he moves, the meaning of its tricks and turns not escaping the practiced eye. The dance he does is more or less unique among the world's cultures, because the boy is not simply dancing. He is writing. The writing he does with his feet is so subtle that one might miss it altogether. In his dance, the boy spells the initials PJWC, for PJ Watts Crips, or alternatively BSC, for Bull Side Crips, representing the neighborhood and the side of the Imperial Courts housing projects where he is from.

The dance is called the Crip Walk. More generically, I refer to it as gang walking because, as one man told me, "Bloods have they own way of putting it down; Crips have they own way of putting it down. If you a Crip, it's called C-walking; if you a Blood, it's called B-walking." For the purposes of this chapter, he said, "Just call it 'gang walking.'" Sometimes individual neighborhoods have different names for their dances. Blood Stone Villains do the "Villain Dance"; Pueblo Bishops do the "Pueblo Stroll." In gang walking, feet become the media of production as gang members spell out nicknames, affiliations, enemies, or even memorials to the dead. Such mimetic acts anchor signification in rhythm, motion, and emotion. They make writing into an evanescent, gestural performance that works akin to a "physical graffiti" indelibly tied to the body and to broader forms of gang signification.[1] If Robert Farris Thompson regards the art history of Africa as a history of "danced" art,[2] then African American gang history offers the art of danced writing—indeed, with gang walking, they become one and the same thing.

In this chapter, I review three interrelated social locations that frame the multiple, sometimes contradictory meanings of gang walking in Los Angeles. First is the world of African American dance, whose innovations and trends have roots in African and creolized expressive formats. Today, the contexts of violent oppression and overt cultural genocide that made dance a critical medium for survival have changed. But because the gang members who invented gang walks are African Americans themselves, they are cultural inheritors of the strength and position of dance in their communities. They are also physical messengers of a corporeal knowledge that includes specific movements, routines, and dance traditions and that demonstrates remarkable carryover from preslavery Africa to the present. I spend quite a bit of time with this history of danced expression as well as with the white response to and participation in these forms. This history helps frame what happens in Los Angeles through contrast and comparison.

The second social location is the gang life, in which gang members represent a complex written system through multiple media such as hand signing, graffiti, and tattoo. Through these written media, gang members respond not only to one another but to persistent segregation, multiple marginality, and cultural erasure. For gang members, erasure is literally not an option. As Barry Sanders suggests in his book *A is for Ox*, "On the streets, erasure spells death. . . . Street life offers no time for revision."[3] Sanders's concept is supported by the rhythmic physicality of gang dancers, who light up a party, bring challenge to a club, or brighten a florescent dayroom in juvenile hall. Gang walking is nothing if not celebratory and competitive, playful and mournful, written and oral. Because of the pervasiveness of violence and death in gang culture, I also analyze the dance with regard to these concepts.

The third social location I discuss is the co-opted space of popular dance floors, rap music videos, and the Internet, specifically comparing this global aesthetic migration to the dance's aesthetic migration through African American history. Gang members' participation in hip hop through gangsta rap has brought the Crip Walk specifically and gang dancing in general into popular focus, where it has been "discovered" and subsequently "dropped" as a popular dance craze. The C-Walk's depiction in rap music videos played on Black Entertainment Television, MTV, or DVD concert releases in the United States has generated overwhelming popular interest in this "new" form of rap-based movement. The pattern of co-option has perhaps as rich a cultural history as do the dances themselves, even if the process of "taking over" radically shifts or loses meaning along the way.

I examine each of these three social locations in turn to discuss the power of gestural patterns and their migration through urban space and time. Dance historian Thomas DeFrantz has posed the critical question of "where we dance" and its implications for African American culture.[4] During the slave trade and on the plantation, the context of explicit, oppressive violence framed dance as a form of resistance informed by markedly spiritual dimensions of African dance, as well as creolized roots in specific movement traditions: Scotch-Irish jigs, American Indian dance, and West African dance. Within this creolized history, dance is inseparable from other forms of African American expressive culture such as oral tradition, music, and drumming. DeFrantz writes that, "As we recover and interpret details of these processes across historical eras and geographies, we pay homage to an ancestral legacy of direct participation in the arts, to the life-affirming choreographies that have sustained and nurtured African American corporeality."[5] For gangs, the body is both receptor and author of violence as well as creativity, both of which must be considered in any analysis of gang expressive culture.

In the gang world, representing gang affiliation causes conflict that can and does routinely destroy people's lives. Here, violence is directly linked to aesthetic and performative issues. But gang members also experience symbolic and structural violence through the various policies and institutions of the larger society. Included among these institutions is writing itself: an exclusionary practice in which society embeds ultimate control over knowledge systems. Barry Sanders, for example, regards gang violence as a "struggle over literacy" as much it is over territory. Similarly, for anthropologist Dwight Conquergood, "'Local' and 'vernacular' are not strong enough adjectives to capture the moral outrage and repression that this literacy practice provokes. Graffiti writing is a counterliteracy that . . . must be situated within the discursive and visual practices of power and control that it struggles against."[6] Claude Levi-Strauss long ago recognized colonization, control, and enslavement as key aspects of writing.[7] When gang members take writing into their own hands—into their very bodies—they dance a reversal. They reframe Levi-Strauss's equation by turning exclusivity around on those who would usually practice it.

In gang dance, extensive word-based symbolism cross cuts expressive genres, commingling cultural truths about social position. This chapter examines how gang members mix, combine, and repeat fluid forms of expression, paying particular attention to the way that gang dancers embody the production of letters themselves. As writing fuses with the body in this stylized performance, gang members bind what is supposedly insulated from physicality (writing) to the very epicenter of sensation, feeling, and emotion (the body).

From Cake Walk to Crip Walk

What are the historical specificities, aesthetic considerations, and sociopolitical underpinnings of gang dancing in Los Angeles? Here, I am specifically concerned with how people have used dance—particularly strategies of mimesis in dance—to transform would-be moments of cultural erasure and social death into moments of cultural cohesion and social life. Such transformations have occurred throughout the history of African American dance, and they are far from purely oppositional. Just as the slave's body in motion is more than simply a site of labor production, dance allows a complex negotiation between oppression and self-authorship, pain and deliverance, play and sadness. Mimicry and mimesis render these dualities into far more complex cultural histories that people continually reinscribe, reenact, and revisit through gesture. This section examines some threads weaving together the rich gestural history of African American dance to set the stage for its entrance into the gang world.[8]

Many authors have examined how features of African artistic traditions survived the migration from Africa to the United States and how dance and community were transformed by it. During the slave trade, for example, white slave masters and slave-ship captains used dance to reinforce the master–slave relationship. Several authors describe brutal shipboard rituals of "dancing the slaves" by forcing their "cargo" to dance and jump around in order to insure their healthy arrival.[9] Such efforts ultimately were more representative of physical domination than of concern for health when one considers that roughly one-quarter to one-half of a ship's "cargo" died en route. As historian P. Sterling Stuckey has written, ". . . to dance with such scars on one's body meant that no matter how true to traditional dance forms a particular African dance was, a new history of dance had begun."[10] Part of this new history had to do with the white reaction to African dance as entertainment, as an exotic form to be owned, wantonly wallowed in, and sometimes co-opted in a manner that complicated images of alterity between the two populations.

In dance are core issues of African American identity and of the institutionalized violence intertwined with that identity. Violence is an ever-changing symbolic, structural, and physical aspect of American identity. It is also part of the cycle of mimesis and co-option. There are no one-to-one equations here; violence and dance are not equivalent to themselves or to each other through time. Violence, however, necessarily accompanies the fact that identity is self-ascribed. In the Crip Walk, identity—and thus violence itself—are what end up being co-opted through the imitation of physical expression and somatic knowledge.

In the United States, American slave owners ethnocentrically framed slave dances within familiar terms—as a pleasant pastime wholly divorced from daily or religious concerns. For them, dancing was the most popular amusement of the day. It was thus one of the few avenues of expression that slave masters actually encouraged. African slaves, however, had come out of a tradition in which dance was far more than entertainment. Stuckey's treatment of the Ring-Dance, for example, argues that meaning in dance was particularly difficult to "see" because of the links between sacred and secular in African—and now African American—culture, links that remained invisible to slave masters who compartmentalized such aspects of their lives. In the Ring-Dance, American slaves used specific ancestral body movements such as bending knees or shuffling feet to mask sacred concerns from masters who would otherwise prohibit non-Christian styles of worship. Slave masters altogether failed to recognize that dance was an expression of the sacred, or even that the shuffling movements of the feet were dance at all. Such marked cognitive gaps left openings for the genesis of new cultural meanings. Because dancers could silence, halt, or render invisible such dances, dance became a primary vehicle for the continuation of religion, of African community, and in the process, of making identity.[11] "Keep dem knee bones bent," not crossing the feet (as this was how whites danced their jigs), or shuffling (moving without taking the feet off the floor) all recall the sacred nature of daily life that blends sacred and profane concerns. Such seemingly simple motions anchored African American identity in the earth itself.[12]

Slaves also powerfully transformed mimetic dance traditions rooted in Africa to mitigate the corporeal terms of their oppression. According to Katrina Hazzard-Gordon, many slave dances mimed aspects of their daily labors, reclaiming actions of the workday such as "pitchin' hay," "corn shucking," "cutting wheat," and loading cotton. Hazzard-Gordon emphasizes the African roots of this mimetic strategy, noting that many African dances "celebrated through imitation" work routines, changes of season, physical labor of all kinds.[13] Through dance, slaves ritually re-created the work they were being forced to do. In the same motions, then, resided not only a somatic ancestral history but an ongoing motion of labor born and bred from the violent circumstances of their lives. Whereas resistance theory tends to assume any form of difference to be opposition, throughout dance, resistance instead resides in sameness, in imitation. Mimesis here is interesting because of the unresolved questions about its possible interpretive recipe: what parts hostility, anger, love, sweat, tradition, domination, belief, or acceptance reside in this identity? In these gestures? In these dances? In a sense, these aspects of identity are not simply divisible, nor are they shared among all culture practitioners.

Several authors write about balance as a theme within the diaspora and of opposites being rendered into unity.[14] As Hazzard-Gordon writes, a "balance is achieved through the combination of opposites. Although dancers may be performing a fury of complex steps or figures, they must never lose equilibrium or control."[15] Through dance, slaves were thus taking control of what was forced upon them (work) in part by integrating it into traditions rooted in preslavery Africa—a far from simple process informed primarily by the violence of their lives.

Balancing the loss of control was thus a feature of slave life and a key to dance within African American slave communities. Slave masters were aware that indeed any form of communal expression could foment insurrection among slaves; the covert nature of much of African American communication during this time was a prominent survival strategy for slave culture as a whole. Slave owners realized that "drums which beat for dances could also call to revolt,"[16] which caused drums to be outlawed in some states. Slaves adapted "quieter" drums and indeed began to use their very bodies to slap, blow, and clap out a rhythm. Here the balancing act is corporeal as well as visual: the ability to be invisible and visible at the same time.[17] Consider Deborah Gray White, who writes that "the best defense against unpredictability [in the slave world] was silence, the key to secrecy. It kept masters ignorant of everything that went on behind their backs. [. . .] Silence protected the slave quarters. It kept the slave family and the slave's religious life removed from white invasion."[18] But the "invasion" to which White refers could not be staved off for long.

The Cake Walk[19] was the first dance that whites co-opted as their own. It was a popular African American dance form from 1850 to 1920 and would set the trend for futures of dance co-option and the reinterpretation of encoded symbolism eventually found in the Crip Walk. The "Walk" part of the dance had its origins with Seminole Indians in Florida, where couples engaged in a ritual of slow, controlled walking. Transferred to the plantation, the Chalk Line Walk, as it was originally called, featured walkers balancing buckets of water on their heads (a common African dance tradition). They would then walk straight or curvy lines drawn on the floor, attempting to spill as little water as possible. Eventually, the Cake Walk became a ritualized mockery of white high society. The movements that defined the Walk were miming gestures that essentialized the rigid white aristocracy of the "Big House": tipping hats, walking in a dignified manner, bowing, strutting, brandishing canes. Slaves selected movements alien to their own culture: straight, stiff limbs in contrast to their bent, fluid ones. Slave owners naively read these dances as aspiration rather than as parody. For slaves, "gimme dem kneebone bent" was a plea against death itself. The African belief was that straight joints were a likeness of dead bodies. Animating the body was akin to life; stiffening it, to death. In this sense, by taking on the characteristics of white dancers, slaves instead owned white people and controlled the movements of death, thus countering the social death of slavery.

Throughout his work on the Cuna of Panama, anthropologist Michael Taussig emphasizes his interest not in why people engage in mimetic behavior linked to colonial power, such as described previously, but in why whites/colonists are so particularly fascinated by imitations of themselves. "In some way," as Taussig titles his initial chapter in *Mimesis and Alterity*, "one can protect oneself from the spirits by portraying them."[20] On slave plantations in the American South, dance served the dual and contradictory purposes of bonding slaves together and entertaining their masters. This equation perhaps proved true for both blacks and whites alike. African Americans in the United States faced an even more dramatic cultural erasure than the Cuna because of slavery. But slaves' use of the mimetic faculty and their masters' fascination with that faculty is deeply parallel to the Cuna case to the point of explicit co-option. With the Cake Walk began a pattern of co-option through mimesis that would persist throughout slavery to the present day.

With its cotillion-based imitations, the Cake Walk developed to involve weekly contests wherein slaves were summoned to compete before their white audience-masters, fascinated in true Taussigian fashion by imitations of themselves. The finest walkers would "take the cake" as a reward for the best performance. Cake Walks eventually comprised regional or statewide competitions, and popular sheet music of the day featured the "Negro Aristocracy" in full gowns and tuxedos. By the 1900s, the Cake Walk had become a veritable dance "craze"—spreading all over the South and Northeast among blacks and whites alike. While whites had always participated to some degree in slave dances, the Cake Walk was the first that involved a crossover between the two cultures informed by such power-laden mimetic images.

Strategic role reversal and reverse mimicry accompanied this dance craze as practiced by both blacks and whites. For example, whites would sometimes perform the Cake Walk in blackface as part of the larger minstrel project of fascination-cum-rejection of black culture. Postslavery, minstrelsy—like dance before it—had become the single most popular form of entertainment, cementing stereotypes of African Americans in the popular imagination. With the end of slavery, the "official order of white supremacy remained unstable and demanded, as a condition of its continuance, that the grand narrative of racial domination be ritually reenacted."[21] In the case of the Cake Walk, the ritual reenactment involved mimesis at several levels, a changing history of imitation and co-option, and an ever-returning struggle over power concerning the interpretation of racialized place and identity. Through dance, power relations were performed, enacted, reproduced, endlessly twisted. The play twisted yet again as African American Cake Walkers corked blackface over their already dark skins, exaggerating lip size and color with characteristic red and white makeup.

Here, the meaning of segregation was communicated by bodies as entertainment—bodies that moved in particular ways, to particular rhythms, with particular gestures, in front of particular audiences. With the Cake Walk, the pattern of co-option complicated the master–slave legacy through double-reverse mimicry (you imitate me, I imitate you imitating me, you imitate me imitating you imitating me). While slaves mimed their white masters through dance, white masters unwittingly imitated slave parodies of themselves, of their own cotillion-based dances, providing a power-laden intertextuality through movement. When white audience-master crossed over to become practitioner, the white possession of both slave and slave dance cemented positions of alterity in a manner that complicated rather than simplified. The black minstrel in blackface also deconstructed the black–white duality: "Because my feet are gay with dancing, you do not know I die?" writes Langston Hughes in his poem, *The Dream Keeper.*[22] In Hughes's sense, dance conflates play and sadness in a manner that belies the minstrel's simplistic demeanor. It is not simply a question of life and death—of dance or death—but rather the complication of embodying such complex contradictions within one's very soul. Here, a line of gestural sympathy connects white and black—that flash of recognition that Taussig says informs the mimetic faculty. This theme emerges in later forms of gang expression, which I address in a later section.

In the free North, African American dance traditions continued to grow and change as contexts for dancing became increasingly urban. In the twentieth century, violent oppression was no longer institutionalized through slavery but through bureaucracy. The "Big House" was now the prison. African Americans remained racially segregated, marginalized in areas of health, education, economy, and basic infrastructure.[23] Again, the "ghetto" was both damned and strengthened by enforced isolation, and its residents gave rise to expressive traditions that continued to represent the cultural specificities linking creativity and oppression.[24] A host of walks, steps, shuffles, and stomps emerged from the common forms of Jitterbugging and Lindy Hopping, from jazz and blues music. "Walks" continued to be popular forms of dance, and walk names alone attest to the ongoing mimetic quality of dance movements: Camel Walk, Palmer House Walk, Ditty Bop Walk, Pimp Walk, Papa Dee Walk, Lambeth Walk, Pirate's Walk, Continental Walk, and Crab Walk.[25] (Today's Blood gang members would be particularly pleased with this last, as Crab is a derogatory nickname, or "disname," for their archrivals, the Crips.)

The Bronx of the 1970s, with its bombed-out buildings, burned-out cars, vacant lots, and colorless winters gave birth to yet another incarnation of urban expression that had dance as a centerpiece. Artist Claes Oldenberg described the train-based graffiti of the period as a "bouquet from Latin America" lighting up the dank subway interiors.[26] Instead of the slave-era triumvirate of oral tradition, drumming, and music, break dancing entered as part of the infamous threesome of deejaying (scratching records), emceeing (rapping), and writing graffiti.[27] Like its predecessor forms, hip hop was characteristically hybrid and newly spacialized in an urban environment. Instead of laying out planks on dirt, breakers spread out cardboard on blacktop or concrete. Disenfranchized black and Puerto

Rican kids began to focus on the centrality of writing—of the name—which Norman Mailer famously termed the "faith" of graffiti.[28] Tricia Rose writes that the hip hop empowered kids so that "each asserted the right to write—to inscribe one's identity on an environment that seemed Teflon resistant to its young people of color; an environment that made legitimate avenues for material and social participation inaccessible.[29] While everything around them attempted to erase their identity, the city itself became the locus where they began to "talk back" through expressive culture.[30]

Sally Banes's landmark *Village Voice* article, "Physical Graffiti: Breaking Is Hard to Do," begins with an account of two kids being hassled by police. "We're not fighting," they insist, "we're dancing!" The cops look on, scratching their heads. Then they variously demand a "helicopter," "head spin," or "chin freeze." Banes writes that breaking is a "competitive display of physical and imaginative virtuosity, a codified dance-form-cum-warfare that cracks open to flaunt personal inventiveness."[31] Performing the name and linking it to mimetic, freeze-frame strategies becomes part of a competitive tradition between dancers. At the time of hip hop's inception, performance of this kind helped to mediate gang warfare, which New York had been struggling with for decades.

Tricia Rose describes hip hop culture's debt to Afro-diasporic expressive traditions, tracing it through rap music in particular. But she is adamant that rap and related elements are not only about such traditions. She argues that we instead must see the city itself—its streets and technologies, sights and sounds—as a staging ground for hip hop as a whole. In urban space, "Hip hop replicates and reimagines the experiences of urban life and symbolically appropriates urban space though sampling, dance, style, and sound effects."[32] Rose describes how all forms of hip hop share three central principles: flow, layering, and ruptures in line. For break dancing, she writes that "popping and locking are moves in which the joints are snapped abruptly into angular positions . . . creating a semiliquid effect that moves the energy toward the fingertip or toe. . . . Abrupt, fractured yet graceful footwork leaves the eye one step behind in motion, creating a time-lapse effect that not only mimics graffiti's use of line shadowing but also creates spatial links between the moves that gives the foot series flow and fluidity."[33]

In Rose's three principles, planning the rupture on one's own is a manner of taking possession of life in which most ruptures are in the hands of others.

At a literal level, the miming of break dancers took many forms, including agrarian references to rural life (still milking, shucking, pitching, and hoeing after all these years).[34] Breakers pretended to row boats, to perform CPR on one another, or to fight—all mimetic features that merge competition with cooperation. A primary mime within breaking was competition itself, in which "breakers double each other's moves . . . [and] intertwine their bodies into elaborate shapes, transforming the body into a new entity."[35] While the South Bronx gave birth to the Electric Boogie, the West Coast also contributed to the development of breaking. Los Angeles was the infamous home of pop-locking, and according to Robert Farris Thompson, the city of Fresno contributed the Electric Boogaloo, which Thompson linked tentatively to the "jerking and trembling" of church women taken by the Holy Spirit. For a Fresno dancer, according to Thompson, doing the Boogaloo meant that "he could master anything. It meant that he could even mime electricity, pass it through his body and put his own stamp on it."[36]

Thompson describes an encounter with a young man who had just performed at a New York breaking contest he had attended. He describes how the young man used his body to "aim energy at me" in a gesture of hip hop appreciation. Here, breakers use bodily movements to communicate, to spread messages that soon exceed the body's physical sphere. As the dancer pushes messages out of the body, he acts as if the message is independent of a body at all, as if it can move through space to land in the body of another. This bodily articulation and disarticulation allows dancers to create a line of sympathy (in Frazer's terms), an invisible connection that momentarily ties them together and that creates challenge between them. Within such battles, dancers playfully take command of the life force itself: electricity.

When breaking hit the mainstream in 1981, part of its allure was predictably lost. Its pirate electricity had been diverted to the feet and arms of people who were already all paid up. Unlike the Cake Walk, the cooption, this time, was not of a wholly "black" cultural form but of rather a multicultural urban one, which included Puerto Ricans, blacks, and whites alike.[37] By the time the landmark hip hop film *Style Wars*[38] was made, break dancing was performing CPR on itself, reviving itself from a death as sure as that of the writing on the New York subways, whose protectors sought gleaming white protection from the blight, not the bouquet, of graffiti flowers. Despite these localized losses, hip hop underwent a transformation. Begun by primarily black and brown kids in the streets of New York, it had become a truly global medium that comprised both an underground, sometimes illegal culture as well as a semi-sanctified multibillion dollar industry (sacred and profane meet in the postindustrial landscape). Kids from all races and classes, and from most countries of the world, were now finding their own meanings in the movements and strategies of the globalized hip hop movement.

From the slave trade to the present, elements of African dance have been transformed by cities, migrations, and relationships of oppression. In the midst of consistent exclusion, dance complicates social life, reclaims domination, recalls history, and provides cultural cohesion through practice. Within contexts of ever-present change, people use dance to comment on social position, to generate new styles of motion, and to invent new meanings for movements based in older formats. And so the names roll off the tongue: the Walk-Around, Juba, Jim Crow, Kongo, Breakdown, Alabama Kick-up, Ring-Shout, Electric Boogie, Electric Boogaloo, the Freeze. In Los Angeles today we have the Cry-baby, the Clown Walk, the Old Man Walk, the Harlem Shake. Consider briefly one last dance of the 1850s minstrel era, the Essence Dance, which Emery describes as the "movement of the heels and toes without changing the position of the legs so that the performer appeared to glide across the floor."[39] Visualizing this motion helps to recall something, finally, familiar—here is a dance we all recognize. This particular configuration of movement, combined with tracing letter shapes with the right foot while moving across the floor from left to right, is the founding principle of gang walking as practiced in most Los Angeles neighborhoods.

Physical Graffiti West

If Sally Banes used the title "physical graffiti" metaphorically to describe break dancing, then Los Angeles gangs members took her message literally.

As with gang identity itself, gang writing-while-dancing predated the arrival of hip hop to Los Angeles. Members of the Crips, founded in 1969, began doing it during the early seventies. According to one man I interviewed, the dance was simpler then:

> The writing the names been out since the C-Walk been out, since Crippin been out, since they had Crip dances. They always been doin' it like that. Writing names out. They would spell out "Crip," that was their thing. As time change, everything change on it. Now they have a new way that they do. They put a little more jiggy with it, a little more extras on it. The changing of the names to regular names all came out with the new way of C-Walking. They write more specific names, like they sets [gang cliques] out, now. It grew. It went from just doing a regular dance, from regular Crip Walking, to a whole different atmosphere of it, where they putting names in it and spelling they homies' names out. It graduated to a different level.

In the mainstream media, the Crip Walk has been called "dancing on crack" or "the hottest dance craze since the Cabbage Patch."[40] It's rumored that it began as a celebratory dance for gang members who were victorious over rivals in violent confrontation. The dance has been banned at high schools precisely because of its links to gang culture and its presumed relationship to violence. Although police have never been able to link Crip Walking to any specific acts of violence, the ban remains in place. The *Los Angeles Times* quoted the principal at Crenshaw High, for example, as saying, "Crip Walking is a no-no. We tell students you might be somewhere doing that dance and it could end your life, or get you seriously hurt."[41]

People outside of gang culture have learned about the C-Walk through hip hop performers like Kurupt, Snoop Dogg, and Lil Bow Wow. In gang culture, however, Crip Walking is more than just for Crips. It's Blood Walking, it's Coast Walkin, it's Villain dancing, it's Pueblo Strolling. It's C-Walking in the PJ's, or on Grape Street. All of these moves do the work of using dance to write out a particular gang name either as a whole or in initial form. A Blood told me of these dances:

> Really they go by whatever set you claim. If they East Coast Crips, they coast walking. If they 6-0s, they do rollin walking [Rollin 60s Crips]. Gangsters been doing that dance forever, since gang banging started. As far as recalling different sets in different gangs, when we were young, we was always in our neighborhood. But when you start to get out, you start getting to see different things, different neighborhoods.

Gangs in Los Angeles developed as early as the 1940s among primarily Mexican and Black youths. African Americans had more individualized traditions of street hustlers and individual pimp-style daddies, but their proximity to well-established pachuco gangs such as 38th Street offered more collectivized models of street cohesion. But if Mexican kids helped to establish a pattern of collective identity, white kids drove it more forcefully into existence. By the 1950s, gangs in the black community arose in part as a response to white racism, with gangs of whites like the so-called Spook Hunters targeting black kids on their way home from school.[42] Today, gangs are close to what Marcel Mauss termed a "total social system."[43] They have their own internal systems of economy and politics, as well as socialization in the symbols of their culture that often begins in early childhood. Some gang families are now entering their fourth and fifth generations.[44] Within this self-consciously independent social system, gang members have developed a comprehensive system of writing, which also focuses their activities in dance.

The first wave of established gangs in the 1950s and 1960s arose just a stone's throw away from the Central Avenue Jazz district. This area was ruled by racial housing covenants and redlining practices, which kept blacks very firmly in the boundaries of what would later be called South Central L.A. The Slausons, Businessmen, Gladiators, Graduates, Ditalians, and Bishops were gangs from this first generation that eventually morphed into more politicized street entities, this time with the Black Panthers as their model.[45] But even they had their dances. Members of the Slauson Village gang, for example, danced what they called the Slauson Shuffle. It involved no writing but rather shared common movement to a theme song. After the Watts riots in 1965, Black gangs remained unified until 1969, with the birth of the Crips and the present dualistic gang structure.

Among the present generation of African American gangs—Bloods and Crips—dance became a form of symbolism more than just peripherally associated with writing. Instead, gangs took dance to a level at which the body, physically and iconically, represented actual letters. Gang walks are thus quite literally what Michel de Certeau terms "pedestrian speech acts," points "of articulation between human behavior and the built environment . . . [where] bodies follow the thicks and thins of an urban 'text' they write without being able to read it."[46] Gang members have sought and captured social power through the creation of an internalized, blanketing structure that unifies geographically disperse gang entities into sharing a particular culture of gangs. Gang cultural expression is rooted in both the material and the gestural; situated in place and on the body. A complex system of gang writing is represented in tattoo, hand signing (sometimes called "stacking), graffiti, dress, speech, and in manners of gestural storytelling (sometimes also called "stacking") and dance. Even such gestures as nodding the head in specific ways, slamming down dominoes, or gathering in a group to shoot craps all reinforce gang culture and identity—they also weave in and out of African American vernacular culture as a whole. Evidenced in these media is what anthropologist Dwight Conquergood terms "reciprocal doubling," an intermodality whereby identical symbols are repeated in different formats, in a variety of media, or through hostile or affirmative dialogs whose goals are to represent the gang and thus bring it to life.[47]

In the front yard, on the street, at parties or clubs, gang walking is very much part of what Robert Farris Thompson refers to as a "canon of motion" rooted in Afro-diasporic tradition.[48] As with much of vernacular dance in general, gestural strategies such as miming, dancing flat-footed (rarely lifting the feet from the ground), and creative competition all hearken back to decidedly African styles. The name "walk" itself also clearly derives from slave traditions, as detailed in the previous section. But the rich history from slavery through the present is not the only reason gang-expressive culture sometimes seems "African." It is not at all why gang members often discuss in-fighting as "tribalism" or why they trace the violence embedded in their culture to preslave Africa.

Gangs seem African for reasons that have to do with the structural position of gangs themselves within a very modern society. Although they have arisen in a complex, urban society, their own internal structure is generally acephalous, or leaderless. Although these structures are not a direct legacy from Africa, they are classically African in one sense. For if one returns to one's Fortes and Evans-Prichard,[49] one will find that Los Angeles gangs, like the Nuer, are a "type b"—a social group segmented and opposed in much the same manner as are many of the so-called tribes of Africa, New Guinea, Australia, Asia, and indigenous North America. With these groups as with gangs, dance and the arts are seamlessly interwoven with daily concerns, both spiritual and secular. In Africa and Los Angeles, then, dance is one medium that "translates everyday life experiences into movement"[50] and that blends visual, spoken, tactile, rhythmic, and emotive concerns. Its tie to social life is intimate. Seen in this way, gang cultural expression has more in common with artistic traditions among the Maori, Kwakiutl, Maasai, and Bedouin than it does to, say, African American pictorial art in the United States. Conquergood's notion of reciprocal doubling is consistent with Thompson's canon in which similar principles are continually expressed through multiple formats. For Thompson, "[T]he dancer moves, in part, to bring alive their name."[51] To bring the name alive is a key feature of what it means to "represent" a gang. A historical legacy certainly resides in the gestures that comprise gang dancing—that is part of the point of this treatment. But gang-expressive culture seems doubly African for reasons of structure and inequality in addition to this rich somatic history.

Like African American traditions before it, gang dancing houses a mimetic tradition. Through mimesis, gang members integrate myriad concerns into the dance—fighting, death, neighborhood, doing double-Dutch jump rope, writing graffiti, dusting off shoes, shooting craps. At least in one neighborhood, dancers sometimes break away from their routines to mime writing on the floor with their fingers. In the process, gang dancers create an essential set of experiences around which their lives are symbolically anchored. Gang members use feet and hands—alone and in combination—either to trace out letter shapes, to mime the act of writing (spray painting), or even to mime the act of Crip Walking itself by dancing with two fingers, representing another's feet, on the floor. Such practices create a meta-discourse of the dance that comments about positionality, hostility, mourning, and death within gang culture.

At one film shoot in June 2005, a group of "y-g's" (young guns) from the Pueblo Bishops Bloods neighborhood was loosely gathered and partially intoxicated—drawn together haphazardly, almost unwillingly, by speakers pumping homegrown rap. The possibility of a photograph brought the participants into sharper focus, giving them a momentary surge of collective energy. They tightened up, threw up hand signs, and shouted out, creating a *tableau vivant* of gang culture in which each person worked in visual concert with the next. Soon, a man emerged from the group as if from the very fabric of social life. A red bandana covered his face. Even as he fought the constant downward motion of his baggy pants, the man moved fluidly from left to right—the concrete, his canvas; his right foot, a stylus. He spelled the letters P-U-E-B-L-O to represent his neighborhood. All the while, he kept a hand over his crotch—as much a gesture of male identity as to keep his pants from a further slide. He communicated the same identity for which his homies provided the backdrop. His choreography was both written and oral, individual and collective, a complex carnal and semiotic performance that unified literacy with the dance.

Joseph Roach analyzes Kenyan novelist and director Ngũgĩ wa Thiong'o's notion of "orature." According to Roach,

> Orature comprises a range of forms, which, though they may invest themselves variously in gesture, song, dance, processions, storytelling, proverbs, gossip, customs, rites, and rituals, are nevertheless produced alongside or within mediated literacies of various kinds and degrees. In other words, orature goes beyond a schematized opposition of literacy and orality as transcendent categories; rather, it acknowledges that these modes of communication have produced one another interactively over time and that their historic operations may be usefully examined under the rubric of performance.[52]

The rubric of performance to which Roach refers necessitates some thought about what it means to write in a culture that largely acts like an oral one. For gangs, personal prowess is always in the name of something larger, which is the gang. Conversely, the history of hip hop is rife with individuals: names like KRS1, Futura 2000, Crazy Legs. The history of gangs is quite different. The names are all collective: Rollin 60s, East Coast Crips, Bounty Hunters, Pueblo Bishops, Black P. Stones. As with the man who danced the letters P-U-E-B-L-O, individual power generally furthers the goals, name, and reputation of the gang project. Collectivism is again what makes gangs sometimes exhibit seemingly "African" tendencies. They frequently act more like traditional oral or folk cultures because this collectivism saturates every aspect of material and expressive culture, including dance. In spelling out his gang name, the dancer thus demonstrates how gangs ride the line between oral and literate cultures, exhibiting elements of both without completely dissolving the divide.

Recall Tricia Rose's analysis of hip hop in which she determines that flow, layering, and ruptures in line are linking principles across hip hop genres. That hip hop genres include music, movement, and the visual art already links them to the diaspora. But whereas all of Rose's categories are about movement and motion, gang categories are steeped in content—the gang name rules all in the hierarchical scale of identity. Like the breaker who sends out energetic messages as if they exist independent of a body, so gang writers write a system of identity they hold in their heads. If Rose's breakers and b-boys respond to their uncertain surroundings by manufacturing their own disruptions in line and movement, then gangs have done the opposite. They have created a rigid world with rules of comportment, highly conservative tendencies, and a focus on keeping the line in tact.

Now think of the young man from Imperial Courts whose dance began this chapter. If ink were to flow from the stylus of his leg, the initials he spells would read as three-dimensional block letters. The letters would be rendered in space, moving back and up for the W and for the J, whose tips are abruptly shaped by the slap of hand on foot, stopped short by the arrival of toe on floor. The boy's body disciplines the letters, as he himself is disciplined by the rules of writing. Yet he glides through these breaks, he never stops moving, and he renders invisible any ruptures in line by placing them into the broader schema of fluid movement that is what gang walking is all about. Gang walking is again this "balance of opposites" to which Hazzard-Gordon refers. The control necessary for writing letters with footwork counterbalances a literal explosion of energy and whole-body expression mediated by mind and body alike.

One respondent linked the whole-body expression to a recognition that the audience must have to "let the dance take its place." As he said,

> When the music is playing, you got certain songs that'll set people off on doing the C-Walk. It be certain songs that'd be that feelin'. It's something that's not said among each other. It's nothing certain, no certain song that does it. It's something with Snoop Dogg or Nate, certain songs just set 'em off to the point where they know, this is what's crackin'. This is what time it is. Time to dance. Time to C-Walk. Everybody'll move out the way and let this dance take it place.

Several authors point out the critical integration of dance with music—the development of dance and its evolution simply cannot be considered without it. Given this fact, we must further consider music as an animator of writing itself, where corporeal memory, beat, and rhythm motivate the body's motions.

At one party I attended, a boy of fourteen arrived on the scene and began to gang walk on the sidewalk with the assuredness of someone in complete control of both his audience and his moves. The air was charged with his energy, with his proficiency, and with an aesthetic pleasure that I could only compare to seeing a tricked-out lowrider car hopping down the street. Later that night, several women and I discussed gang walking. As they attempted to show me how, the few steps I took that night earned me a dig: "What is that—Riverdance?" Irony suffused the very accusation—the whitest forms of music and dance (Irish and Scottish jigs and reels), seemingly so divorced from African American culture, but actually very much part of its history.

What makes this dance different from something like Riverdance is in fact explicitly represented in the question *What is that—Riverdance?* It is the symbolic intersection between writing and violence and the complex manner in which they are mediated by blackness as opposed to whiteness. Violence, or at least the idea of violence, remains a critical question in gang walks. Its tie to gang culture and thus to a culture of violence is embedded in the act of naming and performing this dance. In a treatment of gangsta rap, Robin Kelley discusses how the metaphorical violence gang members rap about is consistently misunderstood to be based on fomenting actual violent occurrences.[53] With break dancing, it is clear that the dance helped urban kids channel competition from physical violence into creative competition. But for gangs, in rap or in dance, the warfare *is* generally reinforced by creative expression within gang culture because it represents gang symbols.

Violence itself thus becomes a text that is written into the dance, just as it is a core text of black street life. Like the letters that mark identity in gang walking, violence is conscripted, projected not only onto the bodies of the dancers but into and behind the dance itself. As in graffiti, the dance moves are signals of who you are collectively, where you are from, what neighborhood you claim. While no actual acts of violence have been officially tied to the Crip Walk, people at gang parties and gang clubs frequently do break out into fighting. People also routinely die on the streets. One man I interviewed downplayed the possibilities of actual violence, indicating that

> You got one dude out there that'll get down and that'll get down real cool, and you got somebody else that'll challenge his way of doing it. It's not a challenge that's violent, but it's just a challenge of just seeing who can C-Walk the best. Or who can do certain things the best. Like if you have a certain dude from another hood that get down the same way, it don't mean that he disrespecting your neighborhood or that he challenging you as a man because he dancing. It's not like that; it's just like break dancing and pop locking. It's like who can do the best thing. It's a fun thing. It's a dance, you know what I mean?

The same man said in the context of another conversation that Crip Walking in a Blood neighborhood would be "damn near suicidal." Gang members send out both messages because the dance itself is so variable contextually and physically. Some say that creative challenge can sometimes get out of hand and that people who aren't gang members might get themselves hurt doing it ("C-Walking is a Crip thing, and a lot of people haven't been looking at it like that"). Then again, people talk about the precision of representing specific gang affiliations—as well as its combination with other expressive forms such as hand signing—that can create situations of danger or impending conflict ("people would look at a nigga crazy," one man described of his visits to a hole-in-the-wall club). For yet others, the "battling" is symbolic, reminiscent of battling in break dancing and yet another link to diasporic culture.

Gangs comprise an honor-bound culture in which violence plays an accepted role. For gang members, death is the "invisible protagonist."[54] Reminders of the dead are all over neighborhoods as well as on the bodies of gang members. People walk over names of the dead scratched in concrete, pass memorials at places where people were killed, and see pictures of the homies that have been lost in mirrors, on memorial t-shirts, sometimes on their own tattoos. They read "RIP" graffiti on the walls, write poems for lost loved ones, and hold tenaciously to printed programs from ubiquitous gang funerals.

As death is present in all gang media, it should come as no surprise that death is also present in dance through more than just symbolic links to gang warfare. Sharon Holland discusses how blacks have historically occupied the same social spaces as the dead. She indicates that we must view death not as final or complete, generating instead "discontinuous readings of death—as a cultural and national phenomenon or discourse, as a figurative silencing or process of erasure, and as an embodied entity or subject capable of transgression."[55] Death as an embodied entity enters through the body of the dancer. During one videotaping session in 2000, the four boys dancing would continually halt their dance to kneel down on the floor and write the names of the homies who had been lost. They would sometimes also finish their foot-based writing to place two fingers on the ground in rhythmic, alternating touches to mime their dead homies dancing the Crip Walk.

When combined with memorial, gang walks have a pronounced elegiac quality. In western society, outside of gang culture, the elegy has historically functioned as a hagiography—a text that overpraises the departed loved one's character and accomplishments or that declares what the world has lost in the loved one's death. When gang walks integrate memorial, they challenge the convention of written elegy in that they are neither hagiographic nor achievement oriented. What they mourn is community. And it is precisely the notion of community—of the gang collective—that motors the threat and the allure of violence. Because the gang walk draws together violence and writing, it also renders the link between violence and dance. It also draws further links to the diaspora and to the distinctly nonwestern shape of gang representation. Thompson writes, for example, of the ancestorism embodied in African dance that he regards as both "empirical fact" and "mystic assumption." "We realize," he writes, "that Africans, moving in their ancient dances, in full command of historical destiny, *are* those noble personages, briefly returned."[56]

George Lipsitz analyzes the 2005 book by Abdul JanMohamed in which JanMohamed talks about slavery (and subsequent forms of anti-black racism) as "social death, as living at the sufferance of the oppressor, of having to beg for life each new day."[57] For JanMohamed, blacks in America embody what he terms the "death-bound-subject, the subject who is formed from infancy onward by the imminent threat of death."[58] Lipsitz writes, "To be a gangster and somehow stage your own time of death is a logical response. It is ultimately a futile response compared to disciplined collective mobilization, but it is both necessary and understandable given the power realities of our society."[59] As death-bound subjects, gang members, along with many scholars, view the gang life as a form of symbolic suicide. When they point a gun at someone who looks and talks and acts like them, they are actually trying to kill themselves. One man I interviewed said it in this way:

> Honestly, to be truthful with you, just being around here is damn near suicide. As far as people killing themselves, yeah, there's been a few of our homies that did that. But basically just coming out here, just standing around here,

> sitting around here doing nothing. We're actually committing suicide everyday. I knew the life I chose involved murder, robbery, kidnapping, whatever it took to survive. I knew that. And most of these dudes did that, and ultimately they paid the biggest sacrifice there is: their life.

Sharon Holland analyzes gangs and death in her treatment of the film *Menace II Society.* She writes, "[I]n the contemporary terrain there are very few living narratives of black people: we literally speak from the dead. As acts of violence create cultural space in the film, they parallel the force that constructs urban poor areas across this nation; and as we watch we participate in such a making and unmaking of urban territories."[60] Just as gang members themselves assert, for Holland, gang members are the "always already dying," and chance is the only difference between a body bag and prison.

In both Holland's comments and those of the man excerpted previously, spaces of death and cultural erasure are transformed into places of life and community that may be positive but in which death is nonetheless ever present. Unlike slavery, which denied true personhood and thus the experience of death itself, prison offers a reaffirmation of life. As Barry Sanders suggests, "For only a flesh-and-blood person, not a ghost, can be convicted and then confined in a jail cell."[61] Prison is not merely a replay, then, of the slave equation, despite the excellent parallels writers like Angela Davis[62] and David Theo Goldberg[63] make between slavery and prison as institutions. Gang members do not experience prison in the same way. In fact, they have co-opted the entire prison industry to make it a critical locus of social power. In prison, gang members have rigid, daily routines of group-enforced exercise. Some black gang members learn to read and speak Swahili, the pan-African language in which their gang documents are encoded; Chicano gang members similarly read and speak Nahuatl to describe gang names and numbers or to insult correctional officers with terms other than that official one.

Dwight Conquergood is right: gang languages of resistance are far too radical to be simply termed "vernacular." Gang members are so radically counter to mainstream culture that even the most astute scholars of urban culture often fail to address gang cultural expression in its own terms. It is instead hip hop that has carried gang culture into the mainstream and into academia, particularly through the gangsta rap medium. Through hip hop, mainstream people have "discovered" gang walking, and in so doing, they have quite literally erased it.

Co-option: Gang Dances Outside of Gang Culture

"I Need to know how to crip walk hella bad!!!! I really need to know how to C-walk. Please someone E-mail me. PLEASE. Thanx Yall...peace." As this chat room participant from 2000 attests, gang dancing has increasingly caught on in non-gang circles since the late 1990s. People of many classes and ethnicities chat about it on the Internet and perform it at clubs, school dances, and weddings. The so-called C-Walk or Crip Walk I describe in this section is a different beast entirely, as its hallmark characteristics—both writing and death—have been forsaken in the process of co-option. It is an age-old thesis that as something becomes co-opted by the middle classes, its originators must find new forms of expression that more properly signal their outsider status in society. This is only partially true of gang dancing, because gang dancing has been only partially co-opted. Gang dancing and other forms of gang representation have been extended somewhat awkwardly as Crip Walking has traveled outside the gang culture. While the Crip Walk is closely linked to early 1960s traditions of black gang dancing in Los Angeles, new dances have begun to emerge that very purposefully combine elements of hip hop and break dancing. Called Crumpin' or Clown Walking, these forms of dance purposefully further the break with gang traditions. Instead of gang identity polluting hip hop with violence, hip hop sanitizes gang culture with, quite literally in the case of the Clown Walk, a mask of decency.

As with any media-based imitation, much may be lost in the translation. Aspects of memorializing and writing with fingers are completely absent in popular incarnations of the Crip Walk. Even more significant, mainstream copying frequently embodies the loss of semiotic information altogether. In other words, kids do what they call the Crip Walk but have no knowledge that they are supposed to be spelling anything. For them, Crip Walking becomes only a series of stylized movements without the writing or letters that were once a fundamental aspect of what the dance was communicating. With or without writing, the Crip Walk ties kids of all classes to urban culture, to the streets, and to the creativity and antinature of gang culture.

The dance genre invented and honed by gang members since the 1970s has been popularized by rap music videos and Internet Web sites—as well as by gang violence itself. Today, the same technologies that drive the spread of hip hop worldwide have transformed Crip Walking into a genre of dance that has itself begun to migrate in and out of the gang world. Clown Walk and Crumpin' create hybrid genres that blend East Coast traditions of breaking with West Coast traditions that stem from gang culture.[64] Though movement remains vibrant, this dance erases writing as well as violence because it excludes gang identity—either purposefully or simply because of lack of contextual knowledge that writing should be part of the dance.

When I've asked my students at Pitzer College and UCLA about their knowledge of the Crip Walk, they either break out in fits of giggles or they want me to demonstrate it for them right there on the spot. They certainly know what it is, and the more street-oriented students know about the writing: "You can write the word Crip, you can write your name, or you can just battle," as one girl told me. When I've talked to gang members about non-gang members doing the Crip Walk, they are concerned that those folks should not be messing with things they don't know anything about, that it could be dangerous, and that they might accidentally get themselves killed. One non-gang member, immersed in hip hop culture, said he would never disrespect his gang friends in Inglewood by performing the dance when he is not a gangster himself. He looks down at those who do, saying, "They're trying to be something they're not." On the other hand, the co-option of the Crip Walk may be so complete as to be altogether disassociated from local arenas. In a chat room in Canada, where questions of potential violence came up, people were wondering about whether Bloods and Crips still really existed. For those outside of gang culture, the mystery of encrypted letters bears the threat of violence because of the ambiguity of what it is representing.

As the Crip Walk has entered expansive realms of music videos and the Internet, the meaning of this dance begs questions of authenticity: Who has the authentic information regarding this dance? To use hip hop terminology: Where does the "real" reside? As Paul Gilroy asserts, "To be inauthentic is sometimes the best way to be real."[65] Marcyliena Morgan's forthcoming work on the hip hop underground echoes this view that the real is not really real at all. It's a kind of fantasy space in which people can envision themselves or others into arenas that supersede their positions in society.[66] But the real is also a kind of hegemony and its own invented tradition.[67] It creates a realm of authority, another mechanism of exclusion and control. In Crip Walk's case, this authority is not only about what properly constitutes this dance but about who constitutes a proper gangster. The real thus becomes an exclusionary tactic that works at the level of youth globally in a diasporic culture of hip hop. It is based on concepts of status, intangibles, rather than driven by greater political economies in the service of power.

Co-option of a dance like the Crip Walk offers a distinct combination of pleasure and danger.[68] It communicates the strength of expressive media within a broader culture that, bell hooks would contend, has always positioned black people as more body than mind.[69]

Crip Walking is now more than simply part of the culture of gang writing. It has become part of an expansive, underground, street-oriented, and urban-centered youth movement that enters the realm of the global through mediated images that safeguard the difference between them.

Regardless of how much they know about it, people are simply dying to learn the Crip Walk. They practically beg each other for instruction in chat rooms over the Internet. Despite risks of inauthenticity, people approach their acquisition of the Crip Walk both desperately and passionately, as the following chat room examples attest:

CAN YOU SHOW ME HOW TO CRIP WALK : E-MAIL ME IF YOU CAN

Sun Nov 19, 2000 06:43 PM

PLEASE SHOW ME HOW TO CRIP WALK AND I'LL GIVE YOU MONEY

I NEED TO C-WALK!!!

Fri Dec 01, 2000 04:04 PM

I NEED TO KNOW HOW TO CRIP WALK HELLA BAD SO SOMEONE PLEASE E-MAIL ...AND TELL ME SOME INFO.... THANX YALL...PEACE!

yo dog

Tue Nov 28, 2000 08:31 PM

i want to learn to crip walk

me and my niggas just started a cripo gang and we wanna learn

so im me back right

e-mail me

please daWG [please, Dog]

Among the many who need to learn the Crip Walk "hella bad" in this chat room example are some gang members who themselves are lacking in the true Crip Walking knowledge. When some friends, for example, decided to form a "Cripo" gang, they realize that knowledge of the Crip Walk is one of the basics. In another chat room, another young man claims to have been taught the Crip Walk by his homies, but his own ineptitude forced him to turn to the Internet for help.

The body's movement during the Crip Walk is about control and subtle messaging. It is distinct as a dance because it is generally performed as a solo routine, and people inside and outside gang culture often engage in competitive dance dueling when performing it. In this, it mirrors African American traditions in break dancing, jazz music improvisation, and other linguistic genres, such as freestyle rapping or playing the dozens.

Because gang members remain in control of ultimate perceptions of gang dancing—as well as the meanings behind them—outsider performances of the Crip Walk are tinged with paranoia. According to Crenshaw High School principal Isaac Hammond, who banned the dance, "The dance glamorizes gang life and could trigger retaliation from rivals such as the Bloods, even if most youngsters C-Walking are not in the Crips, or any gang at all."[70] Performances of the Crip Walk are charged with unknowns.

This is true for youth as well as members of the older generation, as the following chat room example attests:

> **How to C-Walk but why no one will tell you**
> Mon Nov 27, 2000 09:32 AM
> Listen!!! Did you know Crip Walking is for Crips? Did you know Its not a dance for a party? Did you know Bloods hate Crips?
>
> If you didn't know any of the above you shouldn't want to learn because, if you c-walk your a crip if not your ass is on the line in chicago there are FEW crips and lots of bloods in Cali LOTS of crips LOTS of Bloods. See i'm a vicelord and i know how to Crip walk but, because i know lots of crips have been taught and plus i got lots of rythm if you really wanna know how email me....and, i'll send you some pics and, a step by step manuel to spelling and, loccing REMEMBER this if you are ever caught depending where you live dont expose this to anyone because crip walking is SACRED to CRIP so be cool and, dont tell anyone bout this o.k

Debates surrounding the Crip Walk's propriety are well framed within the contradiction of utilizing an expansive medium like the Internet to attempt to control the spread of information: "be cool and dont tell anyone bout this o.k." What interests me here is the ambiguity of the writing itself within co-opted versions of the Crip Walk—the fear generated by doing a gang related dance—representing a gang without affiliation or without precise knowledge of what or how one is doing the representing. Also here is the total loss of semantic context and nearly all contextual knowledge that was so powerful within the Crip performances described in the previous section.

Crip Walking remains potentially dangerous. Regardless of whether their dances spell anything, people on the Internet frequently indicate their discomfort that something about the Crip Walk communicates gang identity. Questions regarding whether gang members "really write" while dancing communicate the inherent dangers of uninformed mimicry. For those outside gang culture to perform a gang-related dance brings back notions of what it means to appropriate the cultural expressions of an excluded social realm. The hidden meanings embedded in danced messages mirror the violence for which Bloods and Crips are known around the world. As Tricia Rose indicates, "Like generations of white teenagers before them, white teenage rap fans are listening in on black culture, fascinated by its differences, drawn in by mainstream social constructions of black culture as a forbidden narrative, as a symbol of rebellion."[71]

For many, Crip Walking should be for gangsters only. Others who attempt it are fake, ain't real gangsters, are not doing it right, are fools, are uninitiated, are wack, and so on. The following, for example, are taken from a chat room discussion surrounding Crip Walking, and they blatantly discourage those seeking Crip Walking knowledge:

> So u wanna C-Walk. . . Let da Cripz do da C-Walkin, aiy't all u fake azz foolz. Only da Cripz C-Walk, n it ain't no damn dance. . . u know y it ain't a dance? It ain't a dance cuz real Gangstaz don't dance, dey boogie. But if u wanna learn den u gotta learn it from da originalz, from L.A. So bring ur azz ova 2 Cali n den go thru da initiationz 4 bein a Crip, den u'll learn da C-Walk (Jan 19, 2001, http://www.dance.net/read.html)

A chat room discussant on another Crip Walk page similarly implores that people "stop telling people how to C-WALK with terrible instructions!"

> none of yal can c-walk
> all of yall [you all] IS WRONG. Please I' m tired of looking at yall wack azz descriptions of the old azz original 1985 C-WALK. If you come to the party doin that wack stuff then you will be laughed at then proceed to get walked on!!!!
> Stop telling people how to C-WALK with terrible instructions!
> Watch XZIBIT'S [a rap performer's] video. Don't ever do what he does. He can't c-walk and that's how these catz is tellin yal how to c-walk.
> Anywayz, the c-walk is Indescribable. It's a combination of foot work with spurts of skipping but overall you jus gotta have groove. What can i say? If c-walkin was eazy then everyone would do it and it would start being weak in about 2 days. If you wanna learn how to walk, come to an L.A. party

> (where it started) wait til some Kurupt come on and find the circle where the real c-walkerz be at.... (March 1, 2001, http://www.dance.net/read.html)

On the one hand is the preoccupation that Crip Walking should not leave the gang community; if it was easy then it "would start being weak in about 2 days." On the other is the notion that to C-Walk incorrectly is to misrepresent it, which is also problematic. Behind all of these questions is the "indescribability" referred to in the last example. Can true C-Walking knowledge be passed through media such as the Internet, music videos, or diagrams rather than from Crip to Crip? According to many who participate in this and other chat pages, the answer is no—even if people were to get the dances right, the gestures are empty if no true gangster identity is behind them.

Co-options of the Crip Walk represent an incomplete border crossing in which the body becomes a primary vehicle for cultural exchange. Crip Walking today is similar to Cornel West's treatment of multiracial involvement in music: "Listening to Motown records in the sixties or dancing to hip hop music in the nineties may not lead one to question the sexual myths of black women and men, but . . . the result is often a shared cultural space where some humane interaction takes place."[72] Outsiders who perform reinterpreted versions of the dance inadvertently cling to existing conceptions of racial identity: prepackaged, predefined. In performing this dance, middle class kids and outsiders to gang culture reenact an adolescent dilemma in the midst of one of the harshest racialized spaces on the globe.

In one conversation, three Bloods gang members were adamant that the co-option of gang dances was a good thing, that they enjoyed the possibilities of gang culture going worldwide, that this was a "beautiful thing." But they were also highly cognizant of the contradictions entailed in such a process. One pointed to the clothes, the gestures, the dances, saying of their would-be imitators: "They try to snatch it from us and, at the same time, they try to knock us for it." In another gang neighborhood, one leader encourages his fellow homies to require payment for anything that comes through the neighborhood—any film crew, documentary photographers, or other people who are trying to "capitalize" on the neighborhood's culture.

He argued, "This is all we got; why would we give this away for free so somebody else can get rich?"

The continued segregation of cultural knowledge between gang and non-gang populations is both enacted and belied through elements like the Crip Walk. Middle-class youth today confront a basic inability to define who they are in a country imprisoned by its own history of racialized class relations. While the privilege to flirt inconsequentially with gang culture is an undeniable aspect of their socially unmarked racial and class categories, the ultimate power that accompanies these dances is not theirs to claim. Gang members remain in control of the definitive authentic cultural form—they provide the impetus for imitation through continual innovation, as well as through their involvement in violent, street-based realms that constantly feed the public-mediated images of a dramatic lifestyle. Perhaps it is optimistic to believe that such embodied practices, shared between cultural practitioners, is one contradictory path against this literal state of apartheid.

The popularity of these dances communicates the power of a subaltern identity within a larger social system with the media power to communicate at a massive scale. Ties to lived experience and body movement make a dance such as the Crip Walk difficult to describe through written language alone. The most we can do is consider this dance within the rubric of its performance, placement, and position in the world. With co-option, dance becomes embedded in forms foreign to gang culture. Instead of being integrated with concepts of writing, death, remembrance, and gang identity, it plays off of those associations in an outsider realm whose status is enhanced by a rough street identity. Miming is no longer about shooting craps or play fighting or walking with the dead. The mime is instead, predictably, of gang culture itself. Instead of being part of a stricter semiotics of gang expression, Crip Walking is now part of a semiotics of global popular culture that extends far beyond gang culture or even the United States.

Conclusion

The Crip Walk's anchoring "sentence" is from the 1850s. Its name and form have roots in Seminole culture, African dance, and the Scotch-Irish jig, which have been carried to the present by dancers who have literally embodied the footwork of oppression. As with all African American dance forms, gang walking "has been an instrument of black survival under the most depressing economic and social circumstances, and continues to be so."[73]

Tricia Rose warns of the dangers of creating too direct a legacy to slavery in urban expressive culture. She contends that overly naïve interpretations of slave linkages might negate African American participation in currencies of technology, power brokering, and cultural innovation, once again relegating African Americans to the same positions of subdominance within a white hierarchy.[74] Paul Gilroy echoes Rose's concerns: "The imagined and sanctified Africans, used to reinstate simple racial dualism in place of an asymmetrical and unfinished political narrative, are not always compatible with the potent residues of Africa's past, let alone the geopolitical agenda set by contemporary Africa. . . . The desire to affirm and celebrate unbroken continuity is clearly a response to racisms that deny any historical currency to black life."[75] My sense is that the pattern of co-option furthers both racist and antiracist goals. But both do what Gilroy suggests: they "deny currency" to black life. When a dance is "discovered" and then "dropped," it has undergone a radical shift in who is giving it meaning, who is charting its direction. Who is crossing whose boundary to get there remains an interesting question here: for there are not one but many current trajectories for this dance. The first resides in popular culture as mediated through rap music videos. The second, however, resides in a gang culture that remains at the edge of acceptable society. It remains as distinct as it has ever been from the larger society; its moves remain as covert. Although the two worlds are not unrelated, they remain at best polite strangers.

In some sense, any act of historical study is also a form of co-option. It's like standing between the two breakers to intercept the moves they shoot at each other, or like entering the circle formed around a Crip Walker with your notebook and pen. When you read about it, it belongs to you, not them. To attribute an outsider value and meaning takes away the ability of dance practitioners to self-describe. In a sense, this self-description is what gang members are already doing in dance for themselves. In other words, they're not talking about it and not writing about it. They're dancing about it. Anyone who does what they didn't do is extending the gaze of co-option. But perhaps that is the point, the inescapable act, the mime once again. One man I interviewed about C-Walking seemed sincerely amused by my questions about miming and imitation. He dismissed them with a laugh: "That's just moves, that's all that is. There's no meaning to it really."

His comment brings a question to the fore: What does it mean to write about a history wholly contextualized within the body itself? Such an embodied history has required not words but images and movement to carry it through multiple lives, neighborhoods, and communities. People continue to define this history through their own embodied actions within myriad social landscapes. For gangs, these social landscapes tie them to African American cultural history and to a nontraditional social system that merges orality with literacy, that struggles with endemic violence, and that creates a culture of loyalties that lie outside of the state. In young bodies, then, reside old stories—stories about race and power, co-option and exclusion, and the struggle to mediate these simplistic dualities through the vibrant, if violent, production of creative culture.

Notes

1. Sally Banes, "Physical Graffiti: Breaking is Hard to Do," in *And It Don't Stop! The Best American Hip-Hop Journalism of the Last 25 Years,* ed. R. Cepeda (New York: Faber & Faber, 2004), 7–11. In my study of gang dance, I am grateful for the support and feedback of George Lipsitz, Sally Ness, Carrie Noland, Kirsten Olson, Sohini Ray, and Deidre Sklar.

2. Robert Farris Thompson, *African Art in Motion: Icon and Act in the Collection of Katherine Coryton White* (Berkeley: University of California Press, 1974).

3. Barry Sanders, *A is for Ox: Violence, Electronic Media, and the Silencing of the Written Word* (New York: Pantheon Books, 1994),184.

4. Thomas F. DeFrantz, "African American Dance: A Complex History," in *Dancing Many Drums: Excavations in African American Dance,* ed. T. F. DeFrantz (Madison: University of Wisconsin Press, 2002), 3–38.

5. DeFrantz, "African American Dance," 27.

6. Dwight Conquergood, "Street Literacy," in *Handbook of Research on Teaching*

Literacy through the Communicative and Visual Arts, eds. J. Flood, S. B. Heath, and D. Lapp (New York: Macmillan Library Reference, 1997), 354–55.

7. Claude Levi-Strauss, *Tristes tropiques*, trans. John Weightman and Doreen Weightman (New York: Atheneum, 1974).

8. For treatment on the history of dance, I am most indebted to Thomas DeFrantz, ed., *Dancing Many Drums: Excavations in African American Dance* (Madison: University of Wisconsin Press, 2002); Lynne Fauley Emery, *Black Dance: From 1619 to Today* (Pennington, N.J.: Princeton Book Company, 1988 [1972]); Katrina Hazzard-Gordon, *Jookin': The Rise of Social Dance Formations in African-American Culture* (Philadelphia: Temple University Press, 2000); and Marshall Stearns and Jean Stearns, *Jazz Dance: The Story of American Vernacular Dance* (New York: Da Capo Press, 1994).

9. Emery, *Black Dance*, 6.

10. Sterling P. Stuckey, "Christian Conversion and the Challenge of Dance," in DeFrantz, *Dancing Many Drums*, 40.

11. Stuckey, "Christian Conversion and the Challenge of Dance," 40.

12. Peter Wood, "Gimme Dem Kneebone Bent: African Body Language and the Evolution of American Dance Forms," in *Free to Dance: Behind the Dance*, retrieved from http://www.pbs.org/wnet/freetodance/behind/behind_gimme.html.

13. Hazzard-Gordon, *Jookin'*.

14. Both Robert Farris Thompson and Katrina Hazzard-Gordon discuss this kind of balance among Yoruba.

15. Hazzard-Gordon, *Jookin'*, 20.

16. Emery, *Black Dance*, here is quoting John Hope Franklin, 83.

17. See also Conquergood, "Street Literacy," for an analysis of how gang members suffer from both a lack of visibility and hypervisibility alike.

18. Deborah Gray White, *Too Heavy a Load: Black Women in Defense of Themselves: 1894–1994* (New York: W. W. Norton, 2000).

19. Information on the Cake Walk is based largely on DeFrantz, *Dancing Many Drums*; Emery, *Black Dance*; Hazzard-Gordon, *Jookin'*; and Stearns and Stearns, *Jazz Dance*.

20. Michael Taussig, *Mimesis and Alterity: A Particular History of the Senses* (New York: Routledge, 1993), 1.

21. Paul Gilroy, "'To Be Real': The Dissident Forms of Black Expressive Culture," in *Let's Get It On: The Politics of Black Performance*, ed. Catherine Ugwu (Seattle: Bay Press, 1995), 21.

22. This poem is used as an epigraph to Emery, *Black Dance*.

23. See, for example, Loic Wacquant, "Ghetto," in *International Encyclopedia of the Social and Behavioral Sciences*, ed. N. J. Smelser and P. B. Baltes (London: Pergamon Press, 2004); James Diego Vigil, *Barrio Gangs: Street Life and Identity in Southern California* (Austin: University of Texas Press, 1988); or James Gilligan, *Preventing Violence* (London: Thames & Hudson, 1998).

24. Robin D. G. Kelly, *Yo' Mama's Disfunktional!: Fighting the Culture Wars in Urban America* (New York: Beacon Press, 1998).

25. List compiled from Stearns and Stearns, *Jazz Dance*.

26. Richard Goldstein, "The Graffiti 'Hit' Parade," *New York Magazine*, March 26, 1973, 34–39.

27. Steven Hager, *Hip Hop: The Illustrated History of Break Dancing, Rap Music, and Graffiti* (New York: St. Martin's Press, 1984).

28. Norman Mailer, "The Faith of Graffiti," in *The Faith of Graffiti*, ed. Mervyn Kurlansky, Norman Mailer, and Jon Naar (New York: Praeger, 1974).

29. Tricia Rose, *Black Noise: Rap Music and Black Culture in Contemporary America* (Hanover, Conn.: Wesleyan University Press, 1994), 60.

30. Robert Farris Thompson, "Hip Hop 101," in *Droppin' Science: Critical Essays on Rap Music and Hip Hop Culture*, ed. W. E. Perkins (Philadelphia: Temple University Press, 1996), 213.

31. Banes, "Breaking Is Hard to Do," 8.

32. Rose, *Black Noise*, 22.

33. Rose, *Black Noise*, 38–39.

34. Katrina (Hazzard-Gordon) Hazard-Donald, "Dance in Hip Hop Culture," in *Droppin' Science: Critical Essays on Rap Music and Hip Hop Culture*, ed. W. E. Perkins (Philadelphia: Temple University Press, 1996), 221.

35. Rose, *Black Noise*, 39.

36. Thompson, "Hip Hop," 215.

37. See, in particular, Henry Chalfant, *From Mambo to Hip Hop: A Documentary on the South Bronx* (New York: City Lore, 2005).

38. Tony Silver, *Style Wars* (New York: Public Art Films, 1983).

39. Emery, *Black Dance*, 194.

40. Erika Hayasaki, "Some Principals Ban Dance with Gang Ties; Teens: Officials Fear That the Crip Walk, a Popular Solo Step, Could Incite Violence," *Los Angeles Times*, B1, June 4, 2002.

41. Hayasaki, "Some Principals Ban Dance with Gang Ties," B1.

42. Mike Davis, *City of Quartz: Excavating the Future in Los Angeles* (London: Verso, 1990).

43. Marcel Mauss, *The Gift: The Form and Reason for Exchange in Archaic Societies*, translated by Ian Cunnison (New York: Norton, 1967).

44. See Vigil, *Barrio Gangs*, and Joan Moore, *Going Down to the Barrio: Homeboys and Homegirls in Change* (Philadelphia: Temple University Press, 1991).

45. Davis, *City of Quartz*.

46. Michel de Certeau, *The Practice of Everyday Life*, trans. S. Rendall (Berkeley: University of California Press, 2002), quoted in Joseph Roach, *Cities of the Dead: Circum-Atlantic Performance* (New York: Columbia University Press, 1996), 13.

47. Conquergood, "Street Literacy," 367–70.

48. Thompson, *African Art in Motion*.

49. E. E. Evans-Pritchard and Meyer Fortes, eds., *African Political Systems* (London: Oxford University Press, 1940).

50. Thompson, *African Art in Motion*, 28.

51. Thompson, *African Art in Motion*, 28.

52. Roach, *Cities of the Dead*, 12–13.

53. Robin D. G. Kelly, "Kickin' Reality, Kickin' Ballistics: Gangsta Rap and Postindustrial Los Angeles," in Perkins, *Droppin' Science*.

54. Barbara Myerhoff, *Number Our Days: A Triumph of Continuity and Culture among Jewish Old People in an Urban Ghetto* (New York: Touchstone, 1980).

55. Sharon Holland, *Raising the Dead: Readings of Death and (Black) Subjectivity* (Durham, N.C.: Duke University Press, 2000), 5.

56. Thompson, *African Art in Motion*, 28.

57. Lipsitz, personal communication, e-mail January 20, 2003.

58. Abdul JanMohamed, *The Death-Bound-Subject: Richard Wright's Archaeology of Death* (Durham, N.C.: Duke University Press, 2005).

59. JanMohamed, *The Death-Bound-Subject*.

60. Holland, *Raising the Dead*, 21–22.

61. Sanders, *A is for Ox*, 179.

62. Angela Davis, *Are Prisons Obsolete?* (New York: Seven Stories Press, 2003).

63. David Theo Goldberg, "Surplus Value: The Political Economy of Prisons and Policing," in *States of Confinement: Policing, Detention, and Prisons*, ed. Joy James (New York: St. Martin's Press, 2000).

64. See David LaChapelle's *Rize* (Santa Monica, Calif.: Lion's Gate Home Entertainment, 2005) for examples of this type of dance.

65. Gilroy, "To Be Real," 29.

66. Marcyliena Morgan, *The Real Hip Hop—Battling for Knowledge, Power, and Respect in the Underground* (Durham, N.C.: Duke University Press, Forthcoming).

67. Eric Hobsbawm and Terence Ranger, eds., *The Invention of Tradition* (Cambridge: Cambridge University Press, 1983).

68. Gilroy, "To Be Real," 21.

69. bell hooks, *Art on My Mind: Visual Politics* (New York: New Press, 1995)

70. Hayasaki, "Principals Ban Gang Dance."

71. Rose, *Black Noise*, 5.

72. Cornell West, *Race Matters* (New York: Vintage, 121).

73. Katherine Dunham, "Forward," in Emory, *Black Dance: From 1619 to Today*, viii.

74. Rose, *Black Noise.*

75. Gilroy, "To Be Real," 23.

CHAPTER 3

Gesture and Abstraction

Blake Stimson

Figure 1. Frontispiece from Thomas Hobbes, *Leviathan* (1651), detail.

The topic that concerns me here sits on a distant horizon of philosophical abstraction, but I make a case for it as lived, bodily experience and thus for its immediate vitality and relevance here and now. Indeed, I argue that it is the process of abstraction itself—that is, the removal of understanding outward from any particular experience to a general, all-purpose explanation or figure or type—that can paradoxically serve as a locus of affective or embodied engagement. The cool, distant, and objective "over there" of theoretical or artistic abstraction, in other words, is considered as the wooly, intimate, and subjective "in here" of fleeting feeling; universality will be understood as the medium of particularity, and embodiment will be seen to be given its lived reality in an idea. We might provisionally refer to this process of corporeal induction, this affective movement from particular to universal and back again, as the *gesture of abstraction* in order to distinguish it from its usual associations with disembodiment or the ideological over-investment in an idea. Just to recall one form of such lived abstraction as illustration, we might look back on the old figure of the "body politic" and imagine what its philosophy once felt like—as a sense of release welling up and out of a newly imagined autonomy, for example, or as a new burden to shoulder with the unwieldy constraints and expectations of modern social being.

The particular universal I have in mind is both different from and the same as the modern one given form in Hobbes's *Leviathan.* My concern is primarily with photography as it is experienced in its broadest and most common sense, that is, experienced as something like a "body photographic," but it is really not limited to that. Put more commonly, the question is really about the lived experience of postnationalist cosmopolitanism, the lived experience of generalizing one's experience of being in the world in a new and greater way, the lived, embodied experience, that is, of *globalization.* Like the social contract for the Leviathan, the moment of collectivization imagined here is attained by a particular relay or switch that defines the terms of participation, and I draw out a simple comparison between the works of Robert Frank and Henri Cartier-Bresson to make this point. I argue that Frank's work effects this switch in a different and more significant way than that of Cartier-Bresson. That said, the meaning of photography that I claim as the housing for this aim is not delimited in any way—as street photography, say, or art photography or photojournalism, much less any notion of good or bad photography. Nor is it my aim to define the meaning of photography around any of its unique or distinctive qualities as a technology: its powerful indexical properties, for example, or its deeply momentary or melancholy vitality, or its mechanical codification of the modern worldview that ascribes to the principle of the individual eye an autonomous point of view, or even according to the easy fluidity and plasticity of its role in the circulation of signs, its role as the ever-shifting and sliding *lingua franca* of our increasingly visual world. Instead, the meaning of photography I have in mind is built on its simple, formal iterability, on the relationship of one photograph to the next and the next and the next onward and outward until, in theory, each and every last photograph and photographic quality has been incorporated like the citizens of a modern state are said to be incorporated as Leviathan.

The abstraction to be taken on board here, in other words, is not photography as representation, style, or brute fact—and in this regard we might distinguish it from later variants on the same theme, such as is evident in Gerhard Richter's *Atlas*—but instead photography as such, photography as idea, photography as it is experienced as a nation unto itself.[1] This all sounds rather ahistorical for the purposes of history writing, I know, but really it is not. Rather, we might imagine it to be meaningfully historical in a manner like the concept "French," say, or "modern," or the concept "art" as used, for example, in the best sort of scholarly studies of French modern art. All such abstractions can be particularized easily by being understood differentially, of course (French is not-German, modern is not-traditional, art is not-craft, etc.), but each might also be taken for qualities that inhere in itself not as spirit or origin or essence but as accumulation or mass. How, we are routinely forced to ask of ourselves (even if we don't always admit to it), is the Frenchness of a French citizen like the Frenchness of a French landscape or the Frenchness of a French painting, and so on? How do these separate experiences, when brought together as a general condition or character, induce a cumulative expression that exceeds the simpler meaning that can be drawn from their place in any differential system? Such an accumulation of individual determinations, after all, is what allows a term like French or modern or art to take on the linguistic form of the proper name and endows it with the great modern promise of autonomy or sovereignty or subjectivity, the great modern promise of Leviathan. It is this power of abstraction that allows one to imagine such things rising to that status once given the magnanimous name of "commonwealth." We can see this old promise well, for example, in one of our founding definitions for the proper name Art: "If you wish to make a beautiful human figure, it is necessary that you probe the nature and proportions of many people: a head from one; a breast, arm, leg from another; and so on through all the parts of the body, front and back, omitting none."[2] This is Albrecht Dürer speaking, and by such technique, he insisted, the beauty that would otherwise be imperfectly "distributed among the multitudes of all people," could be condensed and extracted, and Art, in its great modern sense, given form.[3]

This is all just to say that the habit of mind I wish to call on here is ontological and not semiological—like asking what is red, not as a color differentiable from other colors and circulating in a social system but as red qua red, red as redness rather than red qua blue or green or yellow, say, or red qua lipstick or apples or communism or blood. My goal in doing so is not to be some manner of ersatz philosopher, nor to indulge in flat tautological self-reflexivity, nor to flee from the rigors of properly historical understanding into some ahistorical redoubt of *Sein* or *Dasein* or worse. Instead, my goal is to use the opening given by ontology to look back to a different intellectual-historical origin point, one that might be characterized as "prestructuralist" but cannot rightfully be characterized as "precritical" or prior to the origin of the concept of critical theory as it has come to find its institutional legs in the postwar period. Put another way that is certainly far too narrow but may be useful to make my point nonetheless, the understanding of photography developed here does not draw on the sensitive, rigorous, and duly influential reflections of those two greatest touchstones for any critical history of photography: Roland Barthes and Michel Foucault. Or, risking even greater reductivism to make a point, we might see the difference between these two genealogical limbs to sit at a fork bearing another proper name: Hegel. Let me begin, thus, by quickly reminding you of the emergence of the intellectual history of that split.

The Hegel I have in mind, you may have already guessed, is the Hegel of the twentieth century and not that of the nineteenth. More specifically, it is the Hegel who was returned to in the 1930s in response to Stalin's hardening of the Hegelian tradition on the modern ideal of the Leviathan in the doctrines of "Diamat" and "Histomat" and their consequences in the various horrors and delusions of the time.[4] There are two notable points of origin in the early 1930s for the onset of this latter-day Hegel that would come to define the spectrum of "critical theory" that still carries on at present, one in Germany and the other in France. The first might have been voiced by any of the early members of the Frankfurt School, but Herbert Marcuse, perhaps, stated it most concisely in a 1930 book review. Written at the same time that he was working out the problem in greater detail in his *Habilitationsschrift* on "Hegel's Ontology" (a project not surprisingly rejected by his supervisor, Heidegger), he stated categorically "The word and concept, 'dialectic,' has been so abused in recent philosophy and in Marxist theory and practice that it has become unavoidable to come to one's senses again about the origin of dialectics."[5] That is, he was saying, a return to Hegel had been made unavoidable by the philosophical degeneration brought on and institutionalized by Comrade Stalin.

Indeed, such a coming to one's senses seemed equally unavoidable to Alexandre Kojève and the participants in his landmark seminar on Hegel's *Phenomenology*. Allan Bloom put his own distinctive spin on this development in his 1969 introduction to the seminar's lectures: "Kojève," Bloom inveighed with his characteristic mix of cultivated veneration and haughty dismissiveness, "is the most thoughtful, the most learned, the most profound of those Marxists who, dissatisfied with the thinness of Marx's account of the human and metaphysical grounds of his teaching, turned to Hegel as the truly philosophic source of his teaching."[6]

All judgments aside, both groups used Hegel as a turning point, as a pivot out of the endgames of politics, out of Hegelianism-cum-Marxism-cum-Leninism-cum-Stalinism, and back into a more rigorous philosophy, as Bloom suggests. Put in the philosophical language itself, both French and German sons of the 1930s perceived Hegel to be a solution to the problem Hegel called "identity." As Kojève had the core Hegelian thesis in 1936, albeit too flatly, "Freedom = Negativity = Action = History."[7] This rudimentary premise, that negation rather than identity is the active agent of any truth, would form the hub of the broader critical theory concept as it came to be institutionalized in the coming decades by both groups. Against "an enclosed system of propositions"—this is Horkheimer in his

1937 "Traditional and Critical Theory" essay quoting Husserl as his foil, but it could just as well have been Foucault describing any humdrum "discourse" thirty years later—critical theory sought to develop a different sort of system, one "not so much of objects as of subjects."[8] Indeed, the key to a properly critical theory for both—dialectic for the one, difference for the other—was that it reach outside its own self-justifying conceptual parameters to the test of lived experience, and both groups held tight to the check or balance of subjectivity as a safeguard against the false enclosure of objectivity.[9] Kojève's protégé Georges Bataille put this succinctly (albeit with no little self-indulgence) in a 1937 letter to his mentor. "If action ('doing') is (as Hegel says) negativity," he wrote, "then there is still the problem of knowing whether the negativity of someone who 'doesn't have anything more to do' disappears or remains in a state of 'unemployed negativity'. As for me, I can only decide in one way, since I am exactly this 'unemployed negativity' . . . I think of my life—or better yet, its abortive condition, the open wound that my life is—as itself constituting a refutation of a closed System."[10] So too such a sense of purpose drawn from one's own afflictions or traumas might well be said to have been at work in Adorno's "Reflections from a damaged life," as he subtitled his *Minima Moralia* some ten years later.[11] That said, the two groups worked their wounds via two distinct paths.

How those paths subsequently developed into full-fledged programs—"deconstruction" and so on, on the one side, "negative dialectics" or whatever on the other—has been the matter of much discussion, which need not be rehearsed here. The one thing that is worth pointing to for our purposes, however, is the different relationship each of these positions has had to our central ontological question about accumulation. Where the Kojève school, as a rule, relied on differential approaches that measured critical incisiveness locally and in micropolitical dimensions, the Frankfurt school held firm to Hegel's grand principle of totality as the only viable counterweight to the instrumentalism of Stalinism. Both groups embraced the ethical principle of negation, but the Germans also held on to the old promise of synthesis, assuming that criticality could only find leverage by taking on ontological mass.[12] The trauma of one's own "damaged life," in other words, served as the internal principle for the system as a whole, not its refutation or outside. The problem with the "unemployed negativity" thesis, Adorno had argued already in 1931, was that it carried "nominalism so far" that its "concepts become too small to align the others with themselves," that it individualized, localized, and therefore marginalized the Hegelian principle of negation. Negativity, he insisted, could only be properly understood as itself being mediated, as itself being ever in the employ of system.[13]

Thus, it is only in this philosophical opposition that the meaning of photography considered here can be squared historically, because photography as such, or photography qua photography, is only available philosophically to the German critical-theoretical tradition that held fast to the figure of the Leviathan, to the figure of social totality, as its means for "coming to one's senses" in the wake of Stalinism. In this regard, my efforts might be taken as a sympathetic rejoinder to the place of the French critical-theoretical tradition that the history of photography carries forward, an influence seen in the many worthy and productive efforts to parse the operations of mythologies and discourses, on the one hand, and the corresponding dream of release from those operations given by this or that punctum or heterotopia on the other. My goal might be said to provide a different sort of solution to the research problem with which Barthes opens his *Camera Lucida:* that is, his "'ontological' desire" to resolve what he called "the uneasiness of being a subject torn between two languages, one expressive, the other critical."[14]

To put it in another very different terminology, which I will come back to at the end, the French solution to this ambivalence might be said to be about finding the local "decisive moment" when the two languages come into concert by overlapping one another, the moment of a readerly response when the critic places himself or herself both within the discourse or mythology and simultaneously off at some affective remove from that nexus in the imagined freedom of unemployed negativity.[15] Barthes chose the camera lucida metaphor for this reason, after all: it united a vision split into studium and punctum.[16] My alternative ontological aim is to look for the ways in which meaning accumulates as general historical consequence on the level of subjective affect rather than looking for the diacritical marks that pinpoint the cause and response of that affect. Put differently, the goal is not, pace Barthes, to find the meaning of photography in the one exemplary photograph that pierces to the core with its punctum—a photograph of one's mother, for example—and then extend that experience to all of photography as a new universal studium, but instead to gather the experience of each and every photograph into a common understanding, pace Adorno, an understanding of a damaged life, for example, or an understanding of Leviathan. In other words, the critical-theoretical switch of negation is understood to be best directed against the experience of particularity or exceptionality and toward the experience of subjectivity as a "constellation," in Adorno's parlance, or perhaps better for our purposes here, as that densely layered accumulation of affect that we sometimes refer to with the word *baggage*.

There is a specific turning point in the history of photography that I have in mind as a parallel to critical theory's two-sided turn to the subject. This turning point is the moment when, as Jeff Wall once described it, the "gesture of reportage" was "withdrawn from the social field and attached to a putative theatrical element" creating an "introversion, or subjectivization" of documentary photography.[17] Even though Wall had a very different sort of practice in mind, on the broadest level what he described was no different from what John Szarkowski had already observed back in 1967 when he stated categorically that "A new generation of photographers" (meaning first and foremost Lee Friedlander, Diane Arbus, and Garry Winogrand) "has directed the documentary approach toward more personal ends."[18]

The subjectivized gesture that concerned Wall primarily was the one developed by those conceptual artists who, like Friedlander and company, formed their mature sensibilities in the 1960s, photographically oriented artists such as Ed Ruscha, Dan Graham, Robert Smithson, and Douglas Huebler. But we can expand our historical purview without any damage to Wall's useful reasoning in order to make his "subjectivization" consistent with Szarkowski's "personalization" by seeing a foretelling of both developments in the 1950s work of Frank, and before that, of Cartier-Bresson.

If the gesture of reportage had originally been a look outward or a look over there—as in, say, the foundational work of photographer-muckraker Jacob Riis adventuring downtown to where the other half lived—then the introversion of that gesture would look out only to see a mirror or some other device that focuses the gesture of looking back onto the self. Wall describes this redirection as a "fusion of reportage and performance" and, indeed, the cross-country road trip that generated Frank's 1958 or 1959 *Americans* might well be seen as a foundational performance, one that influenced both the conceptual art practices and Szarkowski's "New Documentarians" to come.[19] As Martha Rosler described it, Frank marked a shift "from an outward looking, reportorial, partisan, and collective [enterprise] to a symbolically expressive, oppositional and solitary one."[20] Indeed, the key ingredient in Frank's distinctive approach that appealed equally to both Wall's preferred photographers and Szarkowski's (even if none of these followers could duplicate that ingredient without reducing it to pastiche) was its look outward in the manner of Jacob Riis—its "gesture of reportage," as Wall called it—that seemed in one and the same instant to inscribe or index a corresponding look inward or back onto the self.[21] That said, my sense is that Rosler overemphasizes this shift from outward to inward. Put simply, what Frank did that none of his followers were able to sustain at the same high level was to do both outside and in at the same time in a way that made them seem both fully vested and inseparable. That is, to put it back into the philosophical language, he was able to sustain the mediation. His inimitable appeal seemed to be born of this all happening in the bodily movement of the photographic act itself, in the decisive moment of the click of the shutter. This was the signature accomplishment of his "strong, personal, nonintellectual eye," an eye that was "very fast," as his wife Mary described it, and it is this that I am labeling his "gesture" of abstraction.[22]

When it worked, that complex look came together in an instant as an amalgam of several interrelated gestures that we might artificially separate here as follows: first, the movement of the finger depressing the shutter, an action that might at once be understood as aggressive toward its object, like the squeezing of a trigger, and defensive of its subject, like the nervous blinking of an eye; second, the turning away of the photographer's body and attention from that view as it is being captured on film; and third, the turning inward of the photographer's attention from the world outside to his own affective response. This complex is on view everywhere in Frank's pictures—in their fleeting, reaching, and distancing quality, in their taught mix of fascination and repulsion, in the nervous glance of photography on the run, and in the constant turn of the photographer's and beholder's attention to motifs that carry the aesthetic or affective charge of a void or full stop.

Any conventionalized bodily movement—a salute, say, or a bow, a look upward and out or a look downward and in, a raised finger or fist, or, more pertinent to our concern here, a finger or thumb depressing a shutter-release button—inscribes the social form of lived experience, and that social form has both a discernible structure or a shape and legible meaning and consequence. In some instances, it is a clear expression of conformity with social will (such as with a salute) and in other instances, it seems an expression of individual will defining itself against social constraints (such as, on occasion, with a raised finger). Either way, however, it carries its sociality as a phenomenological index, that is, as the condition of its capacity for perception. Gesture is bound up in a historically specific form of embodiment, a manner of moving through the world that comports itself variously with and against established conventions of looking and, in this sense, carries meaning. This thesis was a commonplace of the period, and on every level. Merleau-Ponty, for example, called it "the structure of the world outlined by the gesture."[23]

Our concern here, however, is not with the meaning of gesture as such but rather with something that might be called a critical gesture, or a gesture that we can associate with the aims of critical theory, or gesture as the intersection of objective understanding and subjective experience. Cartier-Bresson described it as so: "We always want to work with our brains," he allowed, "but we must be available to and let our sensitivity direct us as if we are surfing on a wave. We must be open, open."[24] Then, in so doing, he argued, and others have argued for him since, the "decisive moment" might be perceived and captured in the click of the shutter. All the narrative elements of a scene would be synchronized with the photographer's perception just as the energy and intention of a surfer synchronizes with the energy and aim of a wave. Lincoln Kirstein, for example, described the goal, perhaps a bit floridly, as capturing "the ultimate image, snapped at the peak of choice" and "fixed through a complex chemistry of moral and muscular explosions, like an orgasm."[25] More delicately, Cartier-Bresson himself described it as "recognizing an event, and at the very instant and within a fraction of a second rigorously organizing the forms you see to express and give meaning to that event. It is a matter," he said, "of putting your brain, your eye, and your heart in the same line of sight."[26]

This was the "decisive moment" ideal in the first instance, and it was something like Barthes's punctum after that: lining up all of one's being on a detail and parrying with a rejoinder, Cartier-Bresson argued, subjectivity gets its say by establishing a balance between two worlds—"the one inside us and the one outside us. As the result of a single reciprocal process, both these worlds come to form a single one."[27] This was the moment of the subject's affective movement from particular experience outward toward the universal as a tiny detail comes to transcend itself in subjective experience, the moment when, as Barthes puts it about his fixation on the picture of his mother, "the particular dies for the satisfaction of the universal," or rather, the particular dies in order to be reborn as universal.[28] It was the moment of abstraction, the moment of nation. As Kirstein described it, again colorfully, "The very nature of photography is to be particularized, impermanent and fragmentary, but one can reconstitute a dinosaur from a tooth and a dynasty from a shard."[29]

This connection between the world in here as subjective experience and the world out there as system is just the sort of switch or relay we have been looking for. There is a momentary bodily identification, a gestural engagement with the other that allows for a kind of transcendence, and we can see it everywhere in Cartier-Bresson's photographs. In the dancelike exchange between the movement of the subject and the movement of the photographer's shutter finger or in the exchange of looks between subject, photographer, and beholder, a constellation of forces all line up to a decisively momentary point or punctum that floods over with a universal meaning for photography—the meaning of simple human recognition—

but it is a meaning that passes in a flash. In this way, pitting punctum against studium, decisive moment against all other moments, experience against theory, body against mind, the meaning of photography comes to be the kind of negation we have been looking for: the negation of systemic understanding that critical theory and its critical photographic equivalent has always taken as its task. In so doing, the decisive moment stands in as a figure of abstraction as negation, but it does so in a manner that might well be considered ideological in all the usual liberal humanist senses.

Against this great image of negation-as-release, negation as the simple outside to system, negation-as-nominalism, however, Frank's work took up an alternative critical-photographic enterprise. The subjectivization of the gesture of reportage in Frank's work could not or would not free itself from the burden of systemic understanding, from the burden of abstraction, in the rudimentary bodily pleasure of simple human recognition. He was famously critical of the ideological potential of this pleasure, referring to Steichen's *Family of Man* exhibition as the "tits and tots" show and distancing himself from the easy, humanist gestural economy of Cartier-Bresson's decisive moment.[30] Instead, his work doggedly refused human recognition and persistently turned experience from inside outward rather than seizing on the decisive moment when outside turns in. In this way, by seeing the meaning of photography not as human recognition but instead as a kind of alienation or baggage, by seeing the camera not as a vehicle for connection but instead as a device for distancing, othering, abstracting, a device that throws photographer and beholder back on themselves, we might begin to make out the figure of the "body photographic." Frank's photography was a kind of sink or catch basin or trap for history. It attained its significance only by accumulation, only as the negation or void or full stop of normal human interaction, only as the dissonance of human recognition refused. In this way, Frank's figure of alienation serves to throw us onward to the next photograph and the next and the next until, in theory, we have taken them all on as our burden, our baggage, as our damaged life, as the flesh of our body photographic. Such then, we might conclude, is the measure for a critical embodiment of abstraction: it is that enlightenment only made available by taking on the weight of the world.

Notes

1. On *Atlas* see, for example, Benjamin H. D. Buchloh, "Gerhard Richter's *Atlas*: The Anomic Archive," in *October* 88 (Spring 1999), 117–45.

2. Albrecht Dürer, *Schriftlicher Nachlaß*, ed. Hans Rupprich (Berlin, 1956/1969), quoted in Joseph Leo Koerner, *The Moment of Self-Portraiture in German Renaissance Art* (Chicago: University of Chicago Press, 1993), 191.

3. Dürer, *Schriftlicher Nachlaß*, quoted in Koerner, *The Moment of Self-Portraiture in German Renaissance Art*, 197.

4. This is opposite also to Trotsky's softening of the same legacy into the concept of "permanent revolution."

5. Quoted in Seyla Benhabib's "Translator's Introduction" to Herbert Marcuse, *Hegel's Ontology and the Theory of Historicity* (Cambridge, Mass.: MIT Press, 1987), xiii.

6. Allan Bloom, "Editor's Introduction" to Alexandre Kojève, *Introduction to the Reading of Hegel* (Ithaca, N.Y.: Cornell University Press, 1969), viii. Or we can listen to the tone of a very different sort of player in the development of this latter-day French Hegelianism warning his readers in 1950: "The fact that, for the last two decades, Hegel has had his place in French bourgeois philosophy is not a matter to be treated lightly." This was Louis Althusser, and he concludes with no dearth of period gravitas and desperation, "This Great Return to Hegel is simply a desperate attempt to combat Marx, cast in the specific form that revisionism takes in imperialism's final crisis: *a revisionism of a fascist type*." Louis Althusser, "The Return to Hegel," in *The Spectre of Hegel: Early Writings* (London: Verso, 1997), 173, 183.

7. Kojève, *Introduction to the Reading of Hegel*, 209.

8. Max Horkheimer, "Traditional and Critical Theory," *Critical Theory: Selected Essays* (New York: Continuum International, October 1975), 190, 209.

9. "With Hegel's concept of the dialectic, the French were compelled to recognize that the intimate, private structures of the self were a shared, communal reality." Mark Poster, *Existential Marxism in Postwar France: From Sartre to Althusser* (Princeton, N.J.: Princeton University Press, 1977), 24.

10. Georges Bataille, *Guilty* (Santa Monica, Calif.: Lapis Press, 1988), 123.

11. Theodor W. Adorno, *Minima Moralia: Reflections from a Damaged Life*, (London: Verso, 2005).

12. See the section titled "Ontological Mass" in Antonio Negri, *The Savage Anomaly: The Power of Spinoza's Metaphysics and Politics* (Minneapolis: University of

Minnesota Press, 2000), 39–44, where he writes, "The critique of the universal, then, represents here the central passage of Spinozian analysis in its genetic movement. But also important is the recuperation of Descartes, in an anti-Cartesian sense. Because, in effect, the mechanism of doubt comes to be used not for the idealistic foundation of knowledge but for the passage toward the apprehension of being. The rationalist method comes to be subsumed within the materialist method. Specifically, it lives on the horizon of the totality. And the real concept of potentia constitutes the only mediation, a mediation internal to being and therefore not a mediation at all but a form of the tension, of the life of being. Certainly, here the analysis of potentia is not developed, it is only founded and posed, not resolved. It is necessary to move forward. It is necessary to throw this paradox into reality, to identify its constitutive figure and force, and to measure, along this path, its crisis. And with the crisis comes the possibility of a philosophy of the future."

13. Theodor W. Adorno, "The Actuality of Philosophy," *Telos* 31 (Spring 1977), pp. 130–1.

14. Roland Barthes, *Camera Lucida: Reflections on Photography* (New York: Hill & Wang, 1982), 3, 8.

15. "I had determined on a principle for myself: never to reduce myself-as-subject, confronting certain photographs, to the disincarnated, disaffected *socius* which science is concerned with." Barthes, *Camera Lucida*, 74.

16. Barthes, *Camera Lucida*, 106.

17. Jeff Wall, "Marks of Indifference: Aspects of Photography in, or as, Conceptual Art," in *Reconsidering the Object of Art, 1965–1975*, ed. Ann Goldstein and Anne Rorimer (Cambridge, Mass.: MIT Press, 1995), 253.

18. Even if he slid a bit on the meaning and purpose of their personalization (not "to reform life, but to know it," he said—whatever that means). Wall text for the exhibition *New Documents* (New York: Museum of Modern Art, 1967), quoted in Martha Rosler, "In, Around, and Afterthoughts (on Documentary Photography)," in *The Contest of Meaning: Critical Histories of Photography*, ed. Richard Bolton (Cambridge, Mass.: MIT Press, 1989), 321.

19. Wall, "Marks of Indifference."

20. Quoted in Lili Corbus Bezner, *Photography and Politics in America* (Baltimore: Johns Hopkins University Press, 1999), 178.

21. Wall, "Marks of Indifference." "Reportage," he writes, "evolves in pursuit of the blurred part of pictures" (p. 249).

22. "Mary Frank," in Eleanor Munro, *Originals: American Women Artists* (New

York: Simon & Schuster, 1979). Quoted in "William S. Johnson, History—His Story," in *The Pictures Are a Necessity: Robert Frank in Rochester, NY November 1988*, ed. William S. Johnson (Rochester, N.Y.: George Eastman House, 1989), 39.

23. Maurice Merleau-Ponty, *Phenomenology of Perception* (New York: Routledge, 2002), 186.

24. Cartier-Bresson quoted in Michael Kimmelman, "With Henri Cartier-Bresson, Surrounded by His Peers," *New York Times*, August 20, 1995. Quoted in Gretchen Garner, *Disappearing Witness: Change in Twentieth-Century American Photography* (Baltimore: Johns Hopkins Press, 2003), 99.

25. Lincoln Kirstein, "Henri Cartier-Bresson," *Photographs by Henri Cartier-Bresson* (New York: Grossman, 1963), n.p.

26. Quoted in Alan Riding, "Cartier-Bresson's Instinct for Decisive Moments," *New York Times*, May 27, 2003.

27. Henri Cartier-Bresson, *The Decisive Moment* (New York: Simon & Schuster, 1952), n.p.

28. Barthes, *Camera Lucida*, 72.

29. Kirstein, "Henri Cartier-Bresson."

30. "Frank seems to have felt that movement *within* the frames of his photographs would only disturb their sense and, with a few exceptions, ignored the use of dramatic gesture and motion in *The Americans* (a fact which . . . suggests his feeling about Cartier-Bresson's work)." Tod Papageorge, "Walker Evans and Robert Frank: An Essay on Influence," (New Haven, Conn.: Yale University Art Gallery, 1981), 5.

CHAPTER 4

Remembering Kinesthesia: An Inquiry into Embodied Cultural Knowledge

Deidre Sklar

This chapter begins at ground level, with a nonfigurative treatment of gesture as rooted in embodiment, and particularly in human bodily movement. Bringing out the somatic, or felt, dimensions of movement opens the way for an examination of kinetic vitality as an overlooked aspect of embodied knowledge. Establishing human movement as the organismic foundation for a concept of gesture also offers a determining yet indeterminate source and medium for examining the processes of cultural manipulation. Thus, the chapter addresses the migration of qualities, especially qualities of vitality, across sensory modalities and their configuration as cultural aesthetic schema across media. Basing my discussion on the potential for movement knowledge inherent in embodiment, I find that cultural patterns of kinetic vitality emerge as the "ghost," to borrow Lesley Stern's term, in all gesture.

As the first assignment in an undergraduate Philosophy of Dance course, I ask students to write about a remembered experience, a childhood event that effected them deeply and led them toward dance. On the first day of class, after the logistics, the review of requirements, course readers, criteria for grading, and the rest, we break the mould of classroom protocol and meditate. The meditation is a preparation for the writing. "Let the mind travel with the breath," I instruct, "following its passage as it touches nostrils, throat, chest, belly, through its change of direction from in-breath to out-breath and back. If the mind wanders, gently bring it back to the breath." We go slowly, shifting attention away from the demanding chatter of word-thoughts to the subtleties of somatic sensation. Once I see the students' breath slowing and facial muscles easing, I suggest they allow a memory to arise and fully occupy the landscape of awareness. To thicken the memory, I call attention to the different sensory modes, asking students to "re-view" (seeing the event from different angles and distances, noting particulars of shape, spatial relationships, colors); "re-call" (sharpening hearing to bring up the memory's sounds, including music, voices, words); and "re-member" (letting the memory's kinetic sensations claim the body and awareness). When the students "return," they make notes, inscriptions toward the essay assignment.

Then we review the meditation. What was your dominant mode of remembering? Which sensory modality emerged to trigger memory? Sound, like music or words heard in your mind's ears? A visual image of a setting or of yourself moving? A kinesthetic sensation of movement or of a particular dynamic of movement? And which sense was easiest to fill out once you tried to retrieve the event in detail? Richard Bandler and John Grinder, students of anthropologist Gregory Bateson and originators of the popular therapy neurolinguistic programming, have shown that different people access memory via different sensory modalities. Further, the sensory mode by which an individual *accesses* a memory is often different from the one in which he or she *represents* the memory.[1] All thinking occurs in one or another sensory modality, but the ratios are different for different individuals, and perhaps for the same individual in different circumstances. I first asked students to drop awareness into their bodies through attending to breath, in effect inviting awareness of somatic sensation. If I had asked them instead simply to remember a dance, perhaps they would have called on visual memory and seen it in their mind's eye, since in their training, they are usually taught dances as a succession of body shapes, steps, and spatial patterns. Indeed, several of the students weep reading their kinesthetic autobiographies, realizing that their childhood ecstasies have been "tamed" by technique classes, and that a sense of their bodies as source of kinesthetic pleasure has been transformed into a sense of their bodies as objects for specular display.

"Any culture is an order of sensory preferences," Marshall McLuhan wrote.[2] Following McLuhan, anthropologists David Howes and Constance

Classen suggest that we attend to differences in "sensory profiles," the relative emphasis placed on different sensory modalities in different cultural communities.[3] "What if," Howes writes, "there exist different forms of reasoning, memory, and attention for each of the modalities of consciousness (seeing, smelling, speaking, hearing, etc.) instead of reasoning, memory, and attention being general mental powers?" This is promising, its premise borne out by the work of Bandler and Grinder. However, Howes and Classen omit kinesthesia, the proprioceptive sense of movement within our own bodies.[4] While kinesthesia might be subsumed under touch, as the changing contours of touch within our own bodies, the result of omitting kinesthesia from the sensorium is that we are left with no sensory locus for building an epistemology of movement and no locus for addressing the cultural or symbolic dimensions of kinetic sensation.

Is kinesthesia excluded from the sensorium because it refers to no external object and can be apprehended only proprioceptively, that is, within one's own body? Aristotle divided the "intellectual" or distanced senses (sight and hearing) from the affective and proximate ones (smell, taste, touch).[5] For the Greek philosophers, while all the senses are shared with animals and are therefore more base than the mind, which is unique to humans, touch and taste are especially animal.[6] There has since been a grudging acceptance of sight as the most refined and least bodily sense.[7] It is hard to think of touch or kinesthesia without associations to body parts, but who associates to eyeballs when they think of sight? We imagine the *objects* of sight rather than its organic means. Seeing implies an object, something to see. And in order to see an object, one must be separate from it, at enough distance to bring it into focus. This necessity for receptive distance does not apply for any of the other senses. The close association between seeing and objective distance (as well as objectification) is not accidental. The objectification implicit in seeing is associated with the objectivity of mind, while the somatic sensation implicit in touch is associated with nearness and the subjectivity of proprioception. Kinesthesia, even more proprioceptive than touch, has been entirely omitted from the western sensorium.

Though we cannot separate from our bodies in order to see ourselves in bodily wholeness, the hegemony of objectification nonetheless enables us to visually imagine ourselves as objects. In America, as perhaps in western Europe, "body consciousness" has come to refer not to somatic awareness but to creating ourselves as images, often enhanced by cosmetics, fashions, and body-shaping classes.[8] Even in dance scholarship, both aesthetic and historical studies tend to display a visualist bias, even though the primary media of dancing is movement. Ballet, the most memorialized dance genre of the European diaspora, emphatically privileges visual display and a set of detailed formal and aesthetic conventions concerning spectacles of shape. Other cultural epistemologies, however, offer other "sensory profiles." Perceptual testing has shown, for example, that in general, African cultures emphasize auditory and proprioceptive values rather than visual ones.[9]

The differentiation between visual and somatic, specifically kinesthetic, modalities raises a problem basic to theorizing human movement, that is, whether to treat it as visual or kinesthetic phenomena. In the first case, human movement is taken primarily to be a visual object, its shapes, steps, and choreographic patterns received by observers through the eyes. In the second, movement is a *do*ing, involving not only the shaping of body positions and locomotion through space but also the organization of kinetic dynamics, received by performers through their own bodies, as proprioception. Dance is, of course, both kinesthetic and visual, and whereas felt processes may be dominant for the *do*er and seen products for the viewer, these are always mutually informing.[10] However, while the dynamics of movement are visible to the eye, they are not easily objectifiable in inscriptions. Labanotation can quantify shape, spatial pattern, and duration, but not dynamics such as the changing relation between rhythm and muscular tension. These dynamic contours are critical to memories of movement, to communication via movement, and to the cultural knowledge and values negotiated through movement.

Mirroring the distinction between movement's seen and felt aspects, philosopher Edward Casey distinguishes "body memory" from "memory of the body," the first working primarily through feelings-in-the-body, the second through representations of the body as an object of awareness.[11] For Casey, the first would be properly called remembering, the second recollecting.[12] He suggests that whereas remembering manifests in terms of "its own depth," as a vertical dimensionality, recollection is "projected" at a "quasi-pictorial distance from myself as a voyeur of the remembered."[13] In recollection (as well as in verbal reminiscing), Henri Bergson wrote, we "peer" back toward a past that seems to have independent being distant from the present; in body memory, the past is enacted in the present.[14] Therefore, regarding body memory, Casey suggests, "we should speak of *immanence* rather than 'intersection' . . . immanence of the past in the present and the present in the past."[15] The present and the past cannot be fully identical, Casey concludes, since we would then no longer be dealing with memory. How then is immanence different from a merger of past and present? As my students meditate and re-member, that is, access the somatic sensations of the past, what, then, are they experiencing in the present?

Suzanne Langer's formulation of "virtual gesture" as the "primary illusion" of dance is suggestive. "Gesture is vital movement," Langer writes, known by kinetic experience and secondarily by sight.[16] Gesticulation, as part of everyday behavior, is likewise vital movement, but it is not art. Only when it is imagined apart from the momentary situation is it art. Then it becomes "free symbolic form," or "virtual gesture."[17] Dancers, Langer writes, "for whom the created world is more immediately real and important than the factual world," cannot easily keep virtual and "actual" separate; they experience the feelings engendered through dancing as spontaneous.[18] However, for Langer, the sorrow that emerges as a young woman dances Giselle is different from the sorrow she would feel if someone backstage whispered to her that her boyfriend had just left her. Thus, Langer distinguishes two senses of movement expressivity: spontaneous, or "symptomatic" self-expressions arising unpremeditated out of life circumstances, and "logically expressive" "signs" that may *seem* to spring from feeling but are actually the result of symbolic form. In spite of various problems with Langer's formulation, the idea of virtual gesture is useful in clarifying the experience Casey describes for bodily memory. Just as the sensations that arise for dancers during performance are virtual, in the sense of being both spontaneous—as immediate affects—and also resulting from a temporal displacement, so too is bodily memory virtual, occurring, intentionally or not, as both immediate sensation and, in the terms of this volume, as a migration of somatic memory over time.

Both Casey and Langer consider bodily memory in terms of feeling, but "feelings" may imply complex emotions, as in Langer's Giselle example, or somatic sensations, including kinetic ones. The distinction is critical. Using the same term for both, the English language blurs the difference, giving rise to confusion in discussions of feeling in dance.[19] While kinetic sensations often carry emotional overtones, and emotional states invariably have kinetic sensation components, the two are not the same. Emotions are the complex states Darwin identified as, for example, happiness, anger, and sadness, while kinetic sensations are the somatic effects of movement dynamics as, for example, the feeling of a swift punch, a light, smoothing touch, or a twitching wink. These feelings depend on a combination of kinetic elements such as speed, rhythm, force, and amount of muscular tension or relaxation as well as on the spatial parameters and shapes of movement.

Though she does not distinguish emotional from kinetic feelings, I believe Langer refers, ultimately, to the kinetic sense when she writes that "gesture is *vital* movement."[20] She continues: all life has "vitality"; we have a "consciousness of life," and this "sense of vital power . . . is our most immediate self-consciousness."[21] Gesture works directly with this vitality, these "felt energies" that seem to be physical but are not. Combining the concepts of vital and virtual, Langer concludes that "The primary illusion of dance is a virtual realm of Power—not actual, physically exerted power, but appearances of influence and agency created by virtual gesture."[22] Elsewhere, she identifies dance, in its recognition of personal power through the body, as "the first presentation of the world as a realm of mystical forces" and as "the very process of religious thinking—to beget powers as it symbolizes them."[23] We needn't follow Langer into the "magic circle" she then names and enters. I do want to point out, however, that in pairing the vital and the virtual as the primary tropes of dance, Langer in effect formulates a bridge between phenomenological and semiotic approaches to movement and gesture. In spite of her insufficient treatment of vitality, Langer understood that in virtual gesture, the vital dimensions are as germane as the symbolic ones.

Kinetic sensations, much less their meaning, are rarely the focus of everyday awareness. As Marcel Mauss and, after him, Pierre Bourdieu have pointed out, the bodily patterns we master are then enacted outside of conscious awareness.[24] We remember how to drive a car without focusing on the motor skills needed to turn the key in the ignition, depress the clutch, shift into gear, and rev the accelerator. Dancers step up to the barre and begin a daily routine that includes so many brushes, so many pliés, so many relevés, without needing to relearn each day how to do each move. Bourdieu recognized that the very roteness of the "habitus" disguises cultural and historical predispositions, social schemes of perception and thought sedimented from one generation to the next in patterns of movement. People are not in possession of the habitus; rather, they are possessed by it.[25] In sum, Bourdieu asserts that the unconscious braiding of movement practices and ideologies constrains people to perpetuate social structures at the level of the body.

But the hold of the habitus is not absolute, and we do sometimes transcend its automatic and efficient grip. Pressing the brakes for the tenth time in the middle of a traffic jam, we may question the reason we own cars, calculating the cost and effort of maintaining them, envisioning the natural resources mined to make and run them, seeing the socioeconomic system that requires getting places quickly, and bringing to mind the millions of people in nonindustrial circumstances who don't require them. Performing a plié in the studio, perhaps dancers, too, have lucid moments of seeing themselves, as if from a distance, lined up among the others, holding onto a wooden pole in order to "gracefully" drop and rise over and over again, all agreeing to the perceptual, ideological, and aesthetic conventions of a sociocultural system that values "ballet."[26] Perhaps the lucid moments occur in the opposite direction, consciousness diving inward and immersing in the minute sensations of toes gripping, quads clenching, spine extending, wrist softening, breath suspending. In the first kind of lucidity, one calls on visual imagination to project across distances to "see" the larger system, one's own body bobbing up and down at the barre to keep the system going; in the second, one calls on proprioception, turning awareness inward to "feel" one's body as a continuum of kinetic sensations. In either case, the hold of the habitus is broken, inviting opening beyond routine.

These two imagined possibilities of transcendence correspond to the two major trajectories that I have elsewhere suggested dominate ethnographic studies of dance at the turn of the twenty-first century.[27] Encapsulated in the polarity of "sensibility and intelligibility," the two trajectories loosely represent approaches that emphasize the nature and details of, on the one hand, somatic organizations of knowledge and, on the other, the socially sedimented meanings embodied in movement systems, especially in their political dimensions. The most succinct elaboration of their complementarity is given by psychological anthropologist Thomas Csordas, who weaves together Maurice Merleau-Ponty's phenomenological analysis of perceptual processes and Pierre Bourdieu's sociopolitical analysis of collective practice.[28] Csordas recognizes that the phenomenologists' "lived experience" is never merely individual and subjective but develops as relational and cultural constructions in social space. On the other hand, he understands that the sociologists' "practice" is not only a collective sedimentation passed on through generations but an opportunity for individuality, agency, and somatic awareness.

Distinguishing between "the body" as biological and material and "embodiment" as an "indeterminate methodological field defined by perceptual experience and the mode of presence and engagement in the world," Csordas addresses embodiment as "the starting point for analyzing human participation in a cultural world."[29] He coins the term "somatic modes of attention" to refer to "culturally elaborated ways of attending to and with one's body in surroundings that include the embodied presence of others."[30] I have elsewhere recast Csordas's phrase to apply "a somatic mode of attention," to a *method* of attending to one's own and others' movement with proprioceptive awareness.[31] Here, I want to review and think about the phenomenological pole of embodiment, which, as Csordas recognizes, has been overshadowed by semiotics and therefore not fully developed.[32] In deeply engaging the phenomenological pole, my intention is not so much to point out its limitations as to amplify its possibilities, following Csordas.[33] I offer theoretical justification for attending to the dynamics of embodied knowledge and, in consequence, suggest the methodological importance of qualitative movement analysis in the study of somatic modes of attention.

Following Merleau-Ponty, Csordas takes the primary problem of phenomenology to be the relation between perception and its objects, including especially how we come to perceive ourselves as objects. Traditional philosophers and psychologists progressed from objects, as objectively real, to perceptions, as subjectively responsive to those real objects. The result was the duality of a subjective mental world and an objective physical one, including people's bodies. Merleau-Ponty suggested instead that human perception creates its objects; not that objects are not "real," but rather, their apprehension *as objects* requires subjects. We are first subjects to ourselves in a pre-objective world that experiences embodiment but not "the body."

The work of child psychologist Daniel Stern provides clarification of the problematic term *pre-objective* and supports Merleau-Ponty's ontological order; Stern shows that infants perceive and organize sensory experience before they are able to differentiate objects, including themselves as objects.[34] While it was previously thought that infants developed the senses separately, it is now clear this is not the case. The capacity to "transfer perceptual experience from one sensory modality to another" is innate; infants develop the senses in tandem.[35] For example, presented with different shaped nipples, first felt in the mouth, infants are then able to recognize the shapes visually. Haptic schema (what something feels like) and visual schema (what something looks like) are not developed separately and then united; they are inherently and innately cross-referenced. Before being able to distinguish a nipple as a discrete object, infants can abstract the global shape of nippleness. The same cross-referencing occurs in translating sound intensities (loudness) to visual intensities (brightness) and with recognizing temporal patterns (beat, rhythm, duration) between visual and auditory modes. As a result of this capacity for "amodal perception," before infants recognize that an impression "belongs" to a particular sense or a quality to a particular object, they make global abstractions of shape, temporal pattern, and intensity across the senses.[36] In other words, at the organic level, perceptual experience migrates across sensory modalities.

Philosopher Mark Johnson offers an elegant model for thinking about the pre-objective processes Stern describes.[37] Like Merleau-Ponty, Johnson's context is western philosophy, particularly the separation between a formal, conceptual, and intellectual territory and a material, perceptual, and sensible territory. Johnson challenges objectivism, the notion that meaning occurs as objective structures transcendent of human embodiment and independent of human engagement, recognizing meaning to be an *event* of human understanding. For Johnson, the structures of rationality, including logical thinking, depend on processes of ordering bodily experience via imagination. While Kant hypothesized that imagination mediates between perception and reflection, he "couldn't draw the reasonable conclusion that imagination is both bodily and rational."[38] What, then, is imagination?

For Johnson, it is the prelinguistic, as well as pre-objective but nonetheless cognitive, capacity to structure experience by organizing perceptions into patterns. Johnson dubs the figurative patterns that emerge from and give structure to perceptions "image schemata" or "embodied schemata."[39] I understand Johnson's embodied schemata to be the results of the cross-modal extrapolations Stern describes, and imagination names the extrapolating, abstracting, and synthesizing process by which we build embodied schemata. For example, the spatial embodied schema of "up and down" or the dynamic embodied schema of "rushing" are built cross-modally from movement sensations, seeing, and hearing. Embodied schemata are neither perceptions nor representations but cross-modal recognitions of pattern, whether of form or of quality, as Stern describes. Imagination, then, is not merely a mental operation that works reproductively to duplicate or reflect experience; it is a perceptual/cognitive process that works productively and creatively to configure experience.

Consider the embodied schema of *balance*.[40] The *word* "balance" is a symbol referring to an embodied schema abstracted from multiple bodily experiences of balancing. The bodily experience of balancing exists preverbally as a somatic awareness, but the various instances of balancing are ordered by imagination into balance-as-a-kind-of-experience, the embodied schema of balance. The word-symbol "balance" draws metaphorically on the embodied schema and also contributes to structuring it by naming it.[41] The schema incorporates all the sensory modes so that eventually we see balance in works of art, hear it in the construction of an argument, feel it as an emotional as well as kinetic state, and perform it as a mathematical operation.[42] In other words, built upon the hardwired migration of sensory experience across sensory modalities, we construct embodied schema that migrate across media. Thus, Johnson argues, all propositional statements and abstract reasoning depend on the cross-modal metaphoric process of embodied schemata building. So, too, do all abstract structurings in words, images, sounds, and movements.[43]

While, as anthropologist Brenda Farnell notes, a phenomenological approach carries the danger of positing a "universal bodily experience" that separates "the body from language and culture," the combination of Stern's concept of amodal perception and Johnson's of embodied schema offers a framework for understanding how innate perceptual/conceptual capacities are differentially developed right from the start.[44] Specifically, while the capacity to abstract patterns from sensory experience via amodal perception is innate, the metaphoric process of schema-building is creative, indeterminate, open-ended, and continuously active.[45] Sensations in the womb are influenced by a social milieu, even though they are not organized objectively in terms of "my" sensations in "your" womb. In Csordas's words, our bodies, from the beginning, are "in the world," part of "an intersubjective milieu" that includes others' bodies; thus, it is not subjectivity but intersubjectivity "that gives rise to sensation."[46] Pre-objective and prelinguistic do not imply precultural. In different sociocultural and historical circumstances, people learn to emphasize and value different sensory details of form and quality, different perceptual and expressive media, and different ways of processing somatosensory information.[47]

Most relevant to my attempt to understand the somatic dynamics of movement knowledge, Stern reports that infants can and do extrapolate not only quantifiable elements like shape and temporal pattern; they also cross-modally "yoke together" qualities of feeling.[48] Stern is emphatic that these feelings are not "categorical affects" like happiness, anger, surprise, and so on. Rather, they are "vitality affects," the complex qualities of kinetic energy inherent in all embodied activity.[49] In other words, in terms of Johnson's embodied schemata, we create schemata of vitality affects just as we do of shape and temporal pattern, and we are innately capable of doing so. An infant can recognize, for example, the similarly lightly caressing quality of vitality in the way her mother might brush her hair, sing a lullaby, and smile at her, before she can distinguish her mother or herself as an object and before she can recognize singing, hair-brushing, or smiling as discrete actions.

Unlike the terminology of emotion specific to categorical affects, Stern writes, vitality affects are "better captured by dynamic, *kinetic* terms, such as 'surging,' 'fading away,' 'fleeting,' explosive,' or 'crescendo,' 'decrescendo,' 'bursting,' 'drawn out,' and so on."[50] Vitality affects are most revealed, Stern writes, in events like music and dance that have no "content."[51] Indeed, he acknowledges, they are equivalent to what Suzanne Langer calls the "forms of feeling" embodied in dance.[52] As stated earlier, for Langer these are based on the "sense of vital power" as "our most immediate self-consciousness."[53] I understand the "play of powers" Langer took to be the "primary illusion" of dance to be a play with vitality affects. Likewise, if the phenomenologists' "lived experience" is understood to be the ongoing dynamic changes in vitality affects over time, what Stern calls the "activation contours of experience," then lived experience is not, as dance anthropologist Drid Williams protests, "some mystical bodily event of shared experience" but the cross-modal apprehension of kinetic dynamics as they are differentially developed in different cultural communities.[54]

Until we attend to kinetic dynamics, the way vitality affects are organized in specific movement systems and gestures, we lack a crucial dimension in understanding the cultural construction of embodiment.[55] As Howes calls for "sensory profiles," I am calling for "vitality profiles." The dynamic factors of rhythm, speed, and duration; force; degree of muscular tension or relaxation; and degree of giving in to or resisting gravity (weightiness and lightness) encode cultural dispositions as much as the shapes and spatial patterns of movement do.[56] Labananalysis, as Rudolf von Laban's schema of qualitative or "effort" factors is now called, offers a systematic way of observing such dynamics. The system focuses on four core factors: Weight, Space, Time, and Flow.[57] While the system can be oversimplified, and though it awaits further development, especially in terms of social and cultural constructions of embodiment, it is the most potent tool we have for guiding observation beyond the shapes and spatial patterns of action toward kinetic qualities.[58]

Dance anthropologist Cynthia Cohen Bull offers a sampling of how comparisons of sensory and vitality profiles might work, taking as examples ballet, contact improvisation, and Ghanaian dance.[59] About the traditional European-based ballet, she writes:

> Ballet practice and performance hone visual sensibility, giving the dancer an acute awareness of the body's precise placement and shaping in space, and demonstrating to the spectator the remarkable possibilities of bodily design and the architecture of moving people in space and time, often viewed from a distance. . . .[60]

About contact improvisation, developed in the United States as a countercultural response to ballet and modern dance and to mainstream social mores:

> Contact improvisation offers an almost opposite set of experiences, yet, as an oppositional practice, it engages some of the same cultural concerns as does ballet. In order to shift focus from the visual, beginning dancers close their eyes. When they dance, the body, as in ballet, remains the focus, but rather than being objectified as viewed from the outside, the body ideally becomes the subject of experience from the inside. The practice of contact improvisation seeks to create a sensitivity to touch and to inner sensation. . . .[61]

Finally, about Ghanaian dance:

> When the dancers are not improvising variations, they dance in rhythmic unison with each other, matching their movement impulses to those of a drumming pattern. However, while dancers may appear unified, they seldom produce an exact spatial unison because the emphasis of their movement lies in rhythmic, dynamic action rather than on achievement of a shape or line, as in ballet. . . . Thus, choreography becomes shaped by the rhythmic

> interaction of many people rather than by the choreographer's vision (as in ballet) or by the mutual momentum with a partner's touch (as in contact improvisation).[62]

Studies are needed that carry forward what Bull only hints at, that is, the way sensory and vitality profiles are implicated in different epistemological systems. Indeed, I suggest that sensory and vitality profiles are central not only to cultural organizations of movement but also to cultural organizations of thinking, itself.[63]

An earlier comparative study of gesture, conducted in 1941 by anthropologist David Efron, a student of Franz Boas, suggests that the aesthetic dimensions of movement provide clues to differences in the way different cultural communities structure thinking.[64] Efron's work preceded the kinesics work of Ray Birdwhistell, Albert Scheflen, and Edward Hall and also preceded McLuhan's understanding of cultures as orders of sensory preferences. I review his study here in some detail because it is little known.

Undertaken to refute Nazi notions about the inheritance of so-called "racial gestures," Efron challenged, on both logical and empirical grounds, notions such as that Jewishness is detectable in movements that are common to all Jewish groups.[65] Any serious attempt to correlate race with any given form of behavior such as gesture, he argued, must first prove race as a real category and then empirically investigate the specific behaviors claimed to correspond with it. Denying the validity of any physical criteria of race, Efron attested that there is hardly a single human group that is not the result of racial intermixing, especially in Europe. As for physical traits, he pointed out that they must be the exclusive characteristic of all individuals belonging to the group; there is no morphological type that meets this requirement.[66] Drawing on European and American histories of oratorical style, Efron demonstrated the tremendous variability over time of gestural "fashion," thereby exploding the idea of consistency within even one so-called racial tradition.

Efron's major refutation of the correlation between race and gesture, however, rested on his own empirical research in New York City. He studied and compared the conversational gestures of Jewish immigrants from the ghettos of Lithuania and Poland with those of Neapolitan and Sicilian peasant immigrants.[67] While he found marked differences between the groups in the immigrant generation, in the following generation, depending on the degree of assimilation, the original gestural patterns quickly disappeared. Both Jewish and Italian groups' gestures now more closely resembled those of other New Yorkers than those of their immigrant parents. Here, old world gestural systems did not migrate with the people; rather, the immigrants welcomed into their bodies a gestural migration from the new environment.[68] That significant differences in gestural patterns are determined not by inherent physiological, psychological, or mental differences, but by the interaction between learned traditions and social conditions, was predictable even in 1940. But in the course of his study, Efron found something less predictable, that differences in gestural systems embody differences in the aesthetic structuring of thought. A summary of Efron's findings will clarify the significance of this statement.

Imagine, if you will, the Jewish immigrants gesturing close in front of their bodies, usually one hand at a time. If both hands are engaged, the gestures unfold sequentially, one hand after the other in an "ambulatory" pattern.[69] The tempo is sporadic, changeable. Imagine angular or sinuous "zigzags" with frequent changes of direction, resulting in an intricate gestural "embroidery."[70] Regardless of the amount of space available, the Jewish immigrants tend to converse at close range, often in compact groups, talking at the same time. Gestures embroider speaker and listener together in a "'hand to hand' rhetorical skirmish."[71] Touch is frequent, sometimes as interruption, sometimes to capture attention.

By contrast, imagine the shape of the Italian immigrants' gestures as broader, more rounded and less complex in design. Imagine a full sweep of the arm, pivoting from the shoulder as a single unit, or both arms sweeping out together, symmetrically. Unlike the rhythmically complex zigzags of Jewish "embroidery," these gestures are fluid, tending toward continuity in the same direction for their duration. They unfold at an even pace or else build and subside, suggesting to Efron a feeling of "wholeness," even "wholesomeness."[72] Rather than the tight knots of the Jewish conversationalists, Italian speakers and listeners place themselves apart in "a kind of spatial consideration for the body of the interlocutor."[73] Where the Jewish immigrants' gestures are relational, Efron writes, those of the Italians are presentational. Touch occurs here, too, but as an expression of confidence rather than as an interruption or call to attention.

Efron recognized that these two gestural systems represented two different cognitive styles and meaning-making processes. The Italian immigrants employed gestures that embodied the *content* of their thought, like a sign language. Their gestures were largely connotational, referring to something objective, whether they worked as a kind of pointing, as a depiction of a form, a spatial relationship, or a bodily action, or whether they were symbolic, representing some object, visual or logical. Gesturing among the Jewish immigrants was not pictorial or symbolic and did not refer to the objects of their thought. Where the Italian immigrants carried, so to speak, "a bundle of pictures" in their hands, the Jewish immigrants used gestures to "link one proposition to another, trace the itinerary of a logical journey, or to beat the tempo of mental locomotion."[74] Their embroideries and zigzags resembled "gestural charts of the 'heights' and 'lows,' 'detours' and crossroads' of the ideational route."[75] The first kind of gesturing emphasized the "what" of thinking, the second emphasized the "how."

Challenging the popular misconception that gestures are a kind of semiotic hieroglyphics or pantomimic language that occurs "naturally," Efron concluded that pictorial gesturing only occurs among some cultural groups and that nonpictorial kinds of gesturing are of equal epistemological significance.[76] "We conceive of gestural behavior as an intrinsic part of the thinking process," he writes.[77] The comment is significant, suggesting that "mind" is as much a matter of kinesthetic as of verbal or visual organization. This organization occurs, Efron's data show, not only as the symbolic products of thought but as the aesthetic processes of thinking. These aesthetic processes can be analyzed in terms of sensory profiles and formal kinetic elements: the Italian immigrants emphasizing, for example, the visual shapes of thought content, the Jewish immigrants emphasizing the auditory rhythms of thought process. They can also be analyzed in Johnson's and Stern's terms as the embodied schema of "thinking," involving not only different sensory profiles and structural elements but also different activation contours. For example, the Italian immigrants' epistemological processes emphasized continuous flow and direct pathways; the Jewish immigrants', interrupted flow and indirect pathways. Had Efron been skilled in observing qualities of vitality, we might also have learned about the force of the two kinds of gestural thinking, their changing intensities, and their use of weightiness and lightness. What if, then, we conceptualize "thinking" in different cultural communities as different genres of "choreographic" improvisation whose structural rules migrate, organizing and reorganizing sensory modalities, formal elements, and vitality affects? Thus conceived, we would have a model for thinking about thinking as a matter of symbolic and kin-aesthetic migrations and orderings.

I have focused on the kinetic dynamics, in particular the vitality affects and activation contours, of human movement as an overlooked aspect of bodily knowledge and of thinking itself. I have argued that our inherent capacity to extrapolate the qualities of vitality as they migrate across sensory modalities works in the context of embodiment to link cultural patterns of movement sensation to cultural patterns of figurative citation and aesthetic structuring. What are the implications of these ideas for a theory of gesture? "Gesture" as a schema, in Mark Johnson's sense, relies on and is closely associated with human movement. If the dynamic qualities of vitality are the unmarked, even hidden, dimension of movement and cultural movement systems, then those cultural organizations of kinetic vitality occur as a "ghost" in all gesture. Whether the gesture is a verbal figurative statement (gestures of kindness) or a mechanical means (camera pans and tilts), whether the gesture is socially iterated and inscribed in bodies as an unconscious habitus (the shaping regime of ballet or military training) or transformed in meaning through individual bodies (Louis XIV's dancing body), gesture retains this vital and culturally meaningful dimension. Even still representations (a portrait of Louis XIV displaying his gesturing leg) reveal kinetic qualities. (How much muscular tension does the king exert in his pointed foot, and what does this reveal about his self-representation?)

While the capacity to extrapolate across sensory modalities is innate, the resultant structuring of schema, including the general structuring of the senses and of kinetic qualities in particular, is indeterminate, variable across cultures and over time. Particular sensory and qualitative patterns are reiterated and become relatively fixed in particular sociocultural contexts, enabling both communication and unconscious reproduction. Thus, all gesture is informed by the schematic ordering of movement-and-ideology implicit in the concept of embodiment as defined by Thomas Csordas. This pervasiveness of gestural regimes undermines Suzanne Langer's formulation of a distinction between spontaneous and symbolic gesture. Gesture migrates between quotidian and framed performances as well as between media. Indeed, as anthropologist J. Lowell Lewis points out,

> Clarifying the relations between specially marked social genres and unmarked or tacitly marked daily practices . . . illuminates similarities and differences between both frameworks and potentially reveals deep iconic patterns or schemata that inform many social domains and therefore are central to the recognizable, distinctive, stylistic unities of given cultural systems.[78]

In the interplay between everyday life and art, gestural schema migrate. Consider, for example, MTV's mechanical rhythms of cutting, panning, and framing in relation to American teenagers' quotidian bodily practices, including everyday computer, household, and street rhythms. Compare these to the mechanical qualities of early Hollywood dance films, Busby Berkeley's long views and temporally extended sequences, drawing on New York burlesque and European ballet, and resonant with street and home life in a mechanizing metropolis. Filmic conventions participate in the embodied schema of their time and are, in that sense, inherently meaningful.

These latter thoughts have been inspired by my colleagues' provocative discussions of gesture and, regarding quotidian and framed performance, by Akira Lippit's chapter in this volume. His treatment of figurative gestures as "acts or expressions that invoke gestures without returning to bodies" has led me to thinking of gesture in terms of kinetic layerings, or Lesley Stern's "ghosts" of culturally elaborated embodied schema. I would draw attention here not to the production of gesture but to its reception.

The result of the camera's movements is that we are presented with kinetic information, which we receive the way we receive any movement—no matter the medium of its presentation—in its multiple dimensions, as spatial change, rhythmic pattern, intensity, and so on. I especially appreciate Lippit's comment that the filmmaker who remakes earlier filmic sequences by, for example, repeating instants ad infinitum, interrupts the viewer's expectations through a kind of mechanical kinetic subversion. However, whereas Lippitt suggests that it may be impossible to speak of meaningful gestures at all, if we take "meaning" to be, as Johnson suggests, imaginative play with schema, where schema include, as Daniel Stern makes clear, abstract rhythmic and spatial patterns, shapings, and intensities, then the filmic work Lippitt discusses emerges not as meaningless but as a meaningful subversion of the qualitative habits of a conventional gestural system.

From the perspective of movement and embodiment I have laid out here, a concept of gesture emerges that requires a connection with the organic, not in the sense of requiring the literal presence of human bodies but of referring to the capacities inherent to embodiment. In other words, the organic foundation of gesture refers, in Merleau-Ponty's words, to the "I can" of embodiment, including especially the innate capacity for translating vitality across sensory modalities. The concept of embodiment, as Csordas points out, refuses the separation of a material body from either the "can do" of embodied human potential or the social habitus of being-in-the-world. By contrast, this concept of gesture does not require, indeed disparages, connection with "the natural," where natural refers to any specific quality or performative mode considered to inhere in human embodiment. Thus, the notion in much contemporary modern dance training that fluidity of motion and relaxed muscular effort are "natural," whereas the muscular tension and precise gestural positioning of ballet are not, is spurious. The only use I can find for this word would be to equate the natural with the possible, at which point it becomes not natural but organic. Critically, I am suggesting that a concept of gesture requires not only association with movement's kinetic qualities of vitality but also an accounting of the way the sensations of kinetic vitality are socially structured, transformed, and mediated. In other words, far from positing a universal kinetic sense, this formulation calls out for contextual analysis and amplification.

Notes

I am grateful to Olga Najera-Ramirez for giving me the opportunity to present an early version of this paper to the Anthropology Colloquium at the University of California, Santa Cruz. I have been deeply inspired by the members of the 2002 "Gesture and Inscription" group of the University of California Humanities Research Institute and, above all, by its convener, Carrie Noland, and her co-editor, Sally Ann Ness.

1. Richard Bandler and John Grinder, *Frogs into Princes* (Moab, Utah: Real People Press, 1979), 14. Bandler and Grinder assert that the "representational system," the words people use to describe experience or information, is conscious, while the "accessing system," the strategies or sequences people use to retrieve it, is not. Within accessing systems, the "lead system" is the one used to "go after" the piece of information, the "reference system" the one used to check out the information retrieved (14–15).

2. McLuhan quoted in David Howes, "Sensorial Anthropology," in *The Variety of Sensory Experience: A Sourcebook in the Anthropology of the Senses*, ed. David Howes (Toronto: University of Toronto Press, 1991), 172.

3. David Howes and Constance Classen, "Sounding Sensory Profiles," in Howes, *Variety of Sensory Experience*, 257–88. Howes and Classen suggest that sensory orders may be gleaned by asking, for example, which senses are emphasized in talk, in performance, in artifacts and body decoration, in childraising, in media of communication, in the natural and built environment, and in mythology and its representations.

4. While I use the term *somatic sensation* to encompass all proprioceptive awareness, including, for example, touch, movement, balance, pressure, tension, and temperature, I use the word *kinesthesia* to refer specifically to proprioception of the joint and muscle action involved in movement and the word *kinetic* to refer to *any* movement, including but not limited to joint and muscle action.

5. Howes, "Sensorial Anthropology," 177.

6. Anthony Synnott, "Puzzling over the Senses: From Plato to Marx," in Howes, *The Variety of Sensory Experience*, 63.

7. For a consideration of the western emphasis on the visual sense, see, among

others, Anthony Synnott, "Puzzling over the Senses," 61–78; Elizabeth Grosz, *Volatile Bodies: Toward a Corporeal Feminism* (Bloomington: Indiana University Press, 1994); Cynthia Cohen Bull, "Sense, Meaning, and Perception in Three Dance Cultures," in *Meaning in Motion: New Cultural Studies of Dance*, ed. Jane Desmond (Durham, N.C.: Duke University Press, 1997), 269–88.

8. Gil Fronsdal, *The Issue at Hand: Essays on Buddhist Mindfulness Practice* (Palo Alta, Calif.: Gil Fronsdal, 2001), 50. Fronsdal, a Buddhism scholar and meditation teacher, compares this kind of body consciousness with Vipassana practice, which fosters proprioception. So, too, do many of the Asian "in-body disciplines." See Phillip Zarrilli, "What Does It Mean to 'Become the Character': Power, Prescience, and Transcendence in Asian In-body Disciplines of Practice," in *By Means of Performance: Intercultural Studies of Theatre and Ritual*, ed. Richard Schechner and Willa Appel (Cambridge: Cambridge University Press, 1990), 131–48.

9. Mallory Wober, "The Sensotype Hypothesis," in *The Variety of Sensory Experience: A Sourcebook in the Anthropology of the Senses*, ed. David Howes (Toronto: University of Toronto Press, 1991), 31–46.

10. Drew Leder, in *The Absent Body* (Chicago: University of Chicago Press, 1990) points out that for most people, most of the time, the sensations of movement are beneath conscious awareness. J. Lowell Lewis recognizes, however, that it is not uncommon for movement practitioners, including artists, athletes, and others whose main instrument is the body itself, to be in "mediated states of multiple or diffuse awareness." See J. Lowell Lewis, "Genre and Embodiment: From Brazilian Capoeira to the Ethnology of Human Movement," *Cultural Anthropology* 10, no. 2 (1995): 231. I have suggested elsewhere that the reception of dance for the dancer occurs as an ongoing translation between visual and kinesthetic modalities in a process of "kinesthetic empathy." See Deidre Sklar, "Invigorating Dance Ethnology," *UCLA Journal of Dance Ethnology* 15 (1991): 4–15; and "Can Bodylore Be Brought to Its Senses?" *Journal of American Folklore* 107, no. 423 (1994): 9–22. A more detailed discussion of translation between sensory modalities is offered below.

11. Edward S. Casey, *Remembering: A Phenomenological Study* (Bloomington: Indiana University Press, 1987).

12. For varying approaches to embodied memory, see also Paul Connerton, *How Societies Remember* (Cambridge: Cambridge University Press, 1989); Leder, *The Absent Body;* and Elaine Scarry, *The Body in Pain* (New York: Oxford University Press,1985).

13. Casey, *Remembering*, 167.

14. Casey, *Remembering*, 168.

15. Casey, *Remembering*, 168 (emphasis in original). Since completing this essay, I have discovered rhetorician Mary Carruthers's potent work on memory. She suggests that rather than being temporal, memory is locational; the past is "stored" in cognitive "places." While all memories share "pastness," they are "distinguished by place." Mary Carruthers, *The Craft of Thought: Meditation, Rhetoric, and the Making of Images, 400–1200* (New York: Cambridge University Press, 1998), 13.

16. Suzanne Langer, *Feeling and Form: A Theory of Art* (New York: Charles Scribner's Sons, 1953), 174.

17. Langer, *Feeling and Form*, 175.

18. Langer, *Feeling and Form*, 181.

19. See, for example, David Best, *Expression in Movement and the Arts: A Philosophical Enquiry*. (London: Lepus Books, 1974).

20. Langer, *Feeling and Form*, 174 (emphasis added).

21. Langer, *Feeling and Form*, 176.

22. Langer, *Feeling and Form*, 175. Langer's discussion of the "vital" in relation to the "virtual" deserves a more extended and nuanced treatment than I can give here. Brenda Farnell, in *Do You See What I Mean? Plains Indian Sign Talk and the Embodiment of Action* (Austin: University of Texas Press, 1995), addresses the intentionality and agency implicit in Langer's formulation, developing the concept of "powers" in social and semiotic terms. In particular, she links agency with "an immateralist model of substance as a structure of powers and capacities in which the natural powers grounded in the human organism make possible the realization of personal powers that are grounded in, and thus afforded by, social life" (12).

23. Langer, *Feeling and Form*, 190.

24. Marcel Mauss, "Body Techniques," in *Sociology and Psychology. Essays*, trans. Ben Brewster (London: Routledge and Kegan Paul, 1979), 97–123; Pierre Bourdieu, *Outline of a Theory of Practice* (Cambridge: Cambridge University Press, 1977).

25. Bourdieu, *Outline of a Theory of Practice*, 18.

26. Along with Michel Foucault's work on the social disciplining of bodies, especially, "Docile Bodies," Bourdieu's ideas have influenced a generation of cultural theorists in dance, who analyze movement forms and events in terms of the way they perpetuate or challenge social ideals and values. See Michel Foucault, "Docile Bodies," *Discipline and Punish: The Birth of the Prison* (New York: Random House Vintage Books, 1977), 135–69. Susan A. Reed, in "The Politics and Poetics

of Dance," *Annual Review of Anthropology* 27 (1998): 503–32, provides an overview of works addressing the politics of dance.

27. See Deidre Sklar, "Reprise: On Dance Ethnography," *Dance Research Journal* 32, no. 1 (Summer, 2000): 70–77.

28. Thomas J. Csordas, "Embodiment as a Paradigm for Anthropology," *Ethos* 18, no. 1 (March 1990): 5–47, and "Somatic Modes of Attention," *Cultural Anthropology* 8, no. 2 (May 1993): 135–56. For a discussion of "practice" theory in anthropology, see Sherry B. Ortner, "Theory in Anthropology since the Sixties," *Comparative Studies in Society and History* 26, no. 1 (1984): 126–66. Ortner understands the central problem of a practice orientation to be the relationship between social institutions and structures, on one hand, and people and their actions, on the other. She traces the roots of the concept of practice to the symbolic anthropology of Victor Turner and Clifford Geertz, the cultural ecology of Marshall Sahlins, the structuralism of Claude Lévi-Strauss, and the reintroduction of sociology via Peter Berger and Thomas Luckman into anthropology in the 1970s.

29. Csordas, "Somatic Modes of Attention," 135.

30. Csordas, "Somatic Modes of Attention," 138.

31. Sklar, "Reprise: On Dance Ethnography."

32. Thomas J. Csordas, *The Sacred Self: A Cultural Phenomenology of Charismatic Healing* (Berkeley: University of California Press, 1994), 4.

33. Farnell, in *Do You See What I Mean?* criticizes Merleau-Ponty for simply relocating agency away from the mind and "appear[ing] to locate an equally ambiguous notion of agency *in* the body" (12; emphasis in original). Farnell argues persuasively that only a concept of "the person" can resolve the problem of agency, or causality. Her work has informed my discussion here.

34. Daniel N. Stern, *The Interpersonal World of the Infant: A View from Psychoanalysis and Developmental Psychology* (New York: Basic Books, 1985). Stern, like Csordas, is concerned with the processes by which we become objects to ourselves, or, in his terms, how infants begin to have an emergent sense of self. Experiments show that a sense of self first develops, under two months old, in relation to one's body—"its coherence, its actions, its inner feeling states, and the memory of all these," through the process of organizing sensory experience (46). This is the framework for his discussion of pre-objective organizations of sensory experience.

35. Stern, *The Interpersonal World of the Infant*, 47.

36. Stern, *The Interpersonal World of the Infant*, 57.

37. Mark Johnson, *The Body in the Mind: The Bodily Basis of Meaning, Imagination, and Reason* (Chicago: University of Chicago Press, 1987).

38. Johnson, *The Body in the Mind,* xxvii–xxviii.

39. For Johnson, *image* refers not only to visual representations but to the full range of sensory modalities through which we apprehend and represent the world; however, *image* carries visual connotations, and I therefore prefer the term *embodied schemata.*

40. I expand here on Johnson's example, Johnson, *The Body in the Mind,* 74–75.

41. Elsewhere, I have written: "Words not only symbolize experiences, they participate in the embodied schemata to which they refer. When infants learn to speak, the cross-modal orderings they have already mastered incorporate a verbal dimension, a name, like 'ball' or 'rushing.' The name is associated to the schema so that it both evokes and works upon the somatic pattern." Deidre Sklar, *Dancing with the Virgin: The Enactment and Embodiment of Religious Belief* (Berkeley: University of California Press, 2001), 186. In effect, the word or other symbol objectifies the schema.

42. This kind of polysemic meaningfulness in the English language can be compared to Victor Turner's work on the orectic and normative poles of association that come together in Ndembu ritual symbols. See, among other works, Victor Turner, *The Ritual Process: Structure and Anti-Structure* (London: Routledge and Kegan Paul, 1969).

43. Johnson's wording, that "the 'bodily' works its way up into the 'conceptual' and the 'rational' by means of imagination" is unfortunate; Johnson, *The Body in the Mind,* xxi. As Farnell writes, this hierarchical ordering fails to recognize that complex bodily systems, like dance traditions, are both rational and conceptual; Brenda Farnell, "Introduction," *Human Action Signs in Cultural Context: The Visible and the Invisible in Movement and Dance* (Metuchen, N.J.: Scarecrow Press, 1995), 10. A better way to cast the argument would be to say that abstract concepts (in any modality) depend on perceptual/conceptual capacities inherent in human embodiment, and further, that the resultant conceptual structures, whether in logic, psychology, or art, can be analyzed as metaphoric acts of imagination that connect multiple media of experience.

44. Farnell, *Do You See What I Mean?* 300.

45. Unlike Bourdieu, who sees the habitus as composed entirely of sedimented structures, Johnson recognizes that what we regard as fixed meanings are *simply* the sediments of embodied schemata that are inherently open-ended and

therefore variable, depending upon cultural circumstances. Johnson, *The Body in the Mind*, 175.

46. Csordas, "Somatic Modes of Attention," 138.

47. Sally Ness asks whether I mean to suggest here that "migrating sensations (moving between/around pre-subjective 'milieux') precede sensing locations (individual bodies/subjectivities) in the development of conceptual/perceptual capacities." I would answer that in Merleau-Ponty's sense of an a priori "symbiosis" between perception and its other (the world and its objects), the potential for migratory sensation—via both the world-coming-to-meet and the human capacity for reception and production—precedes specific sensing locations—the individual human body and individual subjectivity. See Maurice Merleau-Ponty, *Phenomenology of Perception*, trans. Colin Smith (London: Routledge, 1962), 317. At the same time, since we are born into specific cultural circumstances, it is impossible to experience either a pre-subjective world or a pre-subjective self; we can only experience the intersubjective migration of sensation through culturally inflected perceptions.

48. Stern, *Interpersonal World of the Infant*, 58.

49. Stern, *Interpersonal World of the Infant*, 53–59.

50. Stern, *Interpersonal World of the Infant*, 54 (emphasis added).

51. Stern, *Interpersonal World of the Infant*, 56.

52. Stern, *Interpersonal World of the Infant*, 54.

53. Langer, *Feeling and Form*, 30.

54. Stern, *Interpersonal World of the Infant*, 57; Drid Williams, *Ten Lectures on Theories of the Dance* (Metuchen, N.J.: Scarecrow Press), 194.

55. I briefly consider qualitative movement analysis in relation to Clifford Geertz's classic discussion of gleaning the social codes lying behind a simple wink in Sklar, *Dancing with the Virgin*, 3.

56. Regarding the importance of temporal factors, see Edward Hall's discussion of rhythm and "synching" in cross-cultural communication. Edward Hall, "Rhythm and Body Movement," in *Beyond Culture* (New York: Anchor, 1977), 71–84.

57. For information on Labananalysis and effort theory, see Ed Groff, "Laban Movement Analysis: An Historical, Philosophical and Theoretical Perspective" (Unpublished Master's Thesis, Connecticut College, New London, 1990); Eden Davies, *Beyond Dance: Laban's Legacy of Movement Analysis* (London: Brechin Books, 2001); and Irmgard Bartenieff and Dory Lewis, *Body Movement: Coping with the Environment* (Amsterdam: Gordon and Breach, 1980). I am grateful to CMA Mary Hayne for these references.

58. For example, the choreometric system, developed by Lomax, Bartenieff, and Paulay and based on Laban principles, attempts to correlate qualitative movement factors with subsistence patterns worldwide. Alan Lomax, Irmgard Bartenieff, and Forrestine Paulay, "Choreometrics: A Method for the Study of Cross-Cultural Pattern in Film," *CORD Research Annual VI. New Dimensions in Dance Research: Anthropology and Dance—The American Indian*, ed. Tamara Comstock (New York: Committee an Research in Dance, 1974): 193–212. Dance anthropologists criticized the distortion of its oversimplified functionalist organization. See, among others, Joann Kealiinohomoku, "Dance and Human History: A Film by Alan Lomax," *Ethnomusicology* 25, no. 1 (1979): 169–76. However, Ness, Novack, and Feld demonstrate the potential of qualitative movement analysis for ethnographic studies. Sally Ann Ness, "Understanding Cultural Performance: Trobriand Cricket," *The Drama Review* 32, no. 4, T120 (Winter, 1988): 135–47, and *Body, Movement, and Culture: Kinesthetic and Visual Symbolism in a Philippine Community* (Philadelphia: University of Pennsylvania Press, 1992); Cynthia J. Novack, *Sharing the Dance. Contact Improvisation and American Culture* (Madison: University of Wisconsin Press, 1990); Steven Feld, "Aesthetics and Synesthesia in Kaluli Ceremonial Dance," *UCLA Journal of Dance Ethnology* 14 (1990): 66–81. For early, non-Laban guidelines for analyzing dance in cultural context, see also Adrienne Kaeppler, "Method and Theory in Analyzing Dance Structure with an Analysis of Tongan Dance," *Ethnomusicology* 16, no. 2 (1972): 173–217; Allegra Fuller Snyder, "Levels of Event Patterns: A Theoretical Model Applied to the Yaqui Easter Ceremonies," in *The Dance Event: A Complex Cultural Phenomenon*, ed. Lisbet Torp (Copenhagen: ICTM Study Group on Ethnochoreology), 1–21; Joann Kealiinohomoku, "Field Guides," *CORD Research Annual VI. New Dimensions in Dance Research: Anthropology and Dance—The American Indian*, ed. Tamara Comstock (New York: Committee on Research in Dance, 1974): 245–60.

59. Cynthia Cohen Bull, "Sense, Meaning, and Perception in Three Dance Cultures," in *Meaning in Motion: New Cultural Studies of Dance*, ed. Jane Desmond (Durham: Duke University Press, 1997), 269–88.

60. Bull, "Sense, Meaning, and Perception," 282.

61. Bull, "Sense, Meaning, and Perception," 283.

62. Bull, "Sense, Meaning, and Perception," 280–81.

63. I was first introduced to the idea of thinking as a process of changing kinetic dynamics by the corporeal mime teacher and theorist Etienne Decroux. Decroux developed a system of movement practice and analysis that combined

spatial "geometry" with what he called *dynamo rhythme*. During the two years I studied with him (1967–69) students applied these concepts in weekly improvisations on the subject of thinking. We also learned to discern, visually, the dynamic nuances in each other's work; see Deidre Sklar, "Etienne Decroux's Promethean Mime," *The Drama Review: International Acting* 29, no. 4 (Winter 1985): 64–75.

64. David Efron, *Gesture, Race and Culture: A Tentative Study of Some of the Spatio-temporal and "Linguistic" Aspects of the Gestural Behavior of Eastern Jews and Southern Italians in New York City, Living under Similar as well as Different Environmental Conditions* (The Hague: Mouton, 1972 [1941]).

65. Efron documents one particularly absurd example: a Nazi apologist argued that each race has a characteristic body-soul and a matching, typical mode of expression so that "a 'Nordic soul' cannot express itself through a non-Nordic body; thus, the gestural style of a Mediterranean is racially linked to 'light [weight] hair,' for only such hair will swing around with the movements of a Mediterranean body"; Efron, *Gesture, Race and Culture*, 25.

66. Efron, *Gesture, Race and Culture*, 39–43.

67. Efron's methods were fourfold and included direct observation, artist's sketches, rough counting of gestural tendencies, and graphs, charts, and measurements drawn from film clips.

68. I am grateful to Sally Ness for suggesting this link to the volume's theme of gestural migration.

69. Efron, *Gesture, Race and Culture*, 83.

70. Efron, *Gesture, Race and Culture*, 73.

71. Efron, *Gesture, Race and Culture*, 92.

72. Efron, *Gesture, Race and Culture*, 115.

73. Efron, *Gesture, Race and Culture*, 121.

74. Efron, *Gesture, Race and Culture*, 123, 98.

75. Efron, *Gesture, Race and Culture*, 99.

76. Efron, *Gesture, Race and Culture*, 95–96.

77. Efron, *Gesture, Race and Culture*, 105n48.

78. Lewis, "Genre and Embodiment," 227.

CHAPTER 5

Digesture: Gesture and Inscription in Experimental Cinema

Akira Mizuta Lippit

The very name of cinema, from kinematics, or "pure motion," alludes to a foundation in movement and gesture; its colloquial synonym makes the relation explicit, "movies"[1]—images that move, that produce and reproduce movement from life itself, animation. The illusion of pure movement in cinema depends on the verisimilitude of the image, on the reproduction of the bodies in motion.[2] The photographic images that form the basis of live-action films refer to a body in space, a body from which the images are drawn indexically. Noting the lengthy exposures required in early photography, Walter Benjamin speaks of the photographed subject as one who "as it were grew into the picture," as if the movement from the world to the photograph entailed a metamorphosis.[3] Susan Sontag and Roland Barthes, among others, imagine the relationship between physical bodies and the photographs they produce as an umbilicus that connects the photographic image to its source. Alluding to Sontag, Barthes says, "A sort of umbilical cord links the body of the photographed thing to my gaze: light, though impalpable, is here a carnal medium, a skin I share with anyone who has been photographed."[4] The idiom of corporeality continues in the discourses of cinema, where André Bazin and Siegfried Kracauer, among other realists, have made similar claims regarding the contact or touch—*punctum*, says Barthes—that connects bodies and photographs in the realm of cinema.[5] The phantasm of photography, haunted by the specter of an irreducibly maternal indexicality, enters with cinema into the secondary fantasy of animation—to make move and make live, to make alive. The body, captured in the photographic crypt (Bazin speaks of photography as embalming) returns to life in cinema; it resumes life, one could say.

The photographic relation between bodies in the world and bodies in film is extended by some film theorists into the registers of movement. Bazin, for example, says of cinema, "Now, for the first time, the image of things is likewise the image of their duration, change mummified as it were."[6] The movements of bodies in the world dictate, through the medium of photographic reproduction, the movement of bodies in cinema. Movement is measured in time and captured in cinema, a feature unavailable in still photography. Unlike photography, which preserves only the body as such, cinema preserves an image of the body in motion. The two instances of movement, physical and filmic, are bound by a photographic logic that transposes the body from reality to cinema. Time animates the photographic body in cinema. For Kracauer, the dimensions of time (duration) and movement in cinema perfect the representation of reality begun in photography: "Films tend to capture physical existence in its endlessness," says Kracauer. "Accordingly, one may also say that they have an affinity, evidently denied to photography, for the continuum of life or the 'flow of life,' which of course is identical with open-ended life."[7] Life flows freely between physical and filmic reality, establishing an endless continuum between the two registers of movement.

But if physical reality, as Kracauer calls it, and photography, or cinematography, are bound by an umbilical line that maintains a "continuum of life" between life and cinema, a unique paradox haunts the articulation of bodies in cinema. Despite the simultaneous presence of two bodies in cinema, one in the physical world, the other on film, the body in film is also a lost body, in some fundamental way, there only as a trace. The powerful force of photographic impression is countered in cinema by an irrecoverable sense of loss. Kaja Silverman describes a tendency throughout the history of film theory to posit a lack that is symbolic but also essential to the phenomenon of cinema. What is missing in cinema, says Silverman, prior to subjectivity is the body itself. It is at the heart of filmic representation: cinema is an apparatus that generates lost bodies. Silverman encapsulates

Bazin's paradoxical logic of photographic indexicality, on the one hand, and the disappearance of real objects, which "is somehow intrinsic to the cinematic operation," on the other:[8]

> Despite Bazin's assertion that the photographic image "is the object itself," and his conviction that the continuum of the image and object is interrupted only by syntax and metaphor, he occasionally concedes that lack is somehow intrinsic to the cinematic operation. In "An Aesthetic of Reality," he speaks of the "loss of the real" which is "implicit in any realist choice," and which frequently allows the artist, by the use of any aesthetic convention he may introduce into the area thus left vacant, to increase the effectiveness of his chosen form of reality." Elsewhere Bazin suggests that one of the sacrifices cinema thus necessitates is the physical presence of the actor—and, by extension, that of any other profilmic event.[9]

Realism is, in Bazin's thought, ultimately an antidotal idiom designed to address a symptom of cinema, which is the inevitable loss of bodies and things in their depiction. Although cinema generates, perhaps more than any other medium, the effect of verisimilitude bordering on hallucination, the perceived proximity of bodies is balanced by the fundamental disappearance of the body as such in cinema, which is to say, the body is both virtually present and absent in filmic representation.

A shift to psychoanalytic registers produces the same paradox: the powerful forces of primary and secondary identification in cinema do not suture, and are in fact dependent on, the phenomenon of lost bodies. Comparing the reality that is "given" in theater, the presence of bodies "in the same space as the spectator," with the slight remove from reality that determines the effect of reality in cinema, Christian Metz says,

> The cinema only gives it [reality] in effigy, inaccessible from the outset, in a primordial *elsewhere*, infinitely desirable (= never possessible), on another scene which is that of absence and which nonetheless represents the absent in detail, thus making it present, but by a different itinerary.[10]

Metz calls the "primordial elsewhere" that renders the absent and the absence of the absent distinctly present ("but by a different itinerary") an "imaginary signifier." No signifier is more imaginary in cinema, more primordially elsewhere, perhaps, than that of the moving body. The moving, gesturing body in cinema signals its presence in the world, a presence transposed in the umbilical, photographic continuum that binds cinema to physical reality, but also its withdrawal, its status as an imaginary signifier that becomes a figure for absence: a figure of the absent figure.

At work in the peculiar phenomenology that renders bodies present and absent at once is a doubling of bodies in cinema, which allows for the paradox to remain intact: the body is there as an animated photograph, carrying with it all of the phantasms of photographic reality, but the body, that same body doubled, is profoundly and irreducibly absent. The body is at once moved into the frame of cinema and removed from it; moved and *removed.* Mixed together are the various systems—machinic, perceptual, phenomenal, psychological, photographic—that create movement in cinema, as well as the various levels of signification—indexical, symbolic, imaginary—that register the movement. But the duality that haunts the movement of bodies in cinema is not restricted to the body in the world and its transposition to film. Movement in cinema also signals the presence of two types of bodies: those profilmic bodies of actors and even objects, which can also be made to move, and the body of the apparatus, which introduces another form of movement into the spaces of the cinema. The apparatus inscribes onto each film a regime of movements that originates in another body. The camera introduces pans, tilts, tracks, cranes, and other types of movement that refer to the body of the camera, even when it serves as an agent for a character in the film (the point-of-view or subjective shot, for example). Editing also introduces movement by forging temporal and spatial flows, usually with the objective of seamlessness and transparency, but not always. The jump cut, for example, and any breach of the 180-degree line of axis, will introduce jarring movements that do not originate in the body of an actor or thing nor in the camera, but so do ordinary edits that generate shifts in time and space. Taken together, the camera and the apparatus of film (even the projection can introduce movement in some instances) can be seen as a separate body distinct from profilmic bodies and capable of gesturing in another register. In every film, two bodies produce gestures and movements and serve as two separate modes of inscription.

To understand movement in cinema, and gesture in particular, one must recognize the activity of two bodies or sources of movement in cinema. The represented movement of profilmic bodies, which are complicated extensions and erasures of bodies in the world, and the movements that are produced as an effect of the apparatus—synthetic movements, or those movements that do not return to *any body in the film*. The latter form of movement suggests the possibility of gestures without a body or of a body defined prosthetically as the cinema apparatus itself. Can gestures take place without a body? Or rather, is it possible to conceive of gestures that are inscribed on a film body from without rather than produced from within a body?

The doubling of bodies that defines movement in cinema follows two economies. The first involves the photographic duplication of bodies in the world, which produces at once an extension of the body indexically from world to cinema and which also generates an absent body, a phantom body that appears in the film under erasure. The second form of movement signals the presence of two bodies of distinct origin: the profilmic body and the apparatus, two bodies capable of producing movement in a film. The two systems work together and at once in cinema, effecting a simultaneous proliferation and disappearance of bodies across the threshold of movement that defines, in its essence, the operation of cinema.

If two bodies inhabit cinema, one transposed from the world, the other formed in and from the apparatus, then it would follow that movement is similarly doubled, as are gestures in cinema. What term can best accommodate the dual, doubled but paradoxical and contradictory forces of movement and gesture in cinema? What expression might best account for the doubled and absent bodies that generate movement in cinema? The prefix *di-* can mean "two" and, as an abbreviation of *dis-*, an antithesis. Two gestures or non-gesture: *disgesture, digesture.* Digestures are doubled gestures that indicate the presence of two bodies, or two bodily systems, and at the same time, the radical negation of the body, its complete erasure, which forges gestures without bodies: digesture.

Although the machinery that produces movement in cinema is visible in many instances, one genre in particular, one practice more than others, illuminates the complex mechanisms of movement and gesture in cinema: experimental film. Of the various moments and modes that define the history of avant-garde and experimental cinema, the structuralist films of the 1950s, 1960s, and early 1970s best illuminate the emphasis on film movement. Michael Snow's films, including *Wavelength* (1967), *Back and Forth* (1969), *La Région centrale* (1971), and *Breakfast* (1976), emphasize the movement of the camera through space. Zooms, pans, tracking, and other motorized camera movements generate a repertoire of camera gestures in Snow's films that return forcefully to the camera, to the site of the camera, as the origin of movement. In Snow's work, the camera assumes the dimensions of a mechanical body, a source of the gestures that fill the nonhuman spaces of his films. By contrast, Tony Conrad, Peter Kubelka, and Paul Sharits, among others, use single-frame editing or "flickers" to generate movement in the dense transitions between frames. Kubelka's *Arnulf Rainer* (1960) and Conrad's *The Flicker* (1965) generate movements of light on the screen, small explosions of light, by alternating rapidly between dark and light frames of film. In *T,O,U,C,H,I,N,G* (1969), Sharits introduces human figures and objects as single-frame still images, which he mixes with colored frames. These abstract and concrete frames generate bursts of movement between colors and images and engender movement where none is discernible.[11] Stan Brakhage, whose later works often consisted of painted or carved films made without cameras, also emphasizes the movement between frames. By painting or scratching the surface of the film, Brakhage extends continuous lines across the limits of the frame, which generates a movement not bound by the alternation of frames and the breaks between them when projected. Ernie Gehr uses the "energies of the projector" in *Reverberation* (1969) to interject random and irregular movement between frames.[12] The energy of the projector and its erratic drives produce movements in *Reverberation* that supersede those of the camera.

Andy Warhol also uses the vagaries of film projection to institute random movement in his split-screen projection of *The Chelsea Girls* (1966), which generates mobile configurations of the screens as the twelve reels of identical length that constitute the film can be projected in any order. Stephen Koch describes the apparatus:

> The film is projected two reels at a time, in a phased relationship that separates the beginning of each by about five minutes. Tradition, rather than Warhol himself, has established the standard sequence of the reels. . . . Theoretically, any arrangement is possible—and since every reel has a soundtrack, that arrangement would permute with any interplay between sound and silence theoretically conceivable. The sequence of the film freely offers itself to tradition or randomness or taste or invention; playing with it, the projectionist at last has his day as *chef d'orchestre.*[13]

In *The Chelsea Girls*, Warhol has established an economy of movement that shifts between the profilmic bodies of the actors, the gestures of the camera, and the actions of the projectionist, whose own body comes to determine the choreography of movements in the projected film. The crucial movement of the film is performed in its projection.

In the contemporary avant-garde, experimental filmmakers and video artists such as Matthias Müller, Douglas Gordon, and especially Martin Arnold have emphasized movement and gesture in a series of works that put into relief the multiple structures and systems of the body in cinema. Matthias Müller's compilation film *Home Stories* (1990) consists of shots of famous women actors, taken from famous Hollywood films, repeating similar gestures in clusters of rapid sequence. Ingrid Bergman, Tippi Hedren, Kim Novak, Lana Turner, among many others, appear to repeat virtually identical gestures in a compulsive and mechanical manner: falling onto a bed, shutting a door, listening at a shut door, turning on and off lights, peering out of windows, being frightened by noises, running to and from rooms in a house. The bodies that Müller animates in *Home Stories*—all women in domestic settings—appear less photographic than automatic.[14] The women become, according to the apparent politics of the film, like automata, no longer in control of their own bodies, moved through threatening domestic spaces by other forces. At work in Müller's film is a tension between the movements of the photographed bodies, the movements that they bring to cinema from the physical world, and the movements that have been imposed on them by the montage, by the generative forces of the apparatus. They have become photographic marionettes, hybrid bodies that oscillate between the physical and cinema worlds.

In his video installations *24 Hour Psycho* (1993) and *Five Year Drive-by* (2001), among others, Douglas Gordon moves in the opposite direction of Müller, reducing film movements to near imperceptibility by slowing them to a virtual standstill. In *24 Hour Psycho*, Gordon projects Alfred Hitchcock's *Psycho* (1960) in its entirety but slowed to last twenty-four hours. (Hitchcock's original runs approximately 109 minutes, so Gordon has stretched the duration by more than 1,300 minutes, or by more than thirteen times its original length.) Gordon's version of *Psycho* appears to be immobile, frozen in particular frames; its movement is perceptible only over extended stretches of time. In *Five Year Drive-by*, Gordon goes further. Using John Ford's *The Searchers* (1956), Gordon stretches the film across several months to approximate in real-time the five-year narrative of the original. Ford's film runs approximately 119 minutes, while Gordon's installation lasts just under seven weeks, meaning that each second of film in the original takes approximately six hours to project in the installation. In these works, Gordon has destroyed nearly all of the movements in the original films. Camera movements and the movements of people are reduced to freeze-frames and tableaus, imposing an overwhelming catalepsy onto the bodies that roam the original, highly agitated works. Gordon has all but annihilated movement, leaving just enough to maintain an umbilical line to the original films and to the worlds they are in turn bound by.

In three found footage films, *pièce touchée* (1989), *passage à l'acte* (1993), and *Alone. Life Wastes Andy Hardy* (1998), and in a digital film installation, *Deanimated* (2002), Martin Arnold creates an entire circuit of bodily inscriptions and gestures that begins with violent animations and concludes with an attempted erasure of not only gestures and bodies but of cinema as such. Arnold's first three films can be seen as a trilogy, since each work explores in progression the relationship between the movements of bodies and film frames in contiguous shots, entire scenes, and ultimately across multiple films.[15] *Pièce touchée* reworks one shot from Joseph M. Newman's *The Human Jungle* (1954), moving forward and backward in small units of space. The result is the expansion of 18 seconds of original footage into 16 minutes of reconstituted movement. The original gestures and movements of the depicted characters, a man and a woman, have been torn from their original worlds and relocated into the synthetic spaces of Arnold's cinema. Their bodies are no longer theirs, as the original film is no longer itself; even the mise-en-scène has been inverted and flipped in Arnold's reconfiguration. (At moments in the film, Arnold reverses the frame, reversing left and right, and at others, he turns the frame upside-down.) The relations between movements and gestures have also been reconstituted in *pièce touchée:* Arnold's version links, for example, the movements of a man entering a room with a seated woman turning her head. The causal relation of the two movements is amplified in Arnold's film, and the synchronicity of the gestures is transformed in Arnold's film into an aggressive economy of force. The man opening the door appears, in Arnold's mix, to be jerking the head of the seated woman.

The other films from Arnold's found footage trilogy sustain the impression that movements in the original works have been dismantled and that new gestures not located in the original bodies have been inscribed over the original cinematography. *Passage à l'acte* reworks a scene from Robert Mulligan's *To Kill a Mockingbird* (1962), stretching the horizon of gestures from contiguous frames to a larger scene with edits and a sustained shot reverse-shot sequence. The breakfast table scene features a stern Atticus Finch (Gregory Peck), who admonishes his two children to get along. The minor disturbance and scolding is enhanced in Arnold's remix into a cacophony of noise and mechanical gestures, which transforms the sensible original into a violent domestic explosion. The family appears to be gripped by a paroxysm of uncontrollable violence. *Alone. Life Wastes Andy Hardy* is drawn primarily from the "Andy Hardy" films, which feature Mickey Rooney and Judy Garland. The prepubescent romantic and sexual awakenings that tend to drive those films and others that Rooney and Garland starred in are transformed in Arnold's remake into libidinal eruptions and a constant flow of aggressive sexual gestures. Brief touches between a mother and son are turned into displays of erotic affection; a father's slap is repeated until it turns from a spontaneous scolding into a sustained beating; a mother's sigh becomes an expression of sexual excitement; and an awkward kiss between two teenagers becomes a frenzy of hisses.

Throughout the trilogy, Arnold generates in his recycled bodies a repertoire of new gestures: nervous ticks, extensive stutters, apparent seizures, involuntary jerks and spasms, exaggerated signals, overexposed affect, and minute movements like the quivering of fingers between two frames. In each instance, Arnold has put into relief the two systems of movement and the two forms of incorporation at work in cinema. Two bodies clash in Arnold's cinema, the body in the world, and by extension the photographed body, and the body of the apparatus, which appears in conflict with the photographed body. The tension between the bodies produces a series of digestures that operate like the nervous movements Arnold inscribes: bodies start, stop, and falter, unable to advance smoothly because of a resistance inscribed in each movement as a countermovement. Every movement is slowed and resisted by countermovements, counterforces, and counterbodies.

The bodies that inhabit Arnold's work are truly lost bodies; he has evacuated them of all personhood and inscribed them into an emptied-out cinema space. Arnold reanimates these bodies, establishing a form of movement but more precisely of gesture, which does not flow from a body in the world but from another body—an inert, static body that only resembles a photographic imprint or index. One gesture inscribed over another, one gesture absorbed by another, digested. Bodies absorbed by the cinema, digested, re-gestured, and reinscribed over other bodies and gestures.

The structural problem of doubled bodies and missing bodies reaches another plateau in Arnold's work, which emphasizes through exaggeration the paradox of bodies and their movements in cinema. The problem concerns the vicissitudes of identification in cinema generally and in Arnold's work specifically. Among the spectral crises that film representation provokes is the indexical presence of the photographed body, which effects an inverse sense of deep absence. The fact that the body is there, that it appears to be there, photographically transposed and cinematographically animated, underscores the realization of its absence. Further complicating this metaphysics of the body is the vector of identification, which invites an affective and psychological investment in the dialectic of presence and absence. Arnold's bodies are devoid of psychology even when the bodies and their identities are recognizable—Gregory Peck, Mickey Rooney, Judy Garland, and Bela Lugosi, for example. Arnold's figures are inaccessible, making identification nearly impossible. That is, they are not open in the way that even phantoms are. They are sealed bodies, impenetrable materially or psychologically. As a result, Arnold's bodies are uncanny: they are recognizable as photographic traces, as intact figures, but they have been severed from the "flow of life" and recast in an irreducibly distant space, cinema. They are there and not there; and their movements are synthetic assemblages of organic and machinic movement. In each work, Arnold illuminates the heterogeneity of movement in cinema, the superimposition of two bodies and two systems of movement that cannot be resolved into a singular form and energy.

Another visual artist has raised similar issues of movement and the figure in an entirely other register, painting. Francis Bacon is described by Gilles Deleuze as the artist who explored the force of movement on immobile bodies. "What fascinates Bacon," says Deleuze, "is not movement but its effect on an immobile body: heads whipped by wind, deformed by an aspiration—but also all the interior forces that climb through the flesh. To make spasm visible."[16] In the static frame of painting, Bacon's figures struggle to release "interior forces," to expose the spasm that explodes onto the surface of the painting not as the liberation of an organic movement but as the expression of a visual force that is *taken out* on the figure. Why compare a painter and filmmaker across the vast divide that separates the arts, that separates their arts? One entry is through the relationship that both establish between figure and movement, between bodies and immobilities, and the effect that this convergence produces on the medium of each artist.

The figure in Bacon's work is "*too* present," says Deleuze; it conveys an "excessive presence."[17] Like the photograph, which plays an important role in Bacon's work, the excessive presence of the figure marks its fragility and its proximity to absence.[18] According to Deleuze, Bacon's figures do not represent attempts to reinscribe the body into the painting, to counteract the forces of abstraction, but rather the means by which invisible forces become visible. The figure is there, as in Arnold's films, to receive the blow of a force, which makes visible the force of movement. The body serves to register the force; any movement or spasm is an effect of this force and not its origin. Deleuze says, "What interests Bacon is not exactly movement, although his painting makes movement very intense and violent. But in the end, it is a movement 'in-place,' a spasm, which reveals a completely different problem characteristic of Bacon: *the action of invisible forces on the body* (hence the bodily deformations, which are due to this more profound cause.)"[19] The body does not generate movement in Bacon's work; it absorbs and registers those movements imposed on it by force. The body makes movement visible but does not initiate it. Movement deforms the body and renders force visible in the figure.

Although the differences between Bacon and Arnold specifically and the distances between painting and cinema more generally are great, cannot one make a similar claim regarding the artificial movements of Bacon's and Arnold's figures? Arnold's figures are, like Bacon's, deformed: the movements that are ascribed to them are not organic, not derived from the flows of life that are said to animate cinema.[20] Rather, Arnold's figures convey a desperate wish to escape from the economies of subjectivity and identification. "It is not I who attempts to escape from my body," says Deleuze, "it is the body that attempts to escape from itself by means of . . . in short, a spasm."[21] The spasms that characterize Arnold's cinema, the seemingly perpetual state of seizure, reveal an inorganic body or other body, doubled and erased, which seeks to escape movement, escape itself, and erupt into the field of a more general force.

In Bacon's painting, Deleuze identifies the mechanism of escape: an opening in the figure through which force escapes and becomes visible. Bacon's figure, says Deleuze, "presses outward, trying to pass and dissolve through the Fields. Already we have here the role of the spasm or of the scream: the entire body trying to escape, to flow out of itself."[22] It is as if the movements of the body enter and exit through a portion of the figure, an intensified locus of the figure that comes at but also leads to the end of figuration. A figure of and at the end of figuration: this is Bacon's strategy for visualizing force, for releasing the body from itself. "Never (except perhaps in the case of Michelangelo) has anyone broken with figuration by elevating the Figure to such prominence."[23] Bacon's figures are situated, for Deleuze, at the limits of figure and field, representation and abstraction, materiality and dissipation, body and energy, and ultimately body and figure.[24] "Painting," says Deleuze generally, "directly attempts to release the presences beneath representation, beyond representation."[25]

The release of force takes place in Bacon through an opening in the figure, a crack or tear, like the mouth. The eruption and visualization of force is, says Deleuze, hysterical.

> The entire series of spasms in Bacon is of this type: scenes of love, of vomiting and excreting, in which the body attempts to escape from itself *through* one of its organs in order to rejoin the field or material structure. Bacon has often said that, in the domain of Figures, the shadow has as much presence as the body; but the shadow acquires this presence only because it escapes from the body that has escaped from itself through some localized point in the contour. And the scream, Bacon's scream, is the operation through which the entire body escapes through the mouth. All the pressures of the body.[26]

All the pressures of the body are released through some localized contour, and even shadows become expressions of this release. In Arnold's cinema, localized points on the body serve as similar mechanisms of release: a twitching finger in *pièce touchée;* the tip of Gregory Peck's finger or the vibrating hand of the boy in *passage à l'acte;* the mother's heaving respiration and Mickey Rooney and Judy Garland's hissing kisses in *Alone,* for example. In each instance, one senses the force of another body that seeks to escape the photographed body—not an original or organic body but a force that refuses to remain within the cinematographic figure. It is a force that ultimately destroys the figure and the film.

And like the elevation of the figure as a means to break with the figure, which Deleuze describes in Bacon's work, Arnold's work refigures a trajectory of largely abstract, formal, and nonfigurative work that includes Stan

Brakhage, Hollis Frampton, Kurt Kren, and Peter Kubelka among many others, who tore the figure from the screen and replaced the movement of bodies with an entirely other body of movement. In contrast to this lineage of experimental filmmakers who introduced a rupture into the illusion of cinematographic movement, Arnold reintroduces the figure not as a means of resinscribing the body but as a way to exhaust it. The photographic body returns in Arnold's work as a figure of exhaustion. Arnold's figures, like the figures that Deleuze describes in Bacon, come at the extreme end of figuration. It is thus logical that the figure starts to disappear in Arnold's first work after his found-footage trilogy, *Deanimated.*

Arnold's digital found-footage installation reworks an entire film, Joseph H. Lewis's *The Invisible Ghost* (1941), which features Bela Lugosi. Arnold has transposed nearly the entire film (with the exception of one scene) but has then erased various figures from the mise-en-scène.[27] Here and there, Arnold digitally removes characters from the film, filling in the evacuated spaces with a digital mat that conceals, at least graphically, the absence. Neither systematic nor consistent, Arnold's digital erasure leaves large holes in the recycled work through which the forces of narrative cohesion, spatial balance and orientation, camera logic, and the economy of bodily movement and gesture escape. Characters are not where they should be, looks remain unreturned; the camera moves through space for no apparent reason and stares at empty furniture; and conversations remain one-sided when queries and attempts at dialogue are left open by unresponsive and empty silences.

In order to avoid the "invisible man effect," as Arnold calls it, Arnold introduces another form of erasure into *Deanimated:* the removal of voices from the soundtrack.[28] In the middle of conversations, Arnold excises the voices from one or more characters. As a result, characters engaged in dialogue remain in view, but their vocal participation in the scene has been suspended, leaving awkward and unmotivated gaps, pauses, and absences in the economy of a conversation. But in order to fill the void left by the erased dialogue, Arnold digitally seals the mouths of the silenced characters, producing an uncanny suture of the orifice where sound was formally located. It is this act of inscription that produces the most disturbing gestures of *Deanimated:* the normal movements of a body in speech remain while its focal point, the mouth, has been paralyzed. Like the focal organs and orifices that Deleuze identifies in Bacon's painting, this inverted orifice—the sealed mouth—in Arnold's cinema serves as a release of force but through an economy of digestion.

The words are literally swallowed by the bodies that produced them, forced back into the figures. The attempts to digest these words are registered by the uncanny movements of the bodies struggling to reabsorb the attempts at expression, in the twitching motions that remain as traces of the original gestures. Arnold has reinscribed the original gestures back onto the photographed bodies; he has rephotographed them, so to speak. Arnold's *deanimated* mouths have become the site of release for his figures: they absorb the forces that deform the figure. In this sense, Arnold's erasures produce a new system of gestures, digested gestures, digestures.

Deanimated gestures produce gestures in reverse. In Arnold's work, the two bodies of photography—one in the world, the other in the photographic impression—and the two bodies of cinema—one cinematographic, the other apparatic—are compressed into the missing body of photography and film, generating a synthetic figure of doubled and absent bodies. This fantastic economy of gesture produces a figure of erasure, a gesture of disappearing gestures that absorbs and digests all figures, including the scene of representation, the spectacle, and even the spectator. As Deleuze says of Bacon's work, "One discovers in Bacon's paintings an attempt to eliminate every spectator, and consequently every spectacle."[29] The force of digesture that Arnold unleashes through the figure and into the plane of representation consumes everything: every system of the body, every form of movement and gesture, and ultimately the spectacle and spectator. Identification remains here only as a kind of absorption, the sealed mouths close off the body and deflect the *punctum.* Nothing is left in Arnold's cinema except gestures without bodies, emphasizing (but also perverting) the original condition in cinema of the lost body. These gestures are not the cinematographic movements of bodies, nor are they the movements of the apparatus; they are the gestures at the end of cinema, gestures that come at the end of cinema and that end cinema. They are gestures that come from no body, digestures.

Notes

1. The Lumière Brothers, Auguste and Louis, called their 1895 invention "the Cinématographe."

2. In contrast to other movement machines, such as the Phenakistoscope, Zoetrope, and Praxinoscope, which brought together pictorial representation and movement, the particular nature of the cinema effect depended on the convergence of pictorial realism—however imaginary—and movement.

3. Walter Benjamin, "A Small History of Photography," in *One-Way Street and Other Writings*, ed. Susan Sontag, trans. Edmund Jephcott and Kingsley Shorter (London: Verso, 1979), 245.

4. Roland Barthes, *Camera Lucida: Reflections on Photography*, trans. Richard Howard (New York: Hill and Wang, 1981), 81. "The photograph," Barthes says, "is literally an emanation of the referent. From a real body, which was there, proceed radiations which ultimately touch me, who am here; the duration of the transmission is insignificant; the photograph of the missing being, as Sontag says, will touch me like the delayed rays of a star" (Barthes, *Camera Lucida*, 80–81).

5. Certain photographs are capable of wounding their viewers. "A Latin word exists to designate this wound," says Barthes, "this prick, this mark made by a pointed instrument: the word suits me all the better in that it refers to the notion of punctuation . . . *punctum*" (Barthes, *Camera Lucida*, 26–27). In *Theory of Film*, Siegfried Kracauer says, "Due to the continuous influx of the psychophysical correspondences thus aroused [between cinema and the physical world], they suggest a reality which may fittingly be called 'life.' *This term as used here denotes a kind of life which is still intimately connected, as if by an umbilical cord, with the material phenomena from which its emotional and intellectual contents emerge*" (*Theory of Film: The Redemption of Physical Reality* [New York: Oxford University Press, 1960]) 71, emphasis added). Similar motifs appear throughout André Bazin's writing. See for example, "The Ontology of the Photographic Image" (in *What Is Cinema?* ed. and trans. Hugh Gray [Berkeley: University of California Press, 1971], vol. I, 9–16), in which he writes, "The photograph as such," says Bazin, "and the object in itself share a common being, after the fashion of a fingerprint" (15).

6. Bazin, "The Ontology of the Photographic Image," 15.

7. Siegfried Kracauer, *Theory of Film*, 71.

8. Kaja Silverman, *The Acoustic Mirror: The Female Voice in Psychoanalysis and Cinema* (Bloomington: Indiana University Press, 1988), 3.

9. Silverman, *The Acoustic Mirror*, 3. Contrasting the uses of reality in cinema and theater, Bazin says: "Not that we are against filmed theater, but if the screen can in some conditions develop and give a new dimension to the theater, it is of necessity at the expense of certain scenic values—the first of which is *the physical presence of the actor*" (André Bazin, "Bicycle Thief," in *What Is Cinema?* ed. and trans. Hugh Gray [Berkeley: University of California Press, 1971], vol. II, 59, emphasis added). Bazin concludes by declaring Vittorio De Sica's *Bicycle Thief* (*Ladri di Biciclette*, 1948) one of the first examples of "pure cinema," achieved in the total disappearance of aesthetic form: "No more actors, no more story, no more sets, which is to say that in the perfect aesthetic illusion of reality there is no more cinema" (60).

10. Christian Metz, *The Imaginary Signifier: Psychoanalysis and the Cinema*, trans. Celia Britton, Annwyl Williams, Ben Brewster, and Alfred Guzzetti (Bloomington: Indiana University Press, 1982), 61, original emphasis. Speaking of the imaginary recess of the image, the illusion of fullness engendered by all forms of looking, Metz notes the specific quality of the imaginary signifier, which installs a *figure* of absence. He says: "It is this last recess that is attacked by the cinema signifier, it is in its precise emplacement (*in its place*, in both senses of the word) that it installs a new figure of lack, the physical absence of the object seen" (Metz, *The Imaginary Signifier*, 63, original emphasis).

11. "Cinema is not movement," says Peter Kubelka. "It can give the illusion of movement. Cinema is the quick projection of light impulses" (Jonas Mekas, "Interview with Peter Kubelka," in *Film Culture Reader*, ed. P. Adams Sitney [New York: Praeger, 1970], 291). For Kubelka, cinema takes place in the movement between frames, in the concentrated time and space of the interval between frames. "Where is, then, the articulation of cinema? Eisenstein, for example, said it's the collision of two shots. But it's very strange that nobody ever said that *it's not between shots but between frames*. It's between frames where cinema speaks" (Mekas, "Interview with Peter Kubelka," 292, original emphasis).

12. Ernie Gehr used the expression the "energies of the projector" to describe his screening of *Reverberation* at the LA Film Forum in Los Angeles, California, March 2005.

13. Stephen Koch, *Stargazer: Andy Warhol's World and His Films* (New York:

Marion Boyars, 1985), 87. Movement in *The Chelsea Girls* is generated further by the interaction between the actors' gestures and those of the camera: "The camera is invariably on a fixed tripod; its entire movement consists of zooms and swiveling on its stand. Each performer is set in front of the camera and told to stay there playing until the reel runs out. And so they do, pinned by the camera against a wall of time" (Koch, *Stargazer*, 87).

14. Müller continues his obsession with found gestures in his homage to Hitchcock, *Phoenix Tapes* (1999), which he directed with Christoph Giradet. The project consists of six videotapes, which are compilations of scenes from forty Hitchcock films. Each tape emphasizes an aspect of Hitchcock's cinema, including mothers, landscapes, and close-ups. One tape is devoted to the movements of hands in Hitchcock's work. The continuous sequence of hands has the effect of foregrounding but also isolating and abstracting the economy of gestures in Hitchcock's cinema.

15. For a sustained analysis of Arnold's trilogy, see Akira Mizuta Lippit, "*Cinemnesis:* Martin Arnold's Memory Machine," *Afterimage* 24.6 (May/June 1997): 8–10.

16. Gilles Deleuze, *Francis Bacon: The Logic of Sensation*, trans. Daniel W. Smith (Minneapolis: University of Minnesota Press, 2003), xxix.

17. Deleuze, *Francis Bacon*, 44, original emphasis.

18. Bacon has spoken at length about his attachment to photography, and he frequently used photographs as sources for his paintings. Of Bacon's fascination with photography, which is tempered by an aesthetic restraint, Deleuze says: "What we see, what we perceive, are photographs. The most significant thing about the photograph is that it forces upon us the 'truth' of implausible and doctored images. Bacon has no intention of reacting against this movement; on the contrary, he abandons himself to it, and not without delight" (Deleuze, *Francis Bacon*, 74).

19. Deleuze, *Francis Bacon*, 36, original emphasis.

20. "Bacon's faces," Deleuze says, "are indeed those of deformation and not transformation" (Deleuze, *Francis Bacon*, 50). Deleuze explains the distinction: "These are two very different categories. The transformation of form can be abstract or dynamic. But deformation is always bodily, and it is static, it happens at one place; it subordinates movement to force, but it also subordinates the abstract to the Figure" (Deleuze, *Francis Bacon*, 50).

21. Deleuze, *Francis Bacon*, 15.

22. Deleuze, *Francis Bacon*, xxx.

23. Deleuze, *Francis Bacon*, xxxii.

24. Deleuze concludes his study of Bacon by positing the presence of a "body

beneath the organism." This other body is neither originary nor primary but a body of force. Deleuze says: "We witness the revelation of the body beneath the organism, which makes organisms and their elements crack or swell, imposes a spasm on them, and puts them into relation with forces—sometimes with an inner force that arouses them, sometimes with external forces that traverse them, sometimes with the eternal force of an unchanging time, sometimes with the variable forces of a flowing time" (Deleuze, *Francis Bacon,* 129). The "body beneath the organism" may be an analogue of or figure for the other body of cinema.

25. Deleuze, *Francis Bacon,* 45.

26. Deleuze, *Francis Bacon,* 16, original emphasis.

27. For more on Arnold's *Deanimated,* see Akira Mizuta Lippit, "——MA," in *Martin Arnold: Deanimated,* ed. Gerald Matt and Thomas Miessgang (Vienna: Springer, 2002): 30–34.

28. From a conversation with author, 2002.

29. Deleuze, *Francis Bacon,* 13.

CHAPTER 6

Miming Signing: Henri Michaux and the Writing Body

Carrie Noland

Henri Michaux, Belgian poet turned painter, belonged to a generation of mid-twentieth-century modernists intrigued by prehistoric inscriptions and their seemingly immediate relation to gestural routines. Studying the visual cultures of the Paleolithic and the Neolithic, modernist prehistorians (from Salomon Reinach to André Leroi-Gourhan) observed that mark-making was clearly a corporeal as well as a graphic practice. The discourses through which prehistoric visual culture was presented to a larger public were diverse and heterogeneous, yet almost invariably they contained an implicit theory of gesture, or of the rhythmic movements of the body, as fundamental to the production, appearance, and social function of marks. Artists and philosophers from Miró to Masson, Bataille to Merleau-Ponty, were exposed to accounts of prehistoric art not only through scholarly tomes but also through articles that appeared in modernist and avant-garde journals such as *Cahiers d'art*, *L'Esprit nouveau*, *Documents*, and *Ipek*. Given the period's primitivist fascination with the body as a resource for cultural renovation, it comes as no surprise that the vigorously corporeal quality of prehistoric markings inspired lively interest in early twentieth-century artists.[1] The gestural energy of prehistoric markings suggested the possibility of spontaneity without convention, a form of expression with roots in the untamed kinetic body.

The modernist interest in cave inscriptions reflected a broader romance with the primordial origins of sign making in general. Similar to other members of his generation, Michaux often expressed a desire to rediscover primordial signs, both plastic and scriptural, as an antidote to the alienation imposed by the visually impoverished and corporeally constraining sign-making practices of modernity. "L'être d'aujourd'hui est mécontent de sa langue" ("humans today are unhappy with their language"), Michaux stated in a 1984 interview. His turn toward painting, he continues, was determined largely by a need to forge a less culturally specific, more universally intelligible medium. According to Michaux, the graphic, which has "tant de rapports avec l'homme" ("multiple relations with man") could offer a solution to modernity's self-alienation, a way of inventing "une langue universelle" at once accessible to all yet viscerally connected to the communicative impulses of a single subject.[2] In *Par des traits (By Way of Lines)*[3] published that same year, Michaux proposed his own primitivist version of Cratylism, the classical theory adumbrating a motivated relation between objects in the world and the signs designating them. As Michaux turned to painting, he sought a set of signs, or simply "traits," continuous with and energized by the body's "gestes." Instead of seeking signs that could mime in iconic fashion the sounds and qualities of phenomenal entities, Michaux wanted to produce graphic signs indexing the tempo and quality of the body's movements. The conceit was that these signs, based on human gestures, would be legible to all. In this dream of a common language, inscription would be an emanation of the organic body; signs would be motivated, registering types and quantities of physical force. "Gestes plutôt que signes" ("Gestures rather than signs") he writes in *Par des traits:*

départs
Éveil
Autres éveils
PAR DES TRAITS
Approcher, explorer par des traits
Atterrir par des traits
étaler
altérer par des traits [. . .]
Insignifier par des traits.[4]

Departures
awakenings
Other awakenings
THROUGH LINES
To approach, to explore with lines
To alight with lines
to display
to alter with lines [. . .]
To not signify [un-signify] with lines.

Michaux may very well have begun with the urge to "find a universal language" by means of "characters [caractères] clear to all without having to pass through words."[5] But what he actually performed was the *disarticulation* rather than the clarification of the written sign. In works such as *Narration* (1927), *Alphabets* (1943), *Mouvements* (1951), *Par la voie des rythmes* (1974), and *Par des traits* (1984), he distorted the characters of various writing systems by repeating patterns of movement modeled on but not coincident with the gestural routines of these systems. The progression from "signes" in the first line quoted above to "Insignifier" in the last is symptomatic of Michaux's development as a whole: the invention of the neologism *insignifier* indicates that Michaux's goal was not to create a universally intelligible written language but instead to bring the written sign to the very edge of its capacity to signify. Ultimately, Michaux had no interest in communicating a specific meaning with his mimed signs; he expended his energy on examining meaning's contours, on discovering what meaning looks like and, more to the point, how meaning *feels* when being made and unmade.

The vehicle for this simultaneous miming of signification without achieving signification was composed of the gestural routines of several inscriptive technologies, not simply one in particular. Michaux's search for an alternative, more primordial and unmediated form of expression led him to combine distinct practices belonging to different writing systems—prehistoric, pictographic, and calligraphic. Drawing attention away from what such signs meant, he approached writing as a performance, a "display" or presentation unfolding in linear time, in three-dimensional space, and engaging a body alive with proprioceptive and kinesthetic sensations. Michaux transformed the act of writing into a practice that demanded a greater physical investment, or, more precisely, he emphasized that which is always present in the act of writing: the investment of corporeal energy in a set of movements combined in numerous ways. For this reason, he considered himself to be a "primitif," destroying, through the force of his movements, the meaning that arbitrary, "civilized" signs possess, while forging a new, motivated meaning that "savage" signs were thought to embody. According to his own admission, however, Michaux never lit upon the ideal embodiment of the perfectly transparent sign. Yet in the process of experimenting with the kinetic, kinesthetic, and graphemic elements of sign making, he managed to offer valuable insights into the performative nature of signing as well as the paradoxical implications of the primitivist project.

It was a common belief during Michaux's period that gestural languages were more "primitive" than verbal languages in the double sense of primitive: (1) "older," "first," "prior," and (2) "rudimentary," "undeveloped," "uncivilized." With respect to the history of human sign systems, languages composed of gestures were thought to have evolved earlier than languages composed of words; their chronological priority also suggested their greater fidelity to, their motivated one-on-one correspondence with, the objects and emotions they signified.[6] Because gestural languages are overtly kinetic, they were considered by modernist painters and writers to be more authentic, closer to the texture, rhythm, and intensity of the feeling or idea being communicated.[7] However, painters such as Michaux were working with inscriptive rather than performance media and therefore could not show the movements themselves, only the imprint or trace of their performance. Foregrounding these traces *as* traces, as remainders of performed gestures, was thus one strategy available to artists invested in the primitivist fantasy of a direct, less arbitrary system of expression. If an artist could associate his or her own marks with the force of hypothetically "prehistoric" gestures, then those marks could share the aura of a language emanating from an earlier, purer source.

Michaux's earliest attempts to mime the gestures of inscriptive systems are contained in *Narration* and *Alphabets*, volumes in which the shapes of Western cursive writing and pictographic (perhaps Native American) systems serve as inspiration. By the early 1940s, however, Michaux was gravitating toward prehistoric makings unearthed in the caves of Southern France and Cantabrian Spain. According to Leslie Jones, Michaux gleaned much of his material for his earliest experimentation with mark-making not from the walls of prehistoric caves themselves but from the pages of scholarly monographs that, according to his own words, he scattered liberally around the space in which he was working.[8] The illustrations found in studies of Paleolithic and Neolithic painting and notational systems were crucial to the development of Michaux's unique vocabulary of forms. By comparing pages from Michaux's *Alphabets*, composed between 1927 and 1943 (Figure 1) to Paleolithic representations of animals (Figure 2; Breuil, *The Cave of Altamira*),[9] it is easy to see how Michaux's ink drawings imitate the graphic disposition of discrete figures as serialized in books on Paleolithic art. (See also Figure 3, harpoon motifs from Aurignacian sites.)

It is likely that Michaux's greatest exposure to Paleolithic art occurred during World War II, when, resettled in the south of France, he acquired numerous back issues of magazines such as *Cahiers d'art* and *Minotaure*.[10] In images from *Alphabets*, produced between 1943 and 1951 (Figure 4), it is possible to see the influence of the Aurignacian harpoon motifs (Figure 3) as well as the symbol-like markings found on cave walls (Figure 2). Reminiscent of these Aurignacian images is the severe horizontality, the insistence upon vigorously repeated patterns of strokes. For images such as "Untitled *(Alphabets)*," (1944) (Figure 5), Michaux also derives inspiration from spear-throwing scenes (Figures 6 and 7) documented by Leo Frobenius and published in French art reviews of the 1920s and 1930s;[11] Michaux's brief vertical strokes approximate the tangential, limblike branchings of the African figures dashing across the page, or lances captured midflight. "Untitled *(Alphabets)*," (1994) (Figure 4), which preserves the serial presentation of archeological documentation, contains isolated sets of markings reminiscent of both symbolic patterning and iconic rendering: on the lowest row, for instance, we see a series of pattern-type constructions drawing on the decorative aspect of the harpoon motifs (Figure 3), whereas

Figure 1. Henri Michaux, "Untitled *(Alphabets)*" (1943). Copyright 2006 Artists Rights Society (ARS), New York/ADAGP, Paris.

elsewhere—on the second row from the bottom, third from left, for instance—we identify the schematic strokes of the anthropoid spear-throwers.

After the 1940s, Michaux reproduced almost exclusively the less rigid, less pictographic and more iconic figures associated with the Neolithic battle scenes. Although still fascinated with the signlike or notational qualities of markings, such as those located on the bottom row of Figure 4, he nonetheless moved increasingly toward the production of thicker, more ink-saturated lines disposed in less regular arrangements. Instead of imitating the *visual* patterns of specific motifs, Michaux in fact attempted to mime, with his own body, the corporeal experience of a certain variety of "prehistoric" mark-making. Michaux sought the experience of executing the strokes themselves, and it was to some extent of secondary concern whether the strokes resulted in signlike configurations or in figures that appeared to be captured in movement.

Yet even as Michaux experimented increasingly with strokes related to figuration and the production of composed scenes (suggesting nonserial

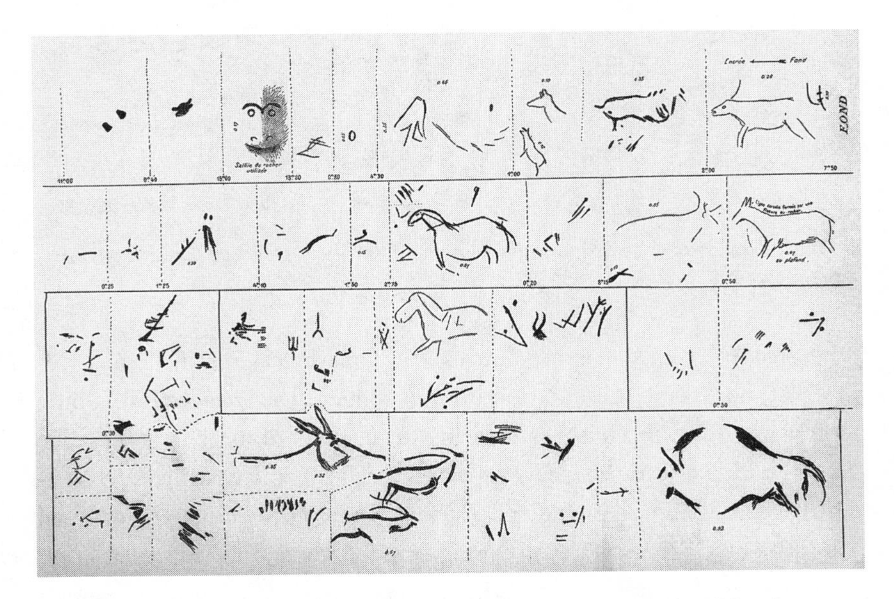

Figure 2. Henri Breuil, signs and engravings, Altamira. From André Leroi-Gourhan, *Préhistoire de l'art occidental* (Paris: Editions Citadelles et Mazenod); reprinted with permission.

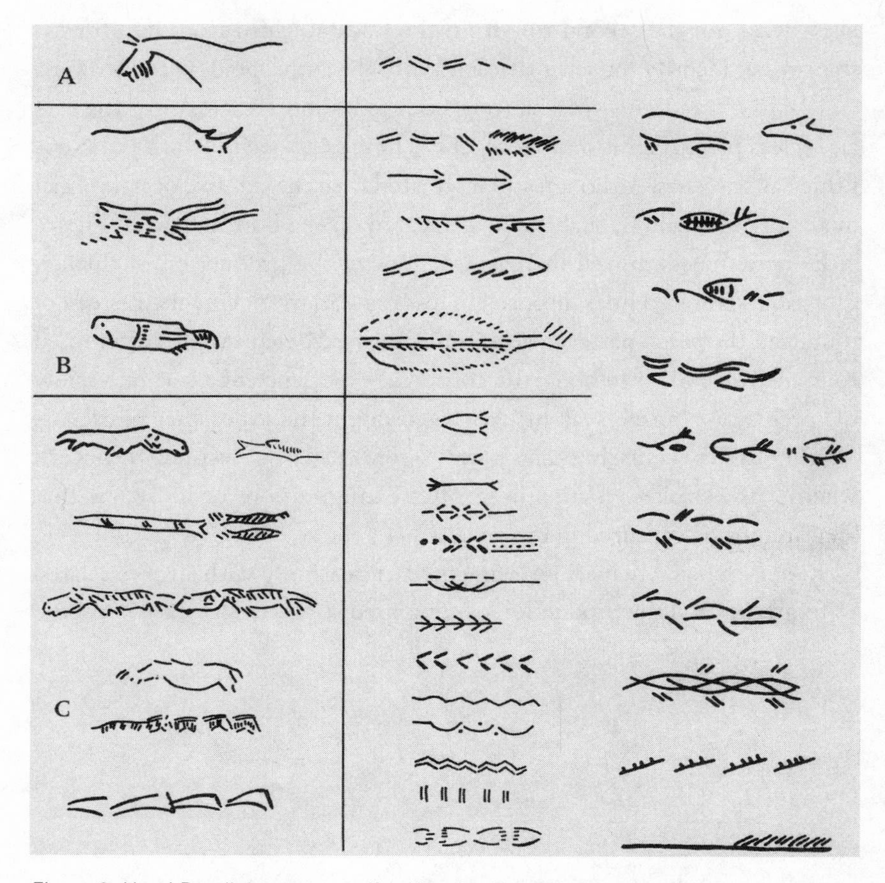

Figure 3. Henri Breuil, harpoon motifs, Altamira. From *Préhistoire de l'art occidental*; reprinted with permission.

relationships among discrete figures), he nonetheless retained the grid-like, flat, nonscenic presentation used in some of the *Alphabets.* By doing so, Michaux was implicitly associating his clusters of marks not with the Neolithic depictions themselves—that is, with the way in which such renderings would appear to the eye of the spectator inspecting the original support—but, alternatively, with the artificial, taxonomic representation of cave art within the format of the scholarly tome. Within these explicit or implicit grids, Michaux traces bovine and equestrian figures in profile, preserving the archeologist's style of rendering the unclosed contours of

Figure 4. Henri Michaux, "Untitled *(Alphabets)*" (1944). Copyright 2006 Artists Rights Society (ARS), New York/ADAGP, Paris.

figures without any visual reference to the irregularities of the actual support. Since cave painters were known to have exploited the accidental irregularities of the support to suggest possible forms, it is clear that Michaux alludes not to the artworks or objects as observed in the cave (or the museum vitrine) but to their reproduction in scholarly formats.[12] In *Alphabets*, the marking hand thus oscillates between two poles of attraction: the gestural and the archival. The artist's hand (and, in some cases, wrist, arm, and torso) is freed from the necessity to make recognizable signs and figures; and yet at the same time, the scope of the artist's movements is tightly restrained by a gestural routine (also executed by the body), one that measures space into predetermined units and subsumes marks within a strict serial formation.

Michaux's critics have attended with enthusiasm to the gestural component of his inscriptive practice and have linked it, with good evidence, to the influence of prehistoric visual culture. What has largely been ignored, however, is the degree to which Michaux maintains a spatial organization that dramatically limits the freedom of his gestures, an organization derived not from the phenomena we call "prehistoric" but from the techniques of archeological documentation forged to preserve those phenomena. The question that must be asked, then, is why, if Michaux were indeed striving to create a language composed entirely of personal signs, did he constrain his gestural, supposedly more spontaneous, practice of inscription within the highly charged disciplinary device of serial organization?

It is clear that Michaux was intrigued not only by prehistoric markings but also by inscriptive systems and supports of many varieties. As critics have noted, he not only took an interest in character sets, pictograms, hieroglyphs, and ideograms associated with specific written languages, he also explored, through an appropriation bordering on *détournement*, a wide variety of formats and technologies of display, such as the abécédaire,

Figure 5. Henri Michaux, "Untitled *(Alphabets)*" (1944). Copyright 2006 Artists Rights Society (ARS), New York/ADAGP, Paris.

Figure 6. Prehistoric rock pictures. From Leo Frobenius and Douglas C. Fox, *Prehistoric Rock Pictures in Europe and Africa* (New York: Modern Museum of Art, 1937).

the chemical table, the geometric diagram, and the classificatory grids of archeological, geological, and botanical manuals.[13] Michaux experiments both with different inscriptive systems *and* the protocols of spatialization associated with each of them. At the heart of Michaux's enterprise is a desire to understand visually, cognitively, and kinesthetically the constitutive elements of inscription both as a set of signs and as a technology of distribution (what the French call a *dispositif*, a systematic means of organizing and circulating signs on a potentially multilayered support).

Mouvements, the next major plastic work Michaux published after *Alphabets*, appeared in 1951 in the form of a polished, coherently conceived artist's book. Measuring 325 by 253 centimeters in format, *Mouvements* was originally an album containing reproductions of sixty-four ink drawings, a prefatory eponymous poem, and a "Postface." Here, the tentative experiment with writing systems and sign-producing gestures initiated in *Alphabets* and *Narration* is pursued in a far more rigorous way. The sixty-four reproductions are divided editorially into four discrete sections, two containing fifteen plates and two containing seventeen plates, each section separated from the next by one blank page. The paper Michaux used for the original pages reproduced in *Mouvements* was cheap, postwar regulation bond, apparently the only ink support he could afford at the time.[14] Michaux was anything but economical in his use of this paper, however: by the time *Mouvements* was published, he had filled over twelve hundred pages with marks, only sixty-four of which would be reproduced on velum for the printed collection (the rest were distributed to friends, sold, or destroyed). In the Postface to the volume, Michaux recounts the story of the volume's genesis: "I had covered twelve hundred pages with these things, and all I saw there were flows ('flots'), when René Bertelé [an editor of artist's

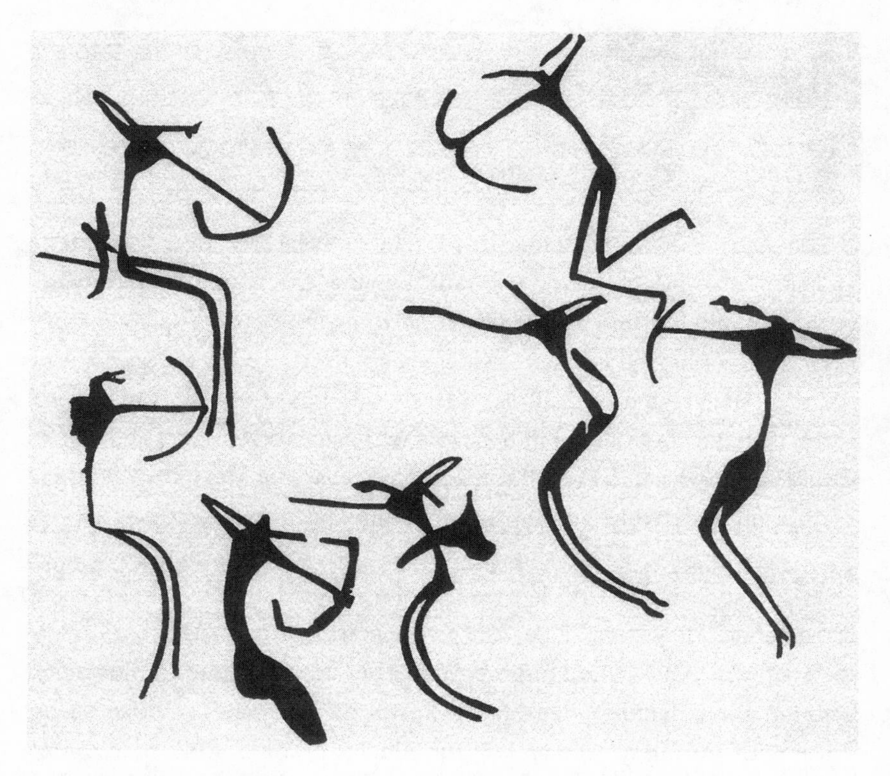

Figure 7. Prehistoric rock pictures. From *Prehistoric Rock Pictures in Europe and Africa.*

books] took hold of them and, gropingly, reflectively, discovered in them sequences [. . .] the book you find here [is] more his work than my own."[15]

The four-part, sequential format imposed by Bertelé provides a particular narrative momentum to the volume. It establishes a sequence in which the reader, moving from one page to the next, is led to observe how an initially constrained—that is, horizontally oriented and consistently spaced—set of signlike marks devolves increasingly toward random configurations. In each of the four sequences, a set of marks similar to those found in Figure 8 (*Oeuvres complètes*, vol. II, 563) leads, seemingly ineluctably, to a set of marks similar to those found in Figure 9 (vol. II, 579). Marks that distantly recall Asian calligraphic characters (while simultaneously maintaining a connection to the Neolithic spear-throwers Michaux copied earlier) evolve slowly but surely toward larger, wilder, unframed doodles (Figures 10 [vol. II, 568] and 11 [vol. II, 569]). The series terminates when the scale is enlarged (Figure 12 [vol. II, 576]) and the implicit grid explodes (Figure 9), giving way to composition, an iconic reading, and the possibility of three-dimensional space. The sequential arrangement works to dramatize the tension between the rhythm of the gesture that marks and the rhythm of the gesture that spaces, or creates, an interval. Eventually, the latter is overwhelmed by the former, as marking gestures transgress the disciplinary and disciplining grid within which the scriptural gesture is supposed to unfold.

I will supply a closer analysis of these mark clusters in a moment, but for now it is crucial to note only that the page sequences of *Mouvements* were constituted not by Michaux but by his editor and promoter, Bertelé. To his credit, Bertelé does manage to create a narrative out of inscriptions; the reader/viewer of *Mouvements* observes if not the actual execution of the strokes, then at least, through the imposed order, evidence of their growing amplitude and intensity. Sequences of signs are arranged in such a manner as to imply that the increasing force and freedom of Michaux's gestures ends up loosening the bonds of the taxonomic imperative in a struggle that ends, time and time again, with the latter's defeat. However, it would be a mistake to ascribe to Michaux the intention to resolve the struggle between the supposedly freer force of gestural marking

Figure 8. Henri Michaux, *Mouvements* (1951). Copyright 2006 Artists Rights Society (ARS), New York/ADAGP, Paris.

and the disciplining force of the archival in quite that way.[16] Bertelé is clearly invested in presenting a particular version of *Mouvements* that might or might not be faithful to Michaux's experience, a version in which the author/painter seeks to break with the constraints of the written in order to create a more organic language, one that veers toward the figural as it reunites the subject with a "primitive" mythographic or pictographic imagination. In Bertelé's words, Michaux was seeking in *Mouvements* a "Writing from the beginning of the world, that of prehistory . . . a Writing taking us back to the primitive sources of communication" ("les sources primitives de la communication").[17]

Bertelé is of course not alone in asserting that Michaux's project—not simply in *Mouvements* but throughout his career as a painter—was to produce an inscriptive system capable of returning to "primal" gestures and marks as a resource for the invention of a universal language. However, Michaux's own comments tend to stress the kinesthetic or sensual pleasures rather than the communicative aims of his procedures. In the poem accompanying the ink drawings of *Mouvements*, for instance, Michaux

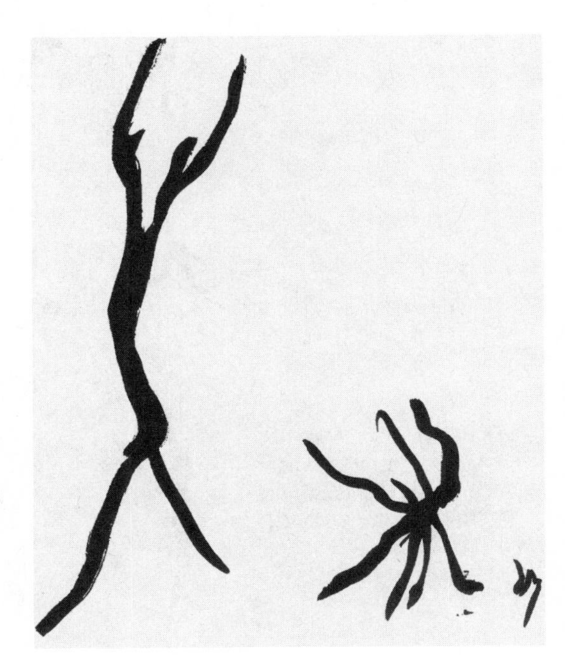

Figure 9. Henri Michaux, *Mouvements*. Copyright 2006 Artists Rights Society (ARS), New York/ADAGP, Paris.

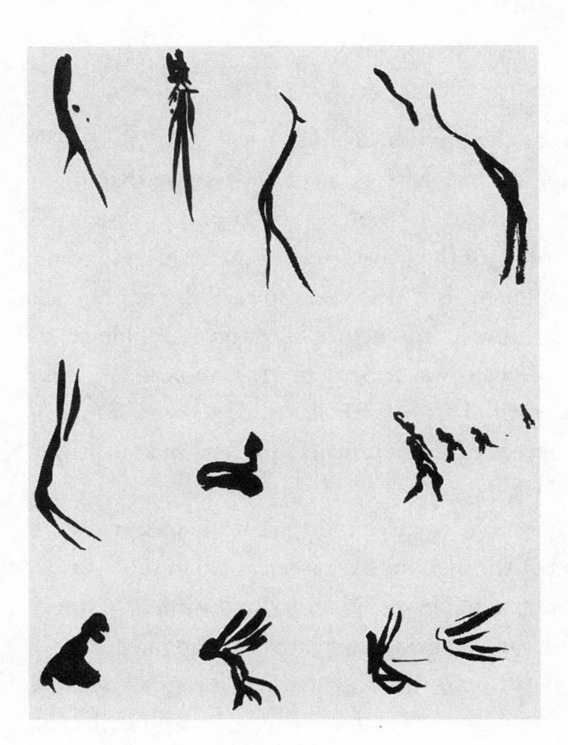

Figure 10. Henri Michaux, *Mouvements.* Copyright 2006 Artists Rights Society (ARS), New York/ADAGP, Paris.

Figure 11. Henri Michaux, *Mouvements.* Copyright 2006 Artists Rights Society (ARS), New York/ADAGP, Paris.

describes his motivation as an "envie cinétique," a kinetic desire, or desire for kinesis. What he does not say, pace Bertelé, is that this desire for kinesis is coextensive with a desire to transmit a universally legible message. "Signs / not of rooftops, of tunics, or of palaces" ("Signes / non de toit, de tunique ou de palais"), Michaux's verse begins, signs "not of archives and dictionaries of knowledge / but of distortions, violence, perturbation / kinetic desire" ("non d'archives et de dictionnaire du savoir / mais de torsion, de violence, de bousculement / mais d'envie cinétique").[18] In other words, the "signs" of *Mouvements* are not intended to decorate a support (one understanding of "Signes . . . de toit"—signs belonging to or found on a roof); nor do they represent, like a courtly hieroglyph, a scene (another understanding of "Signes . . . de toit"—signs depicting a roof). Because they are personal and idiosyncratic, generated by what Michaux calls the "moi-je,"[19] neither are they "Signes . . . de toi[t]" ("*your* signs," a third way the phrase can be interpreted). These signs are decidedly not conventional or designed to be shared. Further, Michaux explicitly remarks that they do

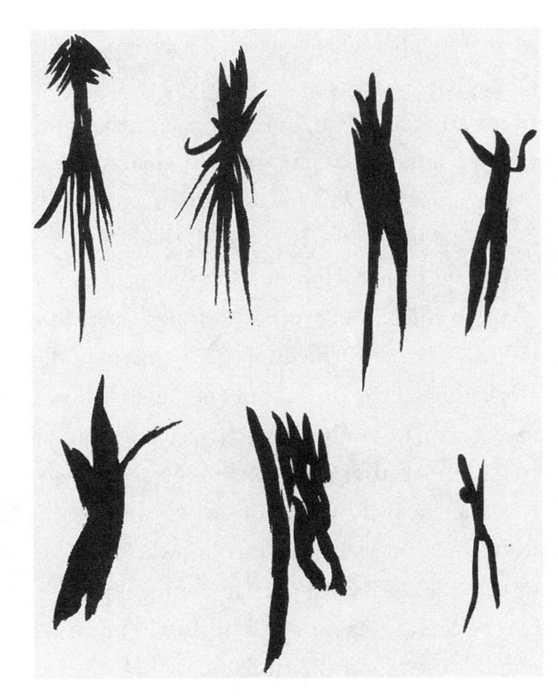

Figure 12. Henri Michaux, *Mouvements.* Copyright 2006 Artists Rights Society (ARS), New York/ADAGP, Paris.

not transmit the kind of knowledge that could be classified: "Signes . . . non d'archives et de dictionnaire du savoir." Instead, they merely evince a desire for kinesis, for motility. They are indexical rather than symbolic or iconic, but only insofar as they register that a movement (the movement that produced them) has indeed occurred. Michaux's "mouvements," as he puts it, are a record only of the impulse to move.

Whereas in his early years Michaux turned to paleographic documentation for examples of a kinetically charged pictographic system, in the 1950s Chinese calligraphy became his major source of inspiration. Michaux owned a copy of Wieger's *Caractères Chinois (Chinese Characters)* in his personal library; as a child, but also later as an adult, he spent many hours attempting to learn the rudiments of Chinese calligraphy (a point that becomes important in a moment).[20] The resemblance between calligraphic scripts and the marks contained in *Mouvements* has been established—perhaps too emphatically—by several of Michaux's critics; Frances Morris, for instance, finds that the collection is "a visual demonstration of [Michaux's] understanding of a Chinese approach. A few deft strokes, swift and spontaneous, identify a character as part of a group or alphabet disposed, like Chinese characters, neatly across the page."[21] As Leslie Jones has observed, however, there are many visual discrepancies that complicate the easy analogy between Chinese characters and Michaux's marks. "The majority of Michaux's 'Mouvements,'" Jones notes, "have a torso-like center from which emanate 'limbs' of all sorts in contrast to the left-to-right, top-to-bottom, exterior-to-interior formation of Chinese characters that often center on an open core or void." According to Jones, instead of laying down strokes "that circulate around the center," as in the calligraphic tradition, "Michaux worked from the center out and never followed a stroke order."[22] On closer inspection, not only do Michaux's "mouvements" fail to bear a resemblance to Chinese calligraphed characters, but also their mode of production differs significantly from that of Chinese calligraphers. Working with the traditional materials of the Chinese form, Michaux "holds the brush as he would a pen—at an angle and resting on the second finger—while the Asian practice requires an artist to hold the brush perfectly upright with the handle resting on the third finger" (156).[23]

These differences in mode of execution must be contrasted with the continuities Michaux obviously wants to preserve. By switching from pen to brush and by working exclusively with "encre de Chine," Michaux underscores his desire to evoke the tools of a practice that is at once writing and drawing, semantically significant and visually compelling. Further, by emphasizing the stroke to the detriment of legibility, Michaux displays his solidarity with practitioners of Chinese cursive or running scripts, forms traditionally achieved only after complete mastery of the rigorously standardized clerical scripts.[24] Michaux obviously wants to align his own efforts with those of innovators in the Chinese tradition who choose expression of individual subjectivity over clarity of communication. By miming only certain aspects of the calligraphic sign-making tradition, Michaux succeeds in maintaining a connection to it while simultaneously putting its methods to new use. For instance, Michaux employs ink and brush, but he manipulates them in a western way. He also follows the calligrapher in combining individual, distinct strokes into characterlike constructions, yet he reverses the orientation that Chinese characters demand. As in his 1975 collection, *Idéogrammes en Chine*,[25] Michaux mixes up the elements of two inscriptive systems, imposing the gridlike distribution associated with East Asian signaries on characters that are not decidedly not East Asian, handling an eastern brush as though it were a western pen, and conducting the business of calligraphy not on a scroll but on a 9 1/2 × 12 5/8 inch western paper support.

This last point is perhaps the most important, for it indicates something about his project that other critics have failed to emphasize. Although in *Mouvements* Michaux may indeed be referencing the traditions of Eastern script, he is also deliberately observing the formatting principles of *western* inscriptive systems. His support is the page; his reception apparatus, the codex. Thus, as figurative as his marks might appear (suggesting at times the shapes of animals, plants, single-celled organisms, or the human body), they are in fact prevented from being received as fully iconic because they are contained within a 9 1/2 × 12 5/8 inch surface inserted into a volume of such surfaces. To this extent, *Mouvements* resembles *Alphabets*, for both reference non-codexical inscriptive supports—the cave wall or the calligrapher's scroll—while clinging nonetheless to a codexical *dispositif*.

The gridlike presentation of Chinese characters echoes the gridlike presentation of paleographic artifacts that served as a compositional model for *Alphabets.* As was the case with the prior volume, here again in *Mouvements,* Michaux is limited by the scriptural economy of the page just as much as he is freed by the gestural possibilities of the body. His "mouvements" are only in part the recorded traces of spontaneous gestures. With the exception of the most extravagant cases, Michaux's marks tend to follow strict and redundant patterns of movement while staying respectfully within their designated squares. The gestural is certainly a crucial component of the exercise; as we shall presently see, gestural energy propels the direction of the strokes and determines the contours of the "signs." However, the space of the page is also strongly present both as a material reality that limits and organizes Michaux's gestures and as a cognitive frame that urges us to "read" these gestures as signs. The format of the page encourages the body to perform gestures that are consequently not those of cave painting or traditional calligraphy but rather those of western writing. If, as critics such as Loreau have strenuously insisted, Michaux's purpose was to "root language and signs in the corporeal gesture [le geste corporel]," why, then, did he preserve and even emphasize the limited space of the page?[26] If he wanted to invent a language true to his own body, why did he discipline this body to perform within such a tight space?

For the space of the page is a tight one indeed. The original brush-and-ink drawings of *Mouvements* were executed on drawing paper somewhat larger than the surface familiar to French schoolchildren but clearly more diminutive than the surface generally employed by painters.[27] The pages of *Mouvements* retain the verticality of writing paper (they are longer in length than in breadth), and the "characters," or what I prefer to call "mark clusters," appear to have been applied from left to right and top to bottom. Michaux's choice of this reduced format places him in stark contrast to other artists of his generation who were also exploring the properties of the sign as a plastic element. At the time *Mouvements* appeared, the Italian painter Capogrossi and the French painter Georges Mathieu, two contemporaries to whom Michaux alludes in a short essay of 1954 entitled "Signes," were engaged in producing signlike figures, but on large canvasses, not codex pages.[28] Even when troping on traditional calligraphy, artists belonging to postwar movements such as *art informel*, *tachisme*, abstract expressionism, and *art brut* tended to move toward more impressive formats, producing their various marks (signlike or not) by means of expansive, theatrical gestures.[29] Michaux's decision to explore the gestural while remaining wedded to the page was quite original; unique in his generation, he combined a surrealist preoccupation with everyday, nonspectacular materials with a clinical interest in his own motility that made him appear closer to artists such as Mathieu, Capogrossi, and Georges Noël than he actually was. Michaux's intervention in the field of painting drew from many sources and resembled that of many contemporaries, and yet he diverged from them all in crucial ways.

I cannot hope to provide here an exhaustive account of mid-twentieth century European and American painting; my purpose is rather to indicate some important points of comparison that will throw the particularity of *Mouvements* into relief. Michaux turned toward painting at a precise moment in the history of the genre, the moment when writing—as inscription, but not necessarily *legible* inscription—emerged as a viable alternative to figuration. His decisive turn toward the visual during the 1940s was neither sudden nor unreflected. He had already tried his hand at watercolors, gouaches, and inks long before 1951, the year he began executing the drawings that would become *Mouvements*. Even during the period when he was known solely as a poet, he took part in small gallery exhibitions, showing, as early as 1937,[30] some of his watercolors and pastels. Unfortunately, Michaux's career as an artist was interrupted by the war and did not really get underway until 1948, when the well-respected Galérie René Drouin displayed a striking collection of his gouaches. At least one significant encounter, however, marked the war years: at the end of 1944, Michaux met Jean Dubuffet for the first time and was "conquered" (his own word) by the energy of his paintings.[31] From that point on, Michaux was drawn into the circle around Dubuffet, exhibiting his works in shows with surrealists like Ernst and Masson and, at the same time, painters of the "new primitivism," such as Dubuffet and Wols.

"New primitivism" is a term coined by Sarah Wilson to characterize a handful of postwar movements that Michel Tapié has referred to, somewhat less convincingly, as *"un art autre."* The pivot between the "old" primitivism and the "new" was arguably provided by a specific event: Artaud's 1947 "conférence" at the Théâtre du Vieux-Colombier, which was responsible for reigniting an interest in earlier aspects of surrealism (Artaud's work in particular) that wartime preoccupations had eclipsed. Wilson describes this "new primitivism" as "divorced from the spoils and the 'anthropology' of the Trocadero, the exotic fascinations of the returning Surrealists" (34). More to the point, the "new primitivism" also differed from the old insofar as it pinned its hopes not on the "talking cure" but on the revealed organic body of the artist. Exposing the supposedly raw impulses, rhythms, gestures, and marks of this body was now seen as a way out of the impasses of cubism, surrealism, and what Michel Leiris diagnosed as the "disillusionment of Western man, ill at ease in his own skin" ("déception d'Occidental mal dans sa peau").[32] In harmony with Brassaï, Luquet, and Bataille, Dubuffet brought attention to instances of inscription not previously considered aesthetically significant. Michaux admired Dubuffet's eccentric visual tastes; in fact, he credited him specifically with teaching an entire generation of artists and writers to "look differently at a wall, a graffiti" ("regarder de façon différente un mur, un graffiti").[33] Dubuffet extended in many directions the interest, initially exhibited by the surrealists, in marginalized art forms. He not only explored the expressive potential of wall inscriptions and uneven, grotto-like supports he also brought greater recognition to the works of the insane and the incarcerated—*"les fous, simples d'esprit, délinquents ou même assassins"*—when he founded the Compagnie de l'Art Brut in 1948.[34]

Michel Tapié, the famous promoter of *art brut,* was instrumental in ushering Dubuffet into the limelight. According to Tapié, Dubuffet placed a greater value on spontaneous compositional methods than did his predecessors; he handled his materials in a way that foregrounds rather than disguises their properties, thereby making the rhythm of application visible, retraceable. In this sense, he theatricalized the painting process itself. Michaux's work was received by gallery owners and collectors as belonging to the emotionally raw aesthetic that Dubuffet and Tapié had championed. In 1948, two years after mounting an important Dubuffet show, René Drouin devoted his entire gallery to Michaux's watercolor washes, thereby underscoring the continuity between Dubuffet's *art brut* and Michaux's own version of working with wet paint. Exhibited in the same spaces as Dubuffet, Michaux was culturally positioned and discursively framed to be heralded as yet another member of the "new primitivism" of the postwar Wols-Fautrier-Dubuffet generation.

It is into this atmosphere of exploratory theatricalizing of the painterly gesture that the drip canvasses of Jackson Pollock and the notion of "action painting" were first introduced. Neither Pollock nor the principles of action painting would have been comprehensible to critics and gallery owners if Dubuffet, Hartung, Mathieu, Wols, and Michaux had not already prepared the French terrain. Michaux had not known of Pollock's paintings until Tapié took him to see them in Paris; in contrast to the prominent art critics of the period, Michaux displayed a marked receptivity to what one reviewer dubbed scornfully "[ces] graffiti d'encres."[35] Apparently, Tapié, as well as many gallery owners, recognized a profound affinity between Michaux's ink marks and the drip paintings Pollock was producing in the late 1940s. From 1952 on, Michaux found his own works hanging in the same galleries as those of Pollock.[36] Given the immediately discernable differences between Michaux's delicate *encres de Chine* and Pollock's explosive "graffiti d'encre," it is surprising that so many critics and art historians—from Geneviève Bonnefoi to Jean Louis Schefer—have insisted upon their resemblance. Pollock poured industrial paint, while Michaux stroked on India ink; Pollock gushed in color, while Michaux dabbled in black and white. And yet, in the discourse of art history, Michaux has found himself most frequently and most consistently compared to Pollock. Why would this be so?

According to the painter Claude Georges, Michaux and Pollock were equally innovative and thus comparable with respect to their "new attitude toward the work."[37] This attitude consisted in allowing the process of painting to assume agency, to dominate the intentionality of the artist; what Georges admired in both Pollock and Michaux was "this way of letting painting itself make the painting, this way of refusing to be obedient and docile with respect to the painter's *ideas.*"[38] In the eyes of Jean Degottex as well, the two painters had embarked on a similar project at approximately the same moment, which was to eliminate the figurative from painting by exploring an "écriture gestuelle."[39] Finally, art critics indebted to Harold Rosenberg, such as Margit Rowell, have placed Pollock and Michaux side by side for the reason that each, in his own way, invests the gestural with the capacity to undo socialization, to return the body to its natural rhythms: "Gesture is a motivation, a tendency," Rowell writes in her chapter on Pollock; the gestural "corresponds to a fundamental human need, and because of this it is parasocial, paracultural. Gesture is the manifestation of a primal state of being."[40] The French poet shares with Pollock this primitivist notion of the gestural, Rowell continues in her chapter on Michaux: with gesture, we find ourselves "at the original source of all . . . creation, at the first, natural and spontaneous manifestation" of being (112). She adds, in conclusion, "More than any other artist, with the exception of Pollock, Michaux sublimated his history in nature."

But if both artists "sublimated" their personal history, drowning the contingencies of their cultural conditioning in a nature they rediscovered through gestural marking (and this is Rowell's contention), they nonetheless did so in utterly different ways. Setting aside for the moment the problematic nature of this primitivist account of Michaux's and Pollock's procedures (according to which both turned to the spontaneity of the gestural to unearth "a primitive state of being"), it is still necessary to account for the striking differences in their choice of format and modes of execution. It may very well be that, as Rowell has insisted, the model for Pollock's drip and splatter paintings was the child's "expérience du griffonnage" (42), the undisciplined enjoyment of materials and the kinesthetic pleasures of their application. However, it is by no means incidental that the deepening of this experience in painterly terms was accompanied, in Pollock's case, by an expansion of the dimensions of the support. Rowell admits that Pollock's paintings of this period (1947–1950) "are of greater dimension than any he had produced before" (47); but for her, nothing was "modified" in the scribbling experience by this "change of scale" ("différence d'échelle") (42). That Pollock took the gestures of the "scribbler" ("griffonneur") and expanded them until they could fill a space ten times bigger than that filled by Michaux's "mouvements" (a painting such as "Number 32" measures 269 by 457.5 centimeters) does not seem to trouble Rowell at all. Even as she underlines the exaggerated dimensions of his support, the magnified scope of his movements—"the pictorial matter follows the movements of his hand, arm, body" (47)—she neglects to consider how the comparison with Michaux's project might have to be revised.

Too often ignored in accounts of Michaux's work is the importance of scale. True, Pollock, similar to Michaux, tended to respect the borders of the support's rectangle; however, in his case, these borders encased and made available a surface (with a horizontal orientation) far larger than that circumscribed by Michaux. The gestures Pollock was referencing are those associated with mural painting or set design; they are larger than the gestures required for writing.[41] In contrast, Michaux not only preserves the scope of the gestural routines of character formation, he also chooses paper and ink over canvas and paint, thereby permitting his tool and his support to limit the variety of movements he can perform. Michaux's choices—to use ink and paper and to distribute the inked figures in rows—are part of a coherent strategy to respect the format of the codex even when venturing out onto the terrain of the painterly stroke. Bertelé's suggestion that the separate pages of "mouvements" be made into a book is thus in keeping with the general thrust of Michaux's procedures. When Bertelé anchored these pages with a spine and assured—by means of a prefatory poem and a Postface—that, as in any codex, the pages of the volume would be turned from right to left, from front to back, he was merely extending the logic of the book that Michaux had established in the first place. Bertelé made sure that the pages of ink drawings would be framed on either end by traditionally laid-out text ("Mouvements" and "Postface"); this *dispositif* prepares the reader to approach the "mouvements" not as a spectator but as a *reader*, one who expects legibility, or at least intelligibility, to emerge from black lines on a white support.

What draws Michaux and Pollock together is perhaps less the formal qualities of their works than the art historical discourse that has been generated about these qualities. Both have been constructed—and at times have constructed themselves—as primitivists, disenchanted westerners searching for the pre-enculturated, primordial self through paint. To the extent that Michaux was indeed seeking to reveal, as he wrote in the poem "Mouvements," a "man, displaying everything, flapping in the wind of his impulses" ("homme, tous pavillons dehors, claquant au vent bruissant de ses pulsions") (436), he can be considered to have operated within the field of what Amelia Jones has called "the Pollockian performative,"[42] a field in which the self and its "pulsions" are *engendered* phenomenologically in relation to a performance situation rather than indexed belatedly by marks on the page.[43] It is clear from Michaux's own statements that he was striving to *produce* a new body through his gestures; it was not a matter of registering graphically the body he already was. A strategy had to be devised that would encourage the performance of spontaneous movements, or at least the performance of movements in a new *sequence* not previously determined by acquired skills. In other words, Michaux, like Pollock, needed to find a way to experience a body in the act of moving—and thus marking—in a new way.

The curious and perhaps singularly modern dilemma facing artists such as Michaux and Pollock was how to set up the conditions, often quite stringent, in which something resembling spontaneity could emerge.[44] As T. J. Clark points out with respect to Pollock's procedures (and in Pollock's terms), a high degree of "de-skilling" was necessary, but, paradoxically, this de-skilling demanded a "battery of techniques."[45] Whereas American artists tended to emphasize the ways in which they exploded previous techniques in order to return to "organic" movements and "authentic" subjectivities, the French of the same generation speak more frequently of the "entraînement," or training in new protocols of execution, required to achieve similar goals. Sloughing off acquired habits of execution was something that could not be done simply by trusting "spontaneous" or "unconscious" impulses; if the French avant-garde had learned one thing from surrealism, it was this.[46] Rather, the artist had to become *more* conscious of habitual ways of doing things: he or she was called on to apprehend the discrete elements in a sequence of linked movements in order to locate and exploit the faultlines between them. As Umberto Eco has written with respect to this period in French cultural history, the aesthetic of the "informel" and the "open work" involved a "rejection of classical forms," to be sure, "but *not* a rejection of that form which is the fundamental condition of communication," or the iterable line itself.[47]

No description could better fit Michaux's project in *Mouvements*, which could be construed as an effort to determine the formal—as well as the gestural—elements that make a mark susceptible to bearing signification. Eco seems to be alluding to Michaux's work even more explicitly (although he was in fact referring to Pollock) when he observes that an "informel" art work "does not proclaim the death of form, rather, it proposes a new, more flexible version of it—*form as a field of possibilities*" (103; original emphasis). In Michaux's case, the forms that served as "fields of possibilities" were not those of the image but of the written character and the spatial conventions of the page. That is, the forms to be "opened" and explored were those of a wide variety of different signaries and formatting systems, and therefore the techniques to be revisited were the gestural routines associated with writing in its many incarnations. Thus, when Michaux began to study Chinese training manuals, filling up the gridded pages of workbooks with calligraphic strokes, he was aiming less at perfecting a new skill than at getting rid of an old one. Accounts of Michaux's attempt to acquire the rudiments of Chinese calligraphy stress that he was a singularly unsuccessful student. The results, apparently, were always inadequate from a technical point of view. But Michaux's purpose was never to attain mastery, to become adept at an alternative but equally traditional and culturally specific gestural routine. His goal was to understand, viscerally, the physical demands of *many* inscriptive systems—Neolithic, calligraphic, pictographic—in order to liberate movement possibilities residing within the anatomical body as it moved to create—or more precisely, to mime—a plethora of forms. In short, the challenge for Michaux was to perform a new gestural routine in order to render less familiar, less necessary, and less *natural* another. In *Mouvements*, Michaux was interested in documenting, encyclopedically, the greatest number of mark-making movements he could execute without exceeding the bounds of an implicit, sign-defining grid. Such an encyclopedic approach might suggest new combinatory possibilities, new choreographies, and these choreographies in turn materialized impulses located less in some unconscious depth of the self or the precultural body than in the body that performs signs.

Mouvements documents Michaux's effort to un-learn how to write; as Michaux himself wrote in 1972, "je peins *pour me déconditionner*" ("I write to decondition myself").[48] To underline that such deconditioning requires an apprenticeship in expressive operations of another variety (rather than the elimination of training altogether), Michaux chooses for *Mouvements* the format of a child's primer. He imposes upon his mark clusters a serial formation drawn not from authentic examples of achieved Chinese calligraphy (scrolls and wall hangings in which characters are rarely justified on both margins) but from the gridded exercise sheets used by Chinese schoolchildren during the apprenticeship phase when they are just *learning* calligraphy. This invisible grid of the primer thematizes visually the fact that Michaux is involved in a process of "entraînement." At the same time, however, this grid also evokes the child's ambivalent experience of learning good penmanship. The child is forced to master the discipline of writing according to linear or other culturally specific spatial conventions, thereby submitting to a limited set of expressive instruments and possibilities. Yet, in the very act of being disciplined, the child is also acquiring the skills necessary to deform the shapes, dislocate the syntax or order, and play with the arrangement of characters on the page, thereby discovering expressive possibilities in the system that cannot be entirely predetermined or controlled. As any parent, schoolteacher, or psychologist can confirm, for many children, learning to write is an experience that incites a good deal of inquisitive experimentation and creative resistance. In *Mouvements*, Michaux is just as interested in the resistance as he is in the discipline.

A closer examination of the mark clusters on a single page of *Mouvements* reveals that the author's impulse to perfect through repetition is challenged by an equally strong impulse to vary and innovate. The single page is a better clue to the nature of Michaux's project than is the sequence of fifteen or seventeen pages, since he alone (as opposed to Bertelé) determined the order of mark clusters on any given page. Therefore, I want to return to a single page from the third sequence briefly discussed earlier, isolating it from the context in which it was placed by Bertelé. Page 2 of the third sequence (Figure 13 [*Oeuvres complètes*, vol. II, 564]) is a good place to begin, for it is fairly representational of a large number of pages found in *Mouvements*. The neat, four-by-four ordering of characterlike marks within the implied grid is typical of many pages, as are the thickness, density, and length of the constitutive strokes. Further, page 2 has the advantage of being neither the first nor the last in a sequence and thus remains unburdened by a significant place in the dramatic arc created by Bertelé. We can attend, then, more closely to the drama taking place within the limits of the individual page.

What is immediately apparent to the eye is the downward, vertical thrust of the primary strokes composing the clusters. Although there are exceptions to the rule (see, in particular, the figures located in the third row/fourth column from the left and third row/first column on the left), most of the mark clusters possess a strong, defining vertical line that thickens as it descends, an attribute that tells us Michaux repeatedly began his stroke from on high and lowered his hand as he proceeded. Alternating with this downward stroke is often a horizontal squiggle or line set (as in figures in the first row/first column and first row/third column). Judging by this group of figures, one is tempted to conclude that in executing the figures on this page, Michaux's hand, wrist, and arm followed a consistent gestural routine, one composed largely of vertical slashes and horizontal swings, with very few meditated circular motions. Visible as well are the types of brush marks made by altering the degree of pressure exerted by the hand as it advances the brush toward contact with the support. In figures in the second row/first column, second row/second column, third row/second column, and fourth row/third column, it is possible to discern the work of a brush that has been pressed to the paper then swiftly lifted, leaving behind a rapidly narrowing trail. Such dramatic marks index the body's movements within a three-dimensional space, as opposed to lateral

Figure 13. Henri Michaux, *Mouvements.* Copyright 2006 Artists Rights Society (ARS), New York/ADAGP, Paris.

or longitudinal movements in a two-dimensional space. Indexes of pressure applied in the three-dimensional space of the human producer are typical (and integral to the legibility) of calligraphic characters but are largely foreign to conventional writing systems of the west.

This page of *Mouvements* is representative of the sequence in which Bertelé has embedded it. It is likely that pages 1, 2, and 3 (Figures 8, 13, 14 [*Oeuvres complètes*, vol. II, 565]) of the sequence were completed if not one after the other then at least closely together in time; the stroke used on page 2 is the type of stroke used to produce many of the other figures in the sequence. And yet the page retains a certain integrity and uniqueness. Just a page later (Figure 15, [vol. II, 566]), Michaux has introduced an entirely new stroke, a new theme, one is tempted to say: the diagonal swing stroke (the entire third row down, for instance), which hardly appears in later pages of the same sequence, such as pages 8 and 9 (Figures 16 and 17 [vol. II, 570, 571]). On the one hand, it would be possible to argue that page 2 contains the germ—the stroke vocabulary or lexicon—of the entire sequence. The diagonal swing can be discerned in the figures located in the third row down/fourth column and fourth row/second and third columns. But then it would be necessary to explain the appearance of a figure such as that found in the lower right-hand corner on page 9 (Figure 16). This cluster of marks is probably not a prolongation or augmentation of any stroke type found on page 2. Its production requires an entirely different movement, a longer, slower, continuous application of ink involving rotation at the level of the elbow. It is probably generated not by any combinatory potential present on pages 1 or 2 of the sequence but rather by a sustained stroke made by exerting uniform pressure as the hand moves across the page. Strokes like these are responsible for the pronounced verticality of all the figures on the page except the horizontal strokes found at its bottom. Those horizontals are a reaction to the verticals above; they maintain the same sort of rhythm, pulse, scale, and scope but simply move in a different direction. Michaux follows the momentum and directionality of the gesture, the same gesture, until the body swerves, a new impulse is manifested, and a new directionality appears.

My reading is intended to emphasize both the integrity of the single

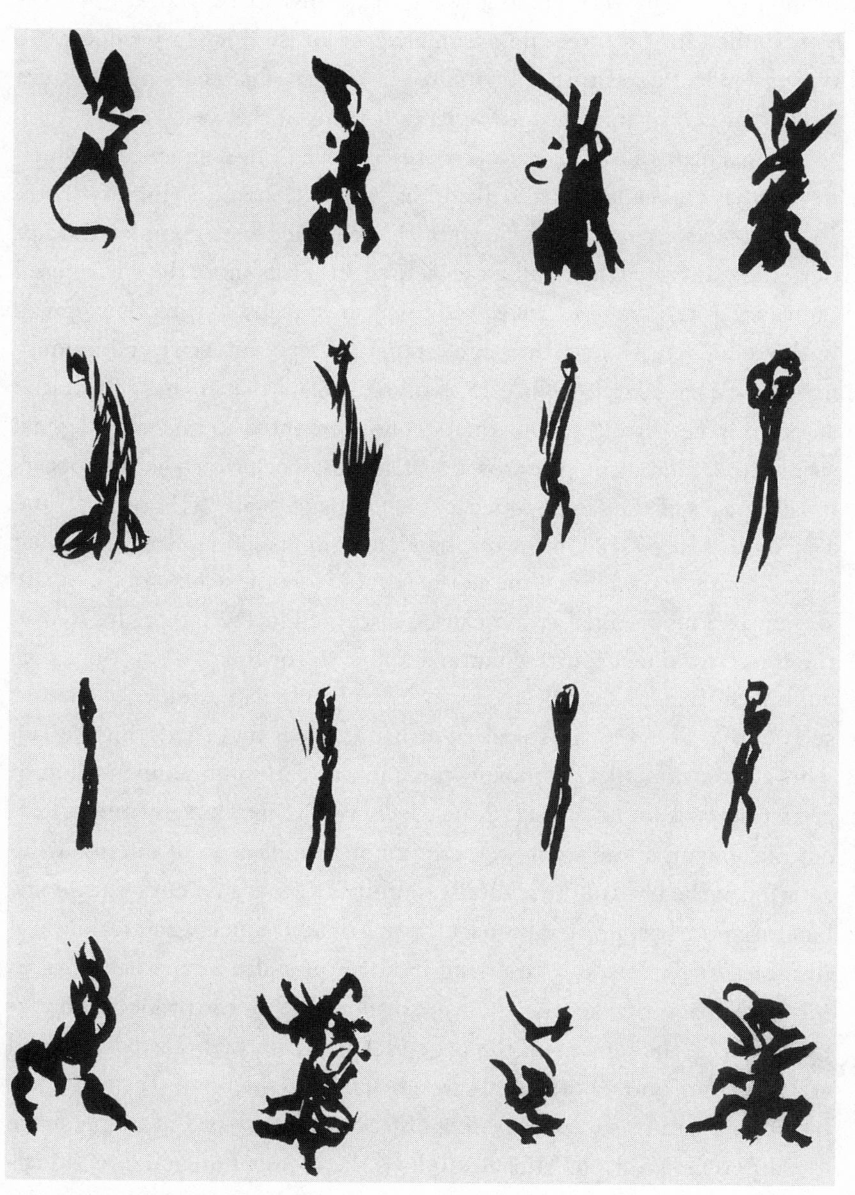

Figure 14. Henri Michaux, *Mouvements.* Copyright 2006 Artists Rights Society (ARS), New York/ADAGP, Paris.

Figure 15. Henri Michaux, *Mouvements.* Copyright 2006 Artists Rights Society (ARS), New York/ADAGP, Paris.

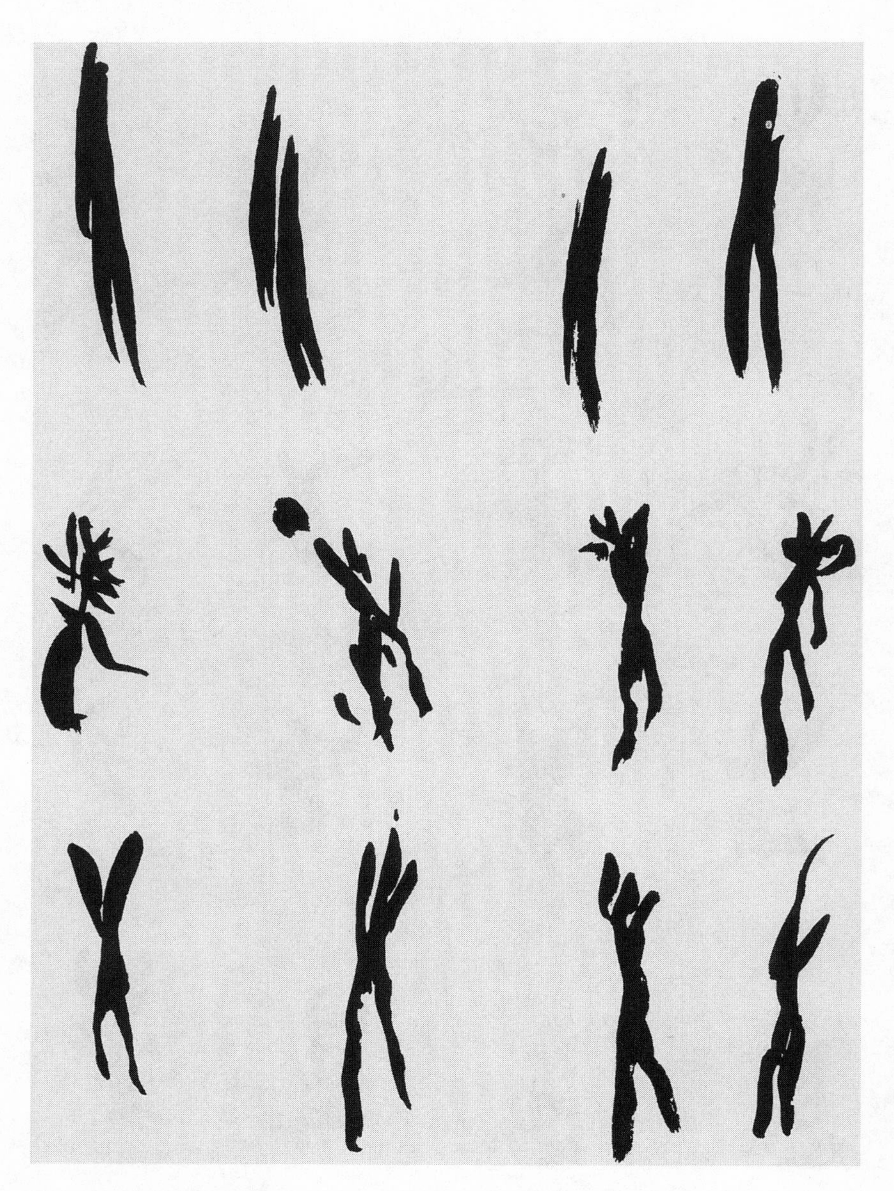

Figure 16. Henri Michaux, *Mouvements.* Copyright 2006 Artists Rights Society (ARS), New York/ADAGP, Paris.

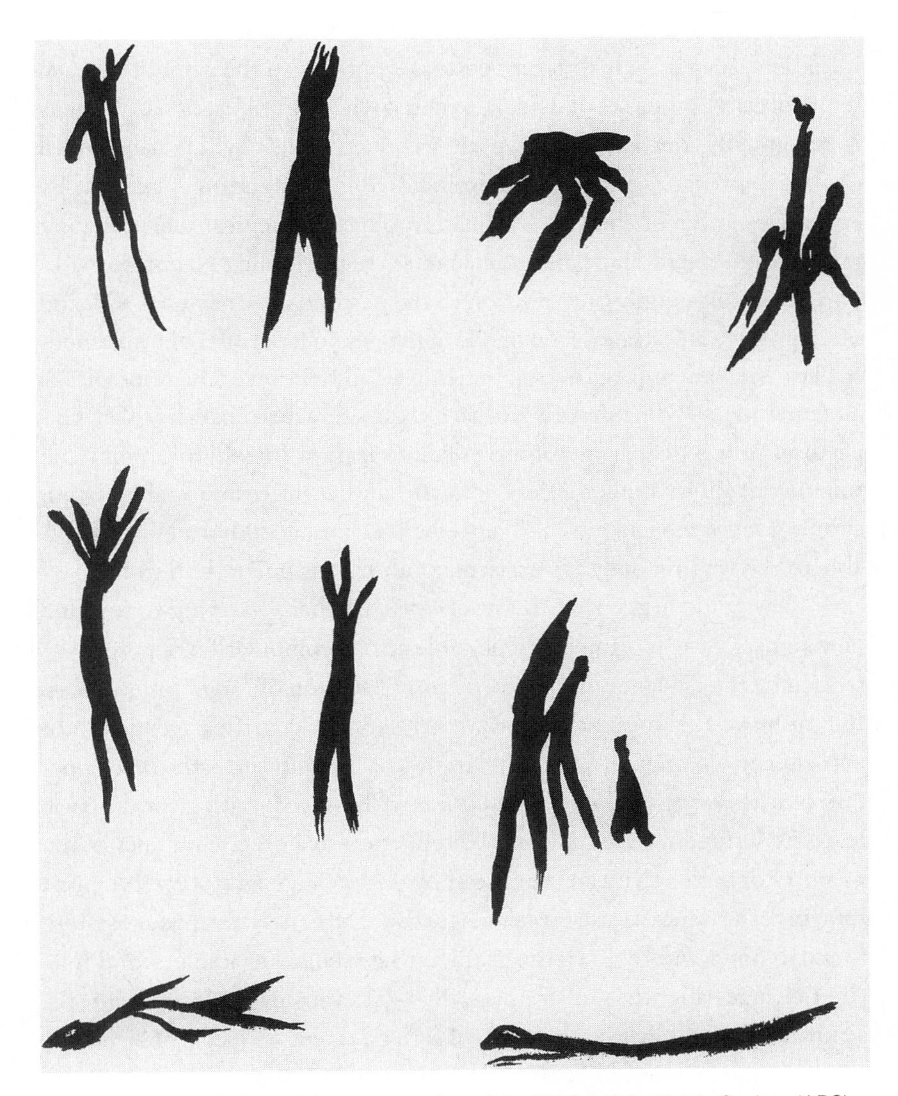

Figure 17. Henri Michaux, *Mouvements.* Copyright 2006 Artists Rights Society (ARS), New York/ADAGP, Paris.

page of markings and the systematicity of the entire approach. Typically, Michaux establishes a gestural routine composed of three to five strokes; he then adds a new element not initially constitutive of the original set, which initiates a substantially different gestural routine. To the extent that each set involves a limited set of strokes executed with slight variations, Michaux is remarkably consistent. However, frequently the new element added (degree of pressure, privileged direction of the thrust) changes the visually evocative power of the strokes entirely. That is, they can change quite rapidly from resembling Chinese characters to resembling Neolithic markings as a result of only one addition to the gestural routine. That addition often involves an extrapolation of one of the possibilities offered by previous strokes. Michaux appears to be practicing an abstraction of the principles—and movements—that make script scriptlike, characters characterlike. This gestural process of abstraction or schematization (through rapidity and repetition) allows him to access not some authentic, primordial body but simply a set of movements (and movement experiences) normally unavailable to the writing body his particular culture has taught him to be.

One could argue that in *Mouvements*, Michaux is trying to invent a new signary by exploring every possible stroke combination, a point buttressed by the evidence of his enormous production of "sign"-filled pages. But to make this argument, one would have to identify a trend toward consistency, a search for regularity. In this respect, however, the mark clusters of *Mouvements* are in contradiction with one of writing's most basic features: limited differentiation, the reduction to a precise number of the quantity of marks that can bear meaning within any one system. No print remains of a single culture (or language) could be as heterogeneous as those found in *Mouvements*. Since the character set (and associated gestural routine) changes slightly—or dramatically—on every page, *Mouvements* resembles more closely a compilation of scripts, an encyclopedia of signaries, than a single, achieved system. Ultimately, what the pages of the volume indicate is that Michaux was less interested in forging a personal character set, "a language all his own," in Bertelé's words, than in using character formation and the generative gestures of inscription to explore untapped gestural and graphic possibilities within the practice of inscription itself.[49]

Thus, despite the critical insistence on language as tool, evidence suggests that Michaux was invested in language as an inscriptive *practice:* he was seeking to discover the essential elements of sign making as a "technique of the body," or a "chaîne opératoire."[50] With respect to the visual phenomenality of the sign, he wished to explore all the potential graphic instantiations of that non-ontological, purely social unit called "the sign," as well as the types of spatial relationships allowed between signs. He knew that he could not transgress the socially determined graphemic and spatial limitations on sign making without losing the formal sign-quality of his marks.[51] What he could do, however, was suggest sign-*ness* (without actually signing) by exploiting the combinatory possibilities provided by signs of all varieties. He therefore mimes the literalness or iconicity of the pictogram, the evocative power of the ideogram, the simplicity and easy iterability of the letter, the discreteness of the cuneiform imprint, and the decorative quality of the hieroglyph. Further, the implicit grid structure Michaux employs not only evokes the child's primer but also establishes an "unnatural" and nonfigurative relation among the various mark groupings on the page.[52] They almost invariably stand in relationships dictated by symbolic rather than iconic representational conventions. The threshold with narrative painting is rarely crossed, and the reader's urge toward a figurative (iconic) reading of the marks is thwarted by the reimposition, either on the page at hand or the next, of a seriality that is inscription's most defining feature.

Michaux thus mimes signing on two levels: he approximates the graphic features of the sign on the level of the visual, and he reproduces the kinetic properties of sign *making* on the level of the gestural. By respecting the rhythms of sequencing or seriality as well as the types and qualities of stroke permitted to character formation within a tight space, Michaux manages to inhabit (in the sense of *habitus*), the gestural routines of not just one but several writing systems. It seems logical that Michaux would turn toward calligraphic and pictographic systems in order to enlarge his field of exploration; such systems generally require more kinetic investment on the part of the writer than do alphabetic systems.[53] In *Mouvements*, especially, the calligraphic allows him to experience his body, as a writing body, in a new way. Michaux seems to have appreciated this augmentation of the choreographic possibilities that were offered to him by alternative writing practices. Flirting with the constraints of these more gestural systems, he often appears to reach a limit point of each routine he initiates; on some pages, his strokes are longer and his characters larger, more figurative, or more schematic than permitted by even calligraphic conventions. But it is perhaps only by experiencing those transgressions physically as well as visually that Michaux's body comes to know what it is to have a signing body, a disciplined body capable of inscribing marks that resemble, or could operate as, signs.

Significantly, in later remarks on *Mouvements*, Michaux tended to stress not the visual qualities of his marks but the kinetic experience of making them. The sheer number of pages Michaux filled with these marks testifies to the aim of the project: to *move* in a sign-making way. Since it is exclusively scholars of literature and art historians (and not dance ethnographers or theorists of movement) who have approached Michaux's ink drawings, it makes sense that an entire aspect—perhaps the most important—of Michaux's practice has until now been ignored.[54] Yet, a mere glance at Michaux's manifold writings on the subject of writing reveals clearly that even if the initial impetus for creating "mouvements" was a desire to invent an ideal signary, in the end it was the opportunity to perform a wide variety of inscriptive gestures that proved the most compelling aspect of the experiment. In "Signes," for instance, Michaux emphasizes the gestural rather than visual motivation while speculating on the genesis of *Mouvements*. "I have to speak now about my signs," Michaux concedes: "But where am I with these signs? Surely not where everyone else is" ("Sûrement pas dans la voie principale").

> I made thousands of them two years ago. But were these really signs? They were gestures, rather, interior gestures [gestes intérieurs] for which we have no limbs, but only a desire for limbs, ways of stretching [tensions], ways of reaching [élans], and all of them executed by lively ligaments, never thick, never weighted down with flesh or closed in by skin [et tout cela en cordes vivantes, jamais épaisses, jamais grosses de chair ou fermées de peau].[55]

When Michaux wrote "Signes," "la voie principale" of painterly experimentation with signlike figures was that cleared by Mathieu and Capogrossi. The latter, Michaux claims, discovered a "signe de base," a schematic cell from which all other signs would issue (430). Mathieu, too, according to Michaux, located something "irreducible": "the final point, the Alpha, the metaphysics of authority" (431). In "Signes," Michaux acknowledges that his experience in *Mouvements* produced something quite different: neither an essential sign (Capogrossi) nor a definitive signature (Mathieu), but instead "movements . . . pieces of movements" ["des émiettements de mouvements"], too numerous and too heterogeneous even to merit the appellative "signs." By leaving "la voie principale," however, Michaux manages to wander into a whole new arena of investigation, one in which gestures and movements become more significant than the marks they leave behind on the canvas or page. Michaux's singular accomplishment is to have relinquished (or at least deferred) the dream of an absolute, essential sign (a dream pursued more rigorously by Capogrossi and Mathieu) in the interest, instead, of reanimating the body's seemingly limitless sign-making capacity.

But this limitless sign-making capacity is a dream of another sort. The marks Michaux leaves on the pages of the *Mouvements* series are not truly produced by "gestes intérieurs." How could they be? If an external body did not execute the gestures, then no marks would remain and there would be no *Mouvements*. "Gestes intérieurs" are imaginative and virtual rather than performed and materialized; as such, they are infinite, or, if not infinite, then at least unhampered by corporeal constraints ("never thick, never weighted down with flesh or closed in by skin"). The "gestures for which we have no limbs but only a desire for limbs" belong to the virtual body, the body before it has been shaped by one—or *any*—culture. Of course, Michaux cannot gain access to this virtual body except in his imagination; the orthography of every character set, in whatever civilization or language, obeys the gestural conventions and regimes of that civilization. Further, the shapes any character set can assume are determined by the physiological limits of human digits, the degree of acceleration wrist movements can attain, the scope of circular flexibility in the joints, and so on. Nonetheless, the virtual body serves as a blueprint for movements beyond those allocated by an individual culture; in the act of trying to execute these imaginary "gestes intérieurs," the real body reaches beyond its cultural conditioning, beyond the disciplines of inscription to which it has been subjected since childhood, and gains the knowledge of what it can and cannot do in its struggle to overcome the routines of a specific practice.

Allusions to this ideal, precultural (virtual) body appear throughout Michaux's works. One of the central themes of his earliest publications is in fact nostalgia for the body before its physical training in pedagogical situations. Michaux taxes his early childhood physical "entraînement" with having severely limited and deformed his potential to move freely in space. In "Observations," a short text published in *Passages* (1950), Michaux attributes his restricted way of moving, and thus his self-alienation, to an elementary school training in "Gymnastique suédoise," "this Western gymnastics with its mechanical gestures which divide the body from itself" ("qui écartent de soi").[56] The Swedish "occidental" training is contrasted with that offered to the Hindu dancer or the African drummer.[57] Michaux's conventional primitivism resurfaces here as he indulges in the fantasy of an alternative physical training that would correspond to, rather than distort, the body's natural rhythms. In an untitled poem immediately preceding "Observations," Michaux explains his recent predilection for playing the tam-tam as an attempt to relocate his own natural rhythm, or pulse ("I play the tam-tam . . . to feel my pulse" ["je joue du tam-tam . . . Pour me tâter le pouls"]).[58] Not that he actually dances to the tam-tam, Michaux assures his reader. Beating, moving to the beat, does not allow Michaux to recover a full, originary freedom of movement he believes forever lost. However, what does return in the process of drumming is an amorphous, unchoreographed wealth of "mouvements": "In the end, I was intrigued . . . by movements, by the influence that movements could have over me." And this wealth of movements, we learn in the footnote Michaux provides, is precisely what had been repressed by an elementary school training in "this damned occidental stupidity, Swedish gymnastics" (344).

The drum thus gives him a sense of what his body, shorn of its western training, might be able to do. A brief glimpse of this virtual body appears as well in "Arriver à se réveiller" ("Managing to Wake Up"), a kind of Proustian recollection of awakening as spatial and temporal but also corporeal disorientation. "Without knowing exactly what kind of being I am [quel être je suis] . . . and moving in contradictory ways . . . I try with my numerous feet to pull myself out of sleep."[59] Michaux's preconscious body appears to him first as an insect body, then an animal or machine body, before losing these potential of ways of being/moving and emerging as a human ambulatory mechanism. The text presents in its own terms an intuition that is far more developed in Eastern religions and spiritually oriented physical practices, namely, that the body is a set of articulations that, with devoted practice, can be sublated into a Divine Body capable of moving in all ways. This Divine Body is associated in Michaux's works either with the preconscious body (caught between sleep and waking) or with that of the child. In "Dessiner l'écoulement du temps" ("Drawing the Passage of Time") (1957), however, he admits that even the child can only experience this "extraordinary," virtually limitless range of movements in fantasy: "In my childhood reveries . . . I never was a prince or a conquerer," he notes, "but I was extraordinary in my movements [mais j'étais extraordinaire en mouvements]. A real prodigy in movements. A Proteus of movements."[60] Once again, as in "Signes," pure freedom of movement is relegated to the virtual; anything visible, performed on the stage of the social, is immediately a reduction of the kinetic possibilities entertained by the mind. The more the child moves internally, virtually (by means of "gestes intérieurs"), the less his real body is displaced ("there was no trace of these internal movements in my attitude/posture" ["on ne voyait pas trace en mon attitude"]). Indeed, his physical apathy grows in direct proportion to his internal agitation. The same ratio holds true for *Mouvements* in which, as the author tells us in his Postface, total indolence germinates an "inouïe mobilité," an unsuspected potential for kinesis, that achieves external form not as dance or athletic movement but as the movement series required to inscribe: "For most of my life, spread out on my bed, for interminable hours during which I never got bored, I brought to life two or three forms. . . . I filled one with an unheard of mobility [une inouïe mobilité] of which I was at once the double and the motor, although I remained immobile and sluggish" (*Oeuvres complètes*, vol. II, 598).

Michaux's description here in the Postface is telling: he describes himself as both the "double" and the "motor" of the "inouïe mobilité" the form achieves. In other words, even while lying in bed (and thus eliminating as many habitual movements as possible), he provides the source of kinetic energy allowing the inscriptive gesture to be performed and the signlike mark to be inscribed. To that extent, he is the "motor," the source of kinetic energy capable of "infusing" the inscriptive form with motility. Yet he is also simultaneously the "double" of this form's motility; he moves according to the way the form moves. As Michaux puts it, "their movement became my movement." As the "motor," then, he is the form's cause; but as the double, *he is the form's effect.* That is, the movements required to make the forms, the signlike marks, actually produce a new moving self and, as a result, a new "technique of the body." The self produced by this technique, this new gestural routine, is not some absolute, essential self, but just that form of being that appears in writing, a *performative* self phenomenalized by a set of inscriptive gestures and the particular quality of movement they require in order to be performed. In short, the performance of inscription offers phenomenological existence (a movement-form) to a kinetic energy that has no single, ontological shape or movement pattern of its own.

But can a movement-form really be called a "sign"? Michaux asks himself this very question in the conclusion of his Postface. "Voilà," he attempts a reply, pointing rhetorically at the volume, Bertelé "urged me to take up once again the composition of my ideograms, resumed time and time again over a period of twenty years and abandoned for lack of success. I tried again," he tells us, "but gradually the forms 'in movement' eliminated the thought forms, the characters of composition. Why? I liked making them more. *Their movement became my movement.* The more I made, the more I existed. The more I wanted. Making them, I became other [Les faisant, je devenais tout autre]" (*Oeuvres complètes*, vol. II, 598; added emphasis).

If there exists a being called "Michaux" at this moment of kinetic possession, one who could be said to exist in ontological terms, it is not a

"Michaux" as Cartesian mind but a "Michaux" as gesturing body. The self revealed is nothing *but* movement, or to put it differently, the self is the way it moves. This does not mean, however, that the self's movements are pure of cultural inflection (or freed from anatomical determination). Michaux, in movement, has not rediscovered some originary, essential way of moving but only a way of moving *as a body that inscribes*. The movements that define him are still those associated specifically with the gestural routines of inscription. and further, the dimensions of the page continue to circumscribe the space within which this self can be performed. Even though Michaux rejects the precise routines of the writing systems to which he has been exposed, the possibilities offered by miming symbol or character formation dictate the scope and type of movements he can execute and thus the being he can be.

Ultimately, Michaux's comments reveal that his lifelong attempt at alphabet invention was less a quest for a universal language of intelligible signs than an exploration of the kinesthetic experience of making them, the experience, that is, of being a *writer* in the most literal sense (an active agent in the act of writing). Michaux was not a dancer or an athlete; he could not explore the sensations of his moving body through practices that were not his own. What he could do was seek to experience the sensation of the moving body by enlarging a practice with which he was all too familiar. Michaux's idea was to experiment not with any gestures whatsoever but specifically with the gestures of sign making, or the gestures of making signlike things. Michaux never achieves an ideal archimedian point beyond culture, beyond history; instead, through operations of skilling and simultaneous de-skilling, he reaches a point where the possibilities within the larger practice we call inscription become more numerous and the movements a sign-making body can make are exponentially increased. Michaux relaunches the energy vectors of a corporeal practice we call writing in order to sound a broader range of the body as an instrument for making marks. To the extent that he practices inscription as disarticulating and recombinatory, a transgressive remixing of the given rather than an ex-nihilo creation of the purely other, he belongs to a radically antiprimitivist tradition of theorizing resistance as parodic citation, or the performative repetition of cultural codes. Michaux's accentuation of the gestural component in inscription has important implications for contemporary theories of subjectivation, such as Judith Butler's theory of the performative construction of the gendered subject or Pierre Bourdieu's theory of subjectivity as constituted through acquisition of a bodily *hexis*. Writing is just one form of practical knowledge, one element of a much larger body of iterable corporeal practices; but what Michaux's experiment suggests is that by exploring writing as a movement practice, we learn that our subjectivity is kinetically as well as discursively conditioned and that we can resist our conditioning through citational practices involving movements as well as words.

Notes

I owe a large debt of gratitude to Leslie Jones, associate curator of prints and drawings at the Los Angeles County Art Museum, for sharing her work and her contacts with me. I would also like to thank Loy Zimmerman of the University of California, Irvine, Visual Resources Collection for spending many hours with me pouring over slides, scans, and illustrations. Micheline Phamkin, Henri Michaux's companion, graciously allowed me to interview her in December 2004, for which I am grateful. Thanks are due as well to the Camargo Foundation, which supported me during the period I composed this essay. My interlocutors, Max and Joyce Kozloff, taught me how to think more deeply about the materials of painting while exploring with me the winding streets of Marseille. Finally, I dedicate this chapter to Francesca and Henry, companions by the sea.

1. Modernist primitivism might be considered an epiphenomenon of industrialization that emerged near the beginning of the twentieth century in Europe. It is characterized by a fascination with "tribal arts" (Picasso and the Surrealists); incantation (Dada); jazz *(tout Paris);* nonwestern dance and ritual forms (Maya Deren, Curt Sachs); and "primitive" peoples (German and French ethnography). For persuasive accounts, see Tyler Stovall, *Paris Noir: African Americans in the City of Light* (New York: Houghton Mifflin, 1996); James Clifford, *The Predicament of Culture: Twentieth Century Ethnography, Literature, and Art* (Cambridge, Mass.: Harvard University Press, 1988); Petrine Archer-Straw, *Negrophilia: Avant-Garde Paris and Black Culture in the 1920s* (London: Thames & Hudson, 2000); William Rubin, *Primitivism in 20th Century Art: Affinity of the Tribal and the Modern* (New York: Museum

of Modern Art, 1984); Carole Sweeney, *From Fetish to Subject: Race, Modernism, and Primitivism 1919–1935* (Westport, Conn.: Praeger, 2004).

2. From "L'Expérience des signes; Entretien avec Henri Michaux" by Jean-Dominique Rey in *Henri Michaux: Oeuvres choisies 1927–1984* (Marseille: Réunion des Musées Nationaux, 1993), 212.

3. The *par* of *Par des traits* is hard to translate: it can mean "with" or "by means of" or "through" or "taking the route of" lines.

4. Henri Michaux, *Oeuvres complètes*, vol. III, ed. Raymond Bellour and Ysé Tran, Mireille Cardot (Paris: Gallimard, Pléiade, 2004), 1249–50.

5. Michaux, in Rey, "L'Expérience des signes: Entretien avec Henri Michaux," 212.

6. Michaux's critics have been anxious to identify his turn toward the gestural with his desire for a liberation of the subject. See, in particular, Loreau, Henri Meschonnic, *La Rime et la vie* (Lagrasse: Verdier, 1989), and Gérard Dessons, "La Manière d'Henry: Prolégomènes à un traité du trait" in *Méthodes et saviors chez Henri Michaux*, ed. Gérard Dessons (Poitiers: La Licorne, 1993).

7. A large body of writing has been devoted to the gestural turn in twentieth-century painting. I will produce my own narrative of the French context, but for more general studies of gestural abstraction, see Margit Rowell, *La Peinture, le geste, l'action: l'existentialisme en peinture* (Paris: Klincksieck, 1972); Michael Leja, *Reframing Abstract Expressionism: Subjectivity and Painting in the 1940s* (New Haven, Conn.: Yale University Press, 1993); Richard Schiff, "Performing an Appearance" in *Abstract Expressionism: The Critical Developments*, ed. Michael Auping (New York: H. N. Abrams with Albright-Knox Gallery, 1987); Mary Kelly, "Reviewing Modernist Criticism" in *Art After Modernism: Rethinking Representation*, ed. and intro. Brian Wallis, foreword by Marcia Tucker (New York: New Museum of Contemporary Art with David R. Godine, Publisher, 1984); Amelia Jones, *Body Art: Performing the Subject* (Minneapolis: Minnesota University Press, 1998).

8. Leslie Jones, "Prehistoric Re-marks: Henri Michaux's Visual Exploration into the 'Origin of Painting'" (unpublished manuscript). Michaux's personal library contained accounts of prehistoric visual culture by Henri Breuil and Hugo Obermaier.

9. Abbé Henri Breuil and Dr. Hugo Obermaier, *The Cave of Altamira at Santillana del Mar, Spain*, trans. Mary E. Boyle (Madrid: Tipografia de Archivos, 1935).

10. See Jones, "Prehistoric re-marks," 3.

11. See, for instance, the 1930 double issue of *Cahiers d'art* (nos. 8–9) devoted

entirely to rock paintings from different regions in Africa with large contributions by Leo Frobenius and Henri Breuil.

12. Thus, Michaux evokes the "primitive"—as a discourse and as a mode of representation—by doing precisely what the prehistorians and ethnographers do: he groups together sequences of seemingly related (visually similar) motifs without taking into account their semantic or syntactic relations, that is, without attending to the meaning or order they might have had within their indigenous cultural environments. As Georges Braatschi has remarked, Michaux's ink drawings possess "the character of collector's cabinets" (see "Michaux, calife de l'intérieur," *Tribune de Genève* [Oct. 26, 1984]: n.p.).

13. I cite Michel Cournot's description of Michaux's work space: "Une table de bois, près de la fenêtre, n'est qu'une confusion de pinceaux chinois, de grattoirs, de revues étrangères de chimie, de géographie, de papier déchirés couverts, de guingois, d'une miniscule écriture illisible. Michaux sur le bout des doigts," *Le Nouvel observateur* (Jan. 11, 1985): 63.

14. From interview with Micheline Phamkin, December 2004. The cheap paper was bought at an art supply store and thus was not intended as a support for writing but as a support for drawing studies and exercises.

15. Henri Michaux, *Oeuvres Complètes*, vol. II, ed. Raymond Bellour and Ysé Tran (Paris: Gallimard, 2001), 598.

16. A similar sequence is repeated in each section, reinforcing the impression that Michaux himself actually drafted the ink drawings in that particular order, that he himself progressed from making small, tightly knit, constrained figures to thrusting greater amounts of ink with greater force onto the page. Michaux obviously approved of the order in which Bertelé arranged the pages, so to some extent he is responsible for it. And yet time and again he refused to take responsibility for Bertelé's choices.

17. René Bertelé, "Préface à Parcours," in Henri Michaux, *Oeuvres complètes*, vol. III, 432.

18. "Mouvements" in *Mouvements* (*Oeuvres complètes*, vol. II, 440); added emphasis.

19. ". . . le signe peut exprimer mieux que n'importe quoi, le 'MOI-JE'" ("Signes," *Oeuvres complètes*, vol. II, 431).

20. Michaux was not alone but rather one of several artists whose impatience with the familiar techniques of Illusionism produced a fascination with exotic alternatives. Michaux first visited China—which is his principal reference for

calligraphy—in 1930. He was also influenced by Paul Klee's line drawings: see "Aventure des lignes" in *Oeuvres complètes*, vol. II, 360–63.

21. Frances Morris, "Introduction," *Paris Post War: Art and Existentialism 1945–55*, ed. Frances Morris (London: Tate Gallery, 1993), 144.

22. Leslie Jones, *"A Barbarian in Asia": Henri Michaux's works in ink, 1927–55* (unpublished doctoral dissertation for the Institute of Fine Arts, New York University, 2003, 155–56). I am not convinced this last point is true; it seems to me that Michaux often does follow a stroke order. I return to this question later on.

23. Jones's account places emphasis on intentional misappropriation: "If Michaux were intending to emulate the practice of Asian calligraphy, why would he consistently break all of its rules? Since we know that Michaux studied Chinese calligraphy as a youth, observed it first hand during his visit to Asia in 1931, and eventually wrote a treatise called *Idéogrammes en Chine* later in his career, it is highly unlikely that these were naïve "mistakes." When Michaux put down the pen and picked up the brush to make "signs," he was undoubtedly aware of the potential associations with Asian calligraphy. Michaux's "mistakes" were thus intentional—a formal display of the artist's self-proclaimed status as "a barbarian in Asia" (156–57). Compare Jones's nuanced appraisal to those included in *Quelques orients d'Henri Michaux* (eds. Anne-Élisabeth Halpern and Véra Mihailovich-Dickman [Éditions Findlay, 1996]), which fail to provide a detailed reading of what, precisely, Michaux appropriates and deforms in the Eastern traditions he emulated. For a more suggestive treatment, see Richard Sieburth, "Signs in Action: The Ideograms of Ezra Pound and Henri Michaux" in *Untitled Passages by Henri Michaux*, ed. Catherine de Zegher (New York: The Drawing Center, Merrell, 2000).

24. For a review of calligraphic script styles and their history, as well as a revealing comparison between calligraphy and the practices of Jackson Pollock and Willem de Kooning, see Robert E. Harrist, Jr., "Reading Chinese Calligraphy," in *The Embodied Image: Chinese Calligraphy from the John B. Elliott Collection* ed. Harrist and Wen C. Fong, (New York: Harry N. Abrams, 1999), 3–27.

25. *Idéogrammes en Chine* is a very strange volume indeed. Michaux betrays the conventions of calligraphy at every turn, all the while miming its elements. For instance, he prints entire pages of calligraphy (not his own) in red ink, a color reserved in China uniquely for the seal that accompanies the black and white ink characters. For an exhaustive overview, see the excellent "Notes" by Yolaine Escande in *Oeuvres complètes*, vol. III, 1658–63.

26. Max Loreau, "La poésie, la peinture et le fondement du langage" in *La Peinture à l'oeuvre et l'énigme du corps* (Paris: Gallimard, 1980), 46.

27. At times, Michaux restrained himself further, using only the center of the paper and leaving large margins on all sides blank. Michaux must have worked as though he were placing ink marks within an invisible rectangle approximately the size of a French (or Belgian) schoolchild's notebook; in some of his later unpublished ink drawings, Michaux even pencils in this square. I thank Micheline Phamkin for showing me a series of ink drawings in the style of *Mouvements* that contain penciled squares inside of which the mark clusters appear. In *Les Années fertiles: 1940–1960* (Villefranche-de-Rouergue: Mouvements Éditions, 1988), Geneviève Bonnefoi explains that French painters of the late 1940s and early 1950s were generally more modest in their formats than were their American counterparts.

28. *Oeuvres complètes*, vol. II, 430–31.

29. For an overview of gestural painting during Michaux's period, see Rowell and Bonnefoi.

30. See Henri Michaux, *Oeuvres complètes*, vol. I, eds. Raymond Bellour and Ysé Tran (Paris: Gallimard, 1998). The editors list Michaux's first exhibition as occurring on June 3–23, 1937 (224).

31. "Chronologie," p. cxxiv. In Michaux's own words: "Vu l'expo Dubuffet. Plein de qualités de peintre ce Dubuffet. J'ai été conquis. Depuis, je me reprends . . . un peu" (quoted p. cxxiv). During 1946–47, Dubuffet made at least seven portraits of Michaux in either India ink, pencil, or oil on canvas. See *Catalogue de travaux de Jean Dubuffet plus beaux qu'il croient: Portraits.*

32. "Préambule," *L'Afrique fantôme* (Paris: Gallimard, 1981; originally published 1934 without the "Préambule"), 7.

33. This is Micheline Phamkin rendering of a sentence Michaux pronounced to her in reference to Dubuffet's works. Interview with the author, December 2004.

34. Bonnefoi, *Les Années fertiles*, 22.

35. Claude Gregory quoted by Alfred Pacquement in Hélène Seikel, Daniel Abadie, and Alfred Pacquement, *Paris–New York* (Paris: Centre Pompidou, 1977), 540.

36. The chronology supplied in *Oeuvres complètes*, vol. II, lists three major exhibits in which Pollock was displayed with Michaux: "Un art autre" (Paris, December 1952); "Vitalita nell'arte" (Venice, summer 1959); and in a Turin exhibition in 1963 that reunited Dubuffet, Fautrier, Mathieu, Wols, Tobey, Pollock, and Michaux (xxx).

37. "Entretiens et témoignages sur l'oeuvre peint [sic] d'Henri Michaux," by Geneviève Bonnefoi in *Cahiers de l'Herne: Henri Michaux*, ed. Raymond Bellour (Paris: Minard, 1966), 377; my translation.

38. Apparently, in contrast, Mathieu and Degottex both gave themselves an intense training in calligraphy and practiced for hours before they placed the definitive paraphe on the canvas.

39. Bonnefoi, "Entretiens et témoignages sur l'oeuvre peint [sic] d'Henri Michaux," 375.

40. Rowell, *La Peinture, le geste, l'action: l'existentialisme en peinture*, 49; added emphasis; my translation.

41. The discovery of a set of small canvases that may have been painted by Pollock during 1944–45 while working with the photographer Herbert Matter complicates the distinction I am trying to support. It may be that, inspired by Matter's abstract light experiments, Pollock tried out his drip techniques on smaller canvasses before moving to the larger scale. See Ellen G. Landau's essay, "Pollock Matters," online at http://www.pollockexhibit.com.

42. See Jones, *Body Art*, especially the chapter entitled "The Pollockian Performative."

43. See Schiff, "Performing an Appearance." As Jones and Richard Schiff have both suggested, the "Pollockian performative" is a painterly utterance in which the artist (here Michaux), rather than leaving traces of his deepest psychological impulses, produces these impulses in the act of inscription itself.

44. Many scholars of modernism have explored this conundrum, which Clement Greenberg characterized in 1948 as distinguishing between "being truly spontaneous" and "working only mechanically" ("Review of an Exhibition of Willem de Kooning" in John O'Brian, ed., *Clement Greenberg*, vol. II, 229). See also Michael Newman, "The Marks, Traces, and Gestures of Drawing" in *The Stage of Drawing: Gesture and Act: Selections from the Tate Gallery*, selected by Avis Newman, curated by Catherine de Zegher (New York: The Tate and the Drawing Center, 2003).

45. T. J. Clark, *Farewell to an Idea: Episodes from a History of Modernism* (London: Yale University Press, 1999), 323.

46. To be fair, de-skilling techniques were prefigured by Breton's technique of changing the speed, or "vitesse," at which he allowed his hand to scribble down thoughts. Breton even differentiated between five different speeds of writing, each of which was identified with another layer of deconditioning.

47. *The Open Work*, trans. Anna Cancogni, intro. by David Robey (Cambridge, Mass.: Harvard University Press, 1989), 103; added emphasis.

48. *Émergences, resurgences* (Geneva: Albert Skira, 1972 and 1993), 9; original emphasis.

49. "Préface à Parcours," *Oeuvres complètes*, vol. III, 432.

50. This phrase is borrowed from André Leroi-Gourhan's groundbreaking study of gesture and its relation to language, *Le Geste et la parole*, vols. I and II (Paris: Albin Michel, 1964); the phrase "technique of the body" is another appropriation, this time from Marcel Mauss's essay, "Techniques du corps," reprinted in *Anthropologie et sociologie* (Paris: Presses Universitaires de France, 1950); originally presented to the Société Française de psychologie in 1934.

51. For instance, a full-fledged scene, a composition—a relationship among individual figures/marks—would collapse signifying into resembling. On this distinction, see James Elkins, *On Pictures and the Words That Fail Them* (Cambridge: Cambridge University Press, 1998).

52. The grid structure has several implications, only some of which I can evoke here. For a brief but suggestive summary, see Rosalind E. Krauss, "Grids," in *The Originality of the Avant-Garde and Other Modernist Myths* (Cambridge, Mass.: MIT University Press, 1987, 4th ed.): "[G]rids are not only spatial to start with, they are visual structures that explicitly reject a narrative or sequential reading of any kind" (13); "[T]he grid is a way of abrogating the claims of natural objects to have an order particular to themselves" (9).

53. Jean Louis Schefer makes this point in "Sur les dessins d'Henri Michaux": "Michaux a fait ce jeu [to create 'signes dansants'] de façon épisodique. Est-ce que parce que le fantôme de l'alphabet et jusqu'aux variations idéogrammatiques feraient barrière au mouvement? Presque toute notre culture, ou son histoire pédagogique, a pensé une perspective morale de l'alphabet comme celle de la disparition progressive du corps gesticulant et expressif" (*Henri Michaux: Peindre, composer, écrire* [Paris: Gallimard, 1999], 27).

54. Several critics allude to Michaux's kinesthetic experience, mostly with respect to the mescaline drawings, but without applying or generating a theory of kinesthetic experience as central to the act of inscription itself. See Dessons, Loreau, Meschonnic, and the psychoanalytic reading of Michaux's *graphomanie* in Anne Brun, *Henri Michaux ou le corps halluciné* (Paris: Institut d'édition Sanofi-Synthélabo, 1999).

55. *Oeuvres complètes*, vol. II, 429.

56. *Oeuvres complètes*, vol. II, 344. Introduced into France and Belgium at the end of the nineteenth century, Swedish gymnastics was based on medical rather than military principles. See Gilbert Andrieu, *L'Éducation physique au XXe siècle: Une histoire des pratiques* (Paris: Actio, 1993). Ironically, Andrieu compares Swedish gymnastics to hatha yoga, the very form Michaux idealizes as superior to the training he received. "For those who do hatha yoga today," writes Andrieu, "the postures [of Swedish gymnastics] . . . are comparable" (26; my translation). Who knows, however, what the French and Belgian primary school systems made of this rational, more medically sound form of physical exercise.

57. Precisely which form of Hindu dance Michaux is referencing in his footnote to "Observations" is impossible to determine. Similar in this regard to Artaud, Michaux makes the mistake of assuming that Eastern movement traditions remain faithful to the natural body: "Que n'ai-je connu plus tôt la danse de l'Hindou, danse qui se garde bien de le [the body] décentrer, de l'éloigner de lui-même. L'oeil, le cou, les doigts, plutôt que les excentriques jambes, font presque tous les mouvements, les mouvements de la pensée, les mouvements pour n'être pas multiple, en pieces et à la débandade, pour n'être pas distrait, les mouvement pour ne pas se désunir" (344; footnote to text).

58. *Oeuvres complètes*, vol. II, 342–43.

59. *Oeuvres complètes*, vol. II, 313–14.

60. *Oeuvres complètes*, vol. II, 372.

CHAPTER 7

Ghosting: The Performance and Migration of Cinematic Gesture, Focusing on Hou Hsiao-Hsien's *Good Men, Good Women*

Lesley Stern

I had hardly crossed the border when ghosts came toward me.

—Nosferatu

She is woken in the middle of the night by the telephone. Stumbling, groping in the dark, at last she reaches and answers it. The piercing insistent ringing stops, followed by silence. The caller says nothing. The fax machine, which sits on the television, clicks into action. As it starts spewing out pages, images from the past and from another country play on the television: Setsuko Hara cycles joyfully toward us, her hair blowing in the wind in Ozu's *Late Spring*. Throughout Hou Hsiao-Hsien's *Good Men, Good Women* (*Haonan haonü*, Taiwan, 1995), this young woman, Liang Ching, is plagued by these machines, haunted by words and silences and images from the past. Liang Ching (played by Annie Shizuka Inoh, in real life a pop star) is an actress in present-day Taipei, preparing to play the part of a real-life revolutionary Taiwanese figure, Chiang Bi-yu, in a film about her and her husband, Chung Hao-Tung. Someone has stolen Liang Ching's diary and is faxing back to her pages detailing her life in the recent past as a bar hostess, hooked on heroin, and romantically involved with a small-time gangster, Ah Wei (Jack Kao), who was shot in a disco. She repeatedly addresses the anonymous caller, desperately, as though he is Ah Wei, a ghost returned to haunt her. She holds the phone, pulls screeds of paper from the fax machine, crumples it in her arms, hugs the paper to her, and weeps. Her words are insubstantial, detached, copied, voiceless, and at the same time inscribed on her body, registered somatically as grief and desperation. These machines, designed as delivery systems for words and images, do indeed deliver messages, but messages that are often more emotionally loaded than semantically coherent. They not only deliver voices, they animate them; they are not simply a conduit, they are haunting machines; mercilessly repetitive, they deliver memories, they mediate between the past and present. Like the camera.

This chapter, to do with performance and turning specifically on the question of gesture, focuses, via *Good Men, Good Women*, on three gestural regimes and an entailed triadic relationship: (a) the profilmic performance of the film actors; (b) the cinematic performance—how filmic codes are deployed not merely to produce meanings but to generate affects; and (c) the spectatorial performance (mimetic enactment).

In exploring the question of what constitutes cinematic gesture, I highlight a particular conundrum: Can the camera itself gesture? *Good Men, Good Women* enacts, in a metadiscursive way, the notion of gesture as a ghosting. The film is simultaneously about history (the modern history of Taiwan) and about performance, technology, and the body. It puts into play bodily techniques (gestural modalities) and the techniques of a range of communication technologies (cinema, telephone, television, fax) that articulate relations between past and present. If *Good Men, Good Women* is a film about the making of a film, it is equally about the way that memory works through the body, the body politic and the individual body, to make and remake history.

Three scenes from *Good Men, Good Women* haunt this chapter, appearing in glimpses, at times moving in and taking over the discourse, then fading away. Two of these scenes are paired:

> Color: A young woman, in a modern-day bedroom—cool neutral colors, hard lines—crouches outside the bathroom. She lifts an arm, clutching the bathroom door; slowly, with great effort, she pulls herself up. It is as though she's pulling a heavy, inert, weight. She stumbles into the shower; we hear the sounds of vomiting but can see only a blurred figure behind the opaque glass.

Figure 1. Grief—Liang Ching. Still from *Good Men, Good Women.*

Much later in the film:

> Black and white: A young woman in a large house, with timber frames and a dark wooden staircase, begins to climb the stairs. She puts out a hand to steady herself on the banister and then puts out her other hand to hold the banister. The camera is behind her, we see her climb, pull herself up slowly, with great effort, as though pulling a heavy, inert weight. She exits the frame, and the camera holds on the empty scene.

The third scene, a death scene, is not part of a pair. In a nightclub, Ah Wei, the small-time gangster lover of Liang Ching, is shot. This is the scene that prompted this chapter. For years after first seeing *Good Men, Good Women* at a Sydney Film Festival (around 1996), I was haunted by this scene, a vivid and visceral memory of a shocking and particularly gestural death scene. I remembered Jack Kao's performance, in fine gangster tradition, as consummately histrionic; I remembered him falling in slow motion. But when I came to look at the film in detail, I found, as is so often the case, that memory had betrayed me. Jack Kao does nothing—the camera does everything. In the nightclub, he is dancing, a gun shot rings out, in long shot he falls. But the sequencing and rhythm of shots, the articulation of space and bodies in space, is extraordinary. The film got me thinking about the relation between technologies of the body and cinematic technique, and about the relation between gesture and memory, and about that question that started idly and then became insistent: Can the camera gesture? We circle around and in on the question and this particular scene, delaying or holding in suspense a detailed description and analysis. Because of the film's sliding between remembrance and projection, imagination and knowledge, because of the uncertainties raised about acting and action within the personal domain and the public, within a fictional arena and a historical one, I first sketch out some of the moves the film makes, then turn in detail to the three scenes.[1]

Good Men, Good Women is a film about the making of a film, and yet it shares few of the characteristics of this particular genre or cycle. There is very little in the way of rehearsal, and the paraphernalia of camera, lights,

Figure 2. Grief—Chiang Bi-Yu. Still from *Good Men, Good Women*.

and stars is largely absent. Films of this genre usually revolve, dramatically, around an on-set/off-set dynamic (in the tradition of the backstage drama), which provides the canvas for an exploration of performativity and a differentiation of the daily and the extra-daily body. Instead, in *Good Men, Good Women*, the transitions and juxtapositions—both between the daily and the extra-daily, "film" and "life," and between present and past—are decidedly jagged. The film's narrative moves backward and forward between (at least) three time zones without signaling the status of images as flashback or memory or film-within-a-film. The three diegetic time zones are the present, the recent past, and the historical past—the present, that is, of the actress (although there is also the present that is ours, the viewers'), her recent past (which is also generically coded as something like a gangster film), and the historical past (which is coded somewhat as a documentary or as recreation). But these distinctions, which become evident even as one tries to differentiate, soon blur. For one thing, the scenes depicting the historical past, supposedly incarnated in the pseudo-documentary film-within-the-film, are hypothetical: the actress is *preparing* to play the part in a film that will be called *Good Men, Good Women*, but the shooting for this film has not commenced. The scenes we see, then, are Liang Ching's *vision* of how the film will look, her imaginary projection. This past exists in the conditional tense. Or perhaps, insofar as it alludes to a series of real people and historical events as filtered and projected through her imagination, we might say this is a past that exists, paradoxically, in the future perfect.[2]

Over the opening credits, singing voices are faded in. In a black and white landscape, misty and semitropical, a group of men and women walk from the distance toward the camera. They sing joyously: "When yesterday's sadness is about to die / When tomorrow's good cheer is marching towards us / Then people say, don't cry / So why don't we sing." They carry bundles and walking sticks indicating a long journey, but there is no other explanation of who and where they are. The film cuts to color and the present day, to the telephone and the fax and the television. Later, this scene is situated within a historical series of events (albeit narratively dispersed): it represents the arrival of Chiang Bi-yu and Chung Hao-Tung with a small group of young Taiwanese radicals on the mainland (in Guangdong province, Hou's birthplace) during World War II, in order to support the anti-Japanese resistance. The final scene of the film is a repetition of the opening, but this time the image is in color and accompanied by Liang Ching's voice announcing the arrival of the film crew on the mainland: "We have a three-month shooting schedule. . . . The day before we left Taiwan, Chiang Bi-yu passed away." The figures leave the frame and the camera holds on the empty scene. A title is superimposed over the emptiness: "Dedicated to all the political victims of the 1950s."

On one level, or rather through a series of interstices, *Good Men, Good Women* tells the story of these political victims. As the film unfolds, we see that instead of being welcomed by the Chinese, they are treated with suspicion (viewed as possible informers), misunderstood (different languages and dialects jostle), interrogated, and incarcerated by the Chinese. At the end of the war, the Japanese surrendered Taiwan to China, and in 1949, Chiang Kai-shek's Nationalist government was established and propped up by America's foreign policy during the Korean war. When the group of young radicals returns home to Taiwan after the war, they are arrested as Communists by the Kuomintang government, and Chung Hao-Tung is executed. The others are persecuted during the White Terror of the 1950s.

Hou's *Good Men, Good Women* was prompted to some degree by Chiang Bi-yu's political campaign in the mid-1990s to bring to light this repressed history of socialist struggle and persecution in the 1950s. Although martial law ended in 1987, when Hou Hsiao-Hsien made *Good Men, Good Women* in 1995, the Nationalist government, which had instituted an "organized forgetting" through civic education and official culture, was still in power.[3] Annie Shizuka Inoh herself did not know this history. Many young Taiwanese, in 1995, did not know this history. And even Hou's knowledge was recent: "I have lived in Taiwan for over forty years, but only when I made *A City of Sadness* did I begin to learn about Taiwan's history. I read a lot of books on Taiwan, delving consciously into its history, people, and life itself."[4]

In many ways, this film enacts the process by which knowledge of the past is acquired, by which repressed history is brought into the sphere of visualization. Modern Taiwan (in this case Taiwan, but every country has its ghosts) is haunted by its past, and during the course of the film, this past materializes in fragments, symptoms, sensory resonances, emotional dissonance.[5] Above all, it materializes through a circuit of exchange, of conversions, a gestural circuit, a conversion of energies. If we were to focus on the repertoire of characters, we might begin by saying, "a bar hostess converted into a revolutionary, a revolutionary converted into an actor." But it is more likely that it is a circuit of energy that passes through actants, gestures that mobilize bodies, affects that travel between bodies on the screen and bodies in the audience. The film works (like a dream "works") as a patterning of doubles, mimicry, repetitions, returns.[6] Hou's cinema is often characterized as one of stillness, restraint, contemplation, observation, understatement.[7] But this is a film propelled by movement—filmic and bodily movement, mechanical and pathetic, movement to and fro between past and present, here and there. Repetition, resonance, ghosting.

Take the opening and closing scenes, which provide framing but not classical symmetry, as in the neat inversion of *Citizen Kane*, for example. The repetition keeps questions in the air, circulating like angry ghosts: Who are the "real" characters, and who are the actors? How is it that key historical players can move through a landscape and disappear? And conversely, how do the actions and gestures of ordinary people register on the historical stage? This pair—opening and closing—signals a Russian doll structure. The film made by Hou Hsiao-Hsien and called *Good Men, Good Women* contains within it another film, also called *Good Men, Good Women.* But containment is an inappropriate description. There is no hierarchy to dictate original and copy but rather a to-and-fro movement. The series of resonances includes the following scenes: Liang Ching and Ah Wei discuss a possible pregnancy and abortion, rhymed with Liang Ching's pregnancy and the handing over of her child to adoptive parents so that she can serve the cause; the cycling sequence from the opening of *Late Spring* is echoed in a more enigmatic and sinister scene of a bicycle moving over cobbled streets at night followed by an announcement of execution (during the same period in which the Ozu film is set); a meeting of gangsters amidst food and wine is rhymed with a spartan land reform meeting, the former characterized by gestures of consumption, the latter by gestures of argumentation; two scenes (already mentioned) of grieving over slain lovers are counterpoised. Like the woman she is to play, Liang Ching's lover has been killed, and she is in mourning. But as the film unfolds, we discover that the circumstances are profoundly different: Ah Wei has not sacrificed his life for a political cause; he dies because Liang Ching, in the best tradition of the gangster film, has betrayed him to a rival gang for money.

Critics often interpret this relation between past and present as Hou's nostalgic evocation of a generation who lived by political ideals, who sacrificed individual gratification for the greater public good. Against this vision of the past, so the argument runs, he negatively poses the self-interest of contemporary youth, whose relations all fall under the rule of commercial transaction. But the circuits of energy cross time lines and bodies. Hou, I think, is more rueful about "goodness"; while ideological certainty may produce a certain kind of goodness, the film also explores the possibilities of goodness in a nonheroic era.[8] For Liang Ching, the process of performance is a process of entertaining knowledge (in the way that an abandoned house entertains ghosts), of coming to know the past through mimetic enactment. The force of this knowledge, and its energetic circulation, is experienced somatically. She plays Chiang Bi-yu, but equally we might say that the ghost of Chiang Bi-yu comes to inhabit Liang Ching, to prize loose repressed knowledge. Annie Shizuka Inoh plays both of them. Rather than saying that this is a story of an actress who plays a revolutionary, it is more useful to say this film gives us two women, played by the same actress. There are a few scenes involving rehearsal and the staging of poses for production shots, but mostly we simply see two women in their separate diegetic worlds (and the one, Liang Ching, is further divided into two time zones and diegetic realms). This perspective is important: one body, two women; a body divided; a history that is and is not continuous.[9] In terms of acting, it is almost the obverse of the method. In *Good Men, Good Women*, we are not shown the actress Liang Ching calling upon her own experience in order to play the part of the revolutionary heroine, to invest the character with psychological depth and authenticity. Rather, her *experiencing* of the historical past serves to summon up her own personal past. She performs a work of memory, which is to say memory (and its aphasic entailments) works through her, history takes place. And it is history told from below.[10] As Didi-Huberman has said, "Repetitions and differences: moments when the work of memory becomes corporeal, becomes a symptom in the continuity of events."[11] Didi-Huberman was addressing the work not of Hou Hsiao-Hsien but of Aby Warburg on the pathos formula, but the phrase is pertinent and we shall return to it later.

Repetitions and Differences

> Color: A young woman, in a modern-day bedroom—cool neutral colors, hard lines—crouches outside the bathroom. She lifts an arm, clutching the bathroom door; slowly, with great effort, she pulls herself up. It is as though she's pulling a heavy, inert, weight. She stumbles into the shower; we hear the sounds of vomiting but can see only a blurred figure behind the opaque glass.

Much later in the film:

> Black and white: A young woman in a large house, with timber frames and a dark wooden staircase, begins to climb the stairs. She puts out a hand to steady herself on the banister and then puts out her other hand to hold the banister. The camera is behind her, we see her climb, pull herself up slowly, with great effort, as though pulling a heavy, inert weight. She exits the frame, and the camera holds on the empty scene.

The force of the first scene derives most obviously from the gestural impulse, though it is only when this gesture is repeated, in the second scene, that it comes into focus, precisely through the force of repetition, *as a gesture*. And in the moment of its repetition, it reconfigures the earlier iteration. The repetition reflects on the origin, recasting both its semantic and affective valency.

Filming the Emotions: Motility, Transference, and Conversion

"He simply films emotions," says Hou of Godard in *Breathless*. How does he do this? "By editing together long shots, medium shots, and close-ups: independently of the size of the shots," answers Hou. Does this question of filming the emotions, then, have simply to do with montage, with a disavowal of continuity editing?[12] Certainly for Hou it would seem in part to do with film language. But it is also about the gestural modality of the actor. Elsewhere, he remarks that Belmondo seems to be devoid of emotion, but this is because he is getting on with things, it is not that he doesn't have emotions.[13] The emotional valency, conveyed through his quotidian gestures, not through intentionality, is observed and mediated by the camera.

What does it mean to film the emotions? Certainly, it must mean more than depiction. The question evokes the motility of filmed emotion—its propensity for movement, to move from one place to another—but also its capacity to move, to effect a change elsewhere. We have talked of actors or human agents, but what of the spectator? How does the viewer figure within the circuit of gesture and affect? How does the camera figure? How are we moved? First, let us say that the viewer is not a repository, an end point, a destination for a message. In the cinema the viewer—I, you, we—is implicated in a circuit of affects, in a dialectical dance of movement and stillness, posture and motion. Serge Daney argues that the situation in which people are rendered immobile before moving images in a situation of "blocked vision" (as Pascal Bonitzer once referred to it) enables them to see all sorts of things. He evokes "immobile people who become sensitive to the mobility of the world, to all types of mobility, the mobility of fictions (ahead to happier tomorrows and various other dreams), bodily mobility (dance, action), material and mental movements (dialectical and logical games)."[14]

It is in this nexus of the visual image, motion, and emotion that I wish to dwell, or pitch camp for a while: in this space between the screen and the viewing body: on the one hand, mobile images caught in a static frame, and on the other hand, mobile emotions caught in an immobile body.

Film theory has often turned to the Freudian concept of dreamwork as a pertinent and useful model for explicating "film work," for understanding the work of the film as analogous to dreamwork in converting ideas into images, images into ideology, and in the process (through tapping the viewer's unconscious) converting the film viewer into a viewing subject. The privileged topology is one that maps psychic exchanges between conscious and unconscious systems. The objective for film theory has generally been the analysis of representation. Like others before, I am attracted to the Freudian model but less interested in drawing from it a theory of representation. Rather, I am interested in turning again to a fundamental postulate: films and dreams are primarily visual, made up moving images, with an unusual capacity to move—that is, to generate and put into circulation affective energies. In order to discuss the circulation of affective energies, I draw mimesis into the ring.

Philosophers from Plato to Lacoue-Labarthe understand mimesis to refer to the practice of copying. But there is another tradition of thought that comes via *The Golden Bough*[15] and anthropology where mimesis means the direct assimilation of an essential force or attribute. It has a shamanic resonance evoking the transfer of energy from one inanimate "thing" or animate body to another. The concept of mimesis migrated into visual studies via E. B. Tylor and Aby Warburg, who understood that the force of visual images resides not just in visuality but in physiognomic and energetic exchanges, and who both attempted a theory of "emotional and imitative language."[16] Aligned to this trajectory, Adorno utilized the notion of mimesis to elaborate an aesthetics based not in ideality but in the senses.[17] In *Mimesis and Alterity*, Michael Taussig mobilizes this sense of the term[18] and also recruits Walter Benjamin to the project, a project to explore the performative dimension of mimesis as a key to understanding "embodied knowing." Benjamin, of course, is a key figure in this trajectory: he identified the camera as a technology of embodied knowing, as a machine for opening up the unconscious, and also wrote on the mimetic faculty and gesture.[19] It is this broad tradition of thought—where anthropology meets visual studies—that informs my use of the term mimesis. But I am interested here in putting into play a concept of the mimetic that also draws on psychoanalytic understandings of energy and its transfer.[20]

Film is analogous to a dream in that both are ghosted by a latent content belonging to the unconscious. But if, in film theory, we stop here, then we fail to register film as a public and performative medium engaging technology and multiple viewers who were not involved in "dreaming" the film, not implicated in the provision of its latent content. There is an asymmetry between the dreamer and the dream, on the one hand, and the viewer and the film, on the other. Nevertheless, viewers' unconscious desires and fears might well be tapped, during the process of viewing, in a crossing and transference between public and private, personal and social, psychic and somatic. Considerable efforts in film theory have been devoted to the project of delineating and interpreting film dreaming. But if we want to understand the aesthetic dimension of film—how as a visual medium it produces affects that are registered bodily by the viewer, through the senses, then we can usefully engage the notion of mimesis.

Freud talks of the "peculiar propensity of dreams to recast their ideational content into sensory images."[21] He is alluding here to the transfer of energy from one psychic register of representation to another (energy is not transferred from one idea to another but from "ideas" to "sensory images"). Carrie Noland takes this instance of transfer between different systems as a model for the transfer of energy from gestural systems to systems of inscription. Is there a kind of survival or *survivance*, of energy, she asks, even as it gets displaced?[22] Can we approach filmic gestures in the same way? When we examine the gestural (figures gesturing) in film, we don't look to untangle the simple transfer from ideas to bodily actions; rather, we take the manifest gesture or network of gestures as an instance of ideas (or charged motions) and their affects cathected through bodily action. The crucial question, for addressing the performative, is how is this cathected energy transferred from the screen to an immobile body in the theater? How is a moving visual image transferred/converted into bodily inscription? Does energy originate on the screen and travel to a destination in the viewer, or can we more imaginatively think of energy moving in a circuit, a circuit in which the viewer might exercise motility and move mimetically?

Cathexis, a key term for Freud, refers to the investment of energy in some kind of material. Most commonly in a Freudian model, it is perceptions and memory traces that get charged with a certain quantity of mental energy. When they become cathected, they exert pressure on consciousness. To become cathected, then, means to demand attention, to produce affect. Freud lays stress on "the attraction exercised by visual memories in the unconscious."[23] He describes how, in its progress to consciousness, an idea might be impeded by the attraction exercised upon the thought by "memories possessing great sensory force."[24] For Freud, it is always a matter of resistance and attraction. To be particularly charged, images, for example, have to have encountered resistance and to have attracted to themselves enough energy to encounter this resistance. For Freud, this dynamic of attraction and resistance entails a series of opposing terms: ideas and images, psyche and soma, conscious and unconscious. There is a teleological impulse to Freud's project: in converting images and bodily symptoms into ideas, through dream interpretation and the talking cure, he aims for psychic balance. However, his own project (particularly in *The Interpretation of Dreams* and *Instincts and Their Vicissitudes*) curiously mimics the attraction–resistance dynamic he describes. An overwhelming fascination is exerted by visual images and charged memory traces and somatic enactments. Rather than reaching a conclusion, he traces and gets caught up in a circuit of incessantly transposed energies. It is here, at the point where his own systematicity encounters resistance, that we can see the possibility for elaborating the visual. Ideas and images are not necessarily translatable one to the other, nor do images always fall under the sovereignty of ideas.[25]

Let us then take the visual and its affects, particularly the moving image of cinema, as our object of investigation, following Freud's insistence on the power of visual images to cathect and transmit energy. This path deflects us from a formalist or cognitive aesthetics. But in order to explore the mimetic as an impulse that implicates the viewer, I also need to diverge from Freud's hermeneutic turn. The gestural does not invariably fall under the hermeneutic sovereignty of ideas. Gestural enactments are not always to be understood within the framework of repressed or diverted or condensed or displaced ideas.[26]

Passionate Gesticulation

If visual images have a pronounced power to cathect and transmit energy, then it is surely the case that in film the gestural regime constitutes a prime instance of this power. To invoke the term *gestural regime* is to emphasize the *performance* of gestures, the process by which energy is focused and disseminated, assimilated, converted. But it is not to occlude the actants, those with whom performance originates. In film, it is generally human bodies that are charged by gestural potential, which is neither accidental nor inconsequential. Inanimate things, of course, may be similarly charged. Cigarettes in *Entr'acte* seem to acquire autonomous gestural capacity, but their dance (the process by which they are animated) is traced by bodily gesture. Smoking involves a relation between bodily gesture and a thing, a cigarette. Often, the relation between a person and a thing as mediated by gesture is transposed into a relation between camera and thing, as happens in *Entr'acte*.[27] We will return to this, but for the moment let us dwell on bodies.

Gesture is normally understood in the most general sense, as a bodily movement or pose. There are of course long histories of debate (across various disciplines) as to whether an immobile body or even an arrangement of phsyiognomic features can be read as gestural and also whether a bodily movement or pose must be purposive and signifying to be labeled a gesture. In this chapter, I use "gesture" in the most general sense. My concern is not to identify a lexicon of gestures but rather to examine how gestures might function cinematically, how we might think of the "cinematic gesture." The parameters for this investigation are shaped by two limit terms: movement and mimesis, and my discussion is ghosted by work from another discipline, from an area where images do not themselves move but do have the capacity to move emotively: Aby Warburg's work on the "pathos formulae" in Renaissance art. All gestures in cinema, a medium of moving pictures, are informed by movement. If we think of gesture in Freudian terms as a perception or memory trace that has attracted to it a quantity of energy, or if we think of it in performative terms as the crystallization of kinetic energy in an extra-daily body, or if we think of it as a quotidian bodily habit framed by the camera in such a way as to invest it with energy and frame it as a gesture—in all such instances, it is about energy moving through the body. Let us say that the cinematic body possesses motility, the "capability or power of moving" *(Oxford English Dictionary)*; it is agentive: the mover has the capacity to originate movement, it has agency but not intentionality. If movement, then, provides one parameter, the other, the mimetic, although not embedded in movement, is related. The gestural regime is mimetic not only insofar as it pertains to motility but also as it pertains to the emotions, to the generation and transmission of pathos.

Let us think more generally about the mimetic nature of gesture. While it does not seem particularly useful to think of gesturing as either intrinsically expressive or signifying, it does seem useful to posit the gestural as social. In gesturing bodies enact the trace of other bodies, rituals, networks of exchange. Gestures solicit gestures. Someone gives me the finger in traffic and I respond with two fingers; a friend I haven't seen for a while opens her arms and I join the embrace; an enemy I haven't seen for a while proffers an embrace and I put out my arm either to ward off the blow or deflect it with a handshake; a stranger I am interviewing keeps scratching and before long I too am scratching; a parting wave elicits a wave from me and might also be the trigger to unleash tears.

What passes between people when gestures are thus exchanged? What happens in the gestural exchange that occurs when a viewer is transported before an immobile painting or sculpture? What happens in the passage between screen bodies and bodies in the theater? What happens when viewers mimic screen gestures? Clearly, the mimicry involves a degree of conversion. To take an extreme example, in Hong Kong action movies, I do not fly out of my seat and tumble through the air. However, the gestures enacted on screen might well be reenacted by me as a *sensation* of flying, tumbling, falling.

We can begin to think about the gestural exchanges in cinema by backtracking into what Giorgio Agamben has called the "unnamed discipline" inaugurated by Aby Warburg.[28] Warburg coined the term *pathos formulai* at the end of the nineteenth century; his attention to bodies in motion occurred "at the very moment," as Philippe-Alain Michaud notes, that "the first images capable of representing them became diffused."[29] He initiated an intervention in Renaissance studies that has reverberated in the history of art history and that was prescient in anticipating many of the concerns of a more expansive visual studies field. Warburg, like others, was interested in Quattrocento borrowings and duplication of motifs from antiquity. But where the orthodoxy promulgated by aesthetes like Winkelman assumed that Renaissance artists were drawn to the classical body because of its harmony, balance, and tranquil grandeur, Warburg on the contrary identified a series of motifs forming "a primeval vocabulary of passionate gesticulation."[30] He traced, via extensive illustration, innumerable instances of gestural migration, suggesting that certain gestural formations possess peculiar power and so survive through duplication, copying, and quotation. To understand *why* certain gestures possess such power, we should not attempt to decipher the meaning of the gesture but rather look to the intensity of the gestural formation. It is this quality of intensity that impresses itself on our visual memory. In a series of notes from 1890 grouped under the title "Spectator and Movement," Warburg writes that the early Renaissance began to lose its scientific character when it introduced forward-moving characters—the spectator believes in movement when he is induced to move his eyes. The question, writes Warburg, was no longer "What does this expression mean?" but "Where is it moving to?"[31] While the meaning of a gesture might vary considerably (a raised arm, which in a classical statue evokes self-defense, migrates into the Quattrocento where it is copied in a painting of David with the head of Goliath at his feet, now evoking victory and joy), what remains the same is the configuration of movement. This configuration entails a focusing of physical tension and emotive intensity. "Pathos formulae," says Moshe Barash, "record and make manifest the pitch rather than the content of passions and events."[32] Warburg posed the survival—the afterlife—of images of antiquity as a kind of archeological process involving superimposition and transformation, jumps, cuts, montages: "Repetitions and differences: moments when the work of memory becomes corporeal, becomes a symptom in the continuity of events."[33] Didi-Huberman goes on: "Warburg's thought sets art history in motion because the movement it opens up comprises things that are *at once* archeological (fossils, survivals) and current (gestures, experiences)."

Warburg constructed a kind of atlas of images, a board draped in black cloth on which he pinned and constantly changed the arrangement of innumerable images, from popular and high culture, from the past and from contemporary life, famous works of art and unknown scenes, people, gestures. He called this Mnemosyne, or Memory. Warburg's act of bringing together, conceptually, gesture and memory and the spectator and movement is instructive. The capacity of gesture to move can be located in the cathexis of energy, perceived as intensity and mimetically converted by the spectator. Images, gestures, do not mean the same thing twice, but by virtue of their intensity, they persist, triggering somatic memory and producing pathos. In the example of the Hong Kong movies, and in the example of the echoing images in *Good Men, Good Women*, energy is cathected in gesture and transmitted to my immobile body, which mimics the gestures on screen, but in the process of mimicry, the gestural force is converted, distilled, into pathos.

Before turning finally to the question of whether the camera can gesture, let us turn back to the pair of images introduced earlier.

> Color: A young woman, in a modern-day bedroom—cool neutral colors, hard lines—crouches outside the bathroom. She lifts an arm, clutching the bathroom door; slowly, with great effort, she pulls herself up. It is as though she's pulling a heavy, inert, weight. She stumbles into the shower; we hear the sounds of vomiting but can see only a blurred figure behind the opaque glass.

Much later in the film:

> Black and white: A young woman in a large house, with timber frames and a dark wooden staircase, begins to climb the stairs. She puts out a hand to steady herself on the banister and then puts out her other hand to hold the banister. The camera is behind her, we see her climb, pull herself up slowly, with great effort, as though pulling a heavy, inert weight. She exits the frame, and the camera holds on the empty scene.

Watching the first scene, I feel my body as a leaden, inert thing, a crystallization of negative energy, pulling me down, resisting the effort to stand. Against this: a feeble reaching upward, a sense of just hanging on. I feel this sensation, feel the dredging and emptying out of the body that follows, but while watching for the first time, I do not think about why, in narrative terms, I feel this sensation, nor do I wonder how it is that, cinematically, my body assimilates the sensory force of the image. The sensation is more physical than emotive, a generalized misery circulating in a tawdry and humiliating ambience. The narrative ellipses, and non sequiturs make it difficult to "place" the scene in a narrative and psychologically motivated sequence. In part, it is because of this difficulty that the gestural movement, unencumbered by a clear semantic imprint, acquires force. The image attracts a quotient of energy and in the process also attracts a mimetic response from the viewer.

To repeat: the force of the first scene derives most obviously from the gestural impulse, though it is only when this gesture is repeated, in the second scene, that it comes into focus, precisely through the force of repetition, *as a gesture*. And in the moment of its repetition, it reconfigures the earlier iteration. The repetition reflects on the origin, recasting both its semantic and affective valency. It is only when this gesture migrates and returns in "another" body that the generalized misery comes into focus as grief. A vague feeling, or emotion, a sense of suffering in the first scene becomes more nuanced as grief by the second. This gesture of pulling the body up does not "mean" grief any more than it means drunkenness, but through narrative accrual, temporal accumulation, and gestural repetition, the somatic is imbued with or overlayed by the semantic. By the time the second scene occurs, we know that both women have experienced the death of a lover. Chiang Bi-yu has just received the news of her husband's execution, Liang Ching is remembering her own act of betrayal three years after the event. Retrospectively, then, Liang Ching's loss—of a husband publicly executed, sacrificed for political beliefs—is overlaid on the drunken remorse of Liang Ching—for a B-grade gangster lover, a petty gangster whom she has secretly betrayed for a payoff. This is not to say that the tawdriness of Liang Ching's bathroom vomiting is tempered by the nobility of Chiang Bi-yu's suffering; dissonance as well as resonance is introduced by the process of repetition. But it is to say that the generalized somatic misery is sharpened by an emotive intensity. Liang Ching is ghosted by Chiang Bi-yu (whose photograph is taped to the bathroom wall, or rather, it is Liang Ching posing in a production shot as Chiang Bi-yu). The pain and weight of memory. But it works the other way as well: the gestural force of the bathroom scene reverberates through the second iteration. The second iteration (which occurs narratively later, though historically earlier) is cooler in its framing, the camera is more distanced, the acting is restrained. We do not see or hear Chiang Bi-yu's suffering; in keeping with the thematic of sacrifice, she walks slowly up the stairs, unostentatiously placing both hands on the banister. But our mimetic memory (albeit perhaps unconscious) of a much more incarnate suffering apprehends the scene as one of passionate gesticulation. Chiang Bi-yu is ghosted by the memory of terrible loss enacted as a dredging and emptying out of the body.

This is a film about history, about repetition and difference; but it is not merely "about"; it also enacts the process of memory. It is memory, unpalatable knowledge of the past, that makes Liang Ching throw up, and it is the capacity of memory traces to attract energy that calls upon us to engage mimetically. Through the energetic conversions of gestural enactment, we too acquire, in a fragmented, montaged manner, as in Warburg's mnemosyne, a kind of bodily knowledge of the history of Taiwan.

Cinematic Articulation: Can the Camera Gesture?

In these two scenes, the camera movement is restrained. We have seen how the bodily gestures of the actors serve as a medium of cathexis, energizing the sensory image and attracting to it a mode of mimetic engagement. The camera, in both these instances, seems utilitarian and subservient to the performance, hardly gestural. But before looking more closely at the filming of these scenes, let's consider, more generally within Hou Hsiao-Hsien's opus, the relation between quotidian performance and the camera.

In the beginning, Hou Hsiao-Hsien got his friends to act in his movies: "I let them use what they were familiar with—their usual habits and gestures so that they need not 'act': for example, having a meal or smoking under the sun, and so forth. In order not to make them nervous, I would deliberately put the camera quite a long distance away and not move it."[34]

This method of eliciting performance became a habit. Not only does Hou often use nonactors, but he elicits from his actors (professional and nonprofessional, and there seems to usually be a mix) a kind of quotidian, improvised performance.[35] He loves to dwell on scenes of nothing much happening: cooking, eating, tea-drinking, gambling, hanging around, playing.[36] This is not to say that the fictional element is suppressed in favor of the reality effect; in fact, he gives much attention to character, and in an Olivier Assayas documentary, *HHH*, Hou talks of character as a catalyst for developing the film. But what it does mean is that he builds his characters not so much through psychological depth (back story, motivation, through-lines) as through a repertoire of bodily techniques, in this case quotidian techniques, those techniques learned and repeated on an unconscious level, gestures of the everyday. Burdieu refers to Hou's subjects as "energetic facts."[37] What we see in an Hou film is how people act *through* gestures, ordinary people as well as historical characters. Ordinary people act, perform, and generate circuits of energy and exchange through gesturing. Gestures are idiosyncratic, performed individually, but they are agentive and possessed of motility. As a Hou film unravels, so a network of gestures and a network of human relationships, a social milieu, takes shape.

In the first scene, Liang Ching is framed in a midshot for the duration of a single take. The camera is pretty still, but it does reframe slightly as she staggers into the bathroom, and it holds on an empty frame as we see her shadowy presence behind the opaque glass and hear her vomiting. "Empty" is of course the epithet used to describe a cinematic scene in which there is no human figure. There are two observations to make here: the first pertains to restraint, the second to emptiness. First, restraint is not effacement. Hou has developed a style that accommodates quotidian performance and gestural regimes that do not serve the narrative.[38] But in a cinema like Hou Hsiao-Hsien's, the very restraint—an eschewal of editing in favor of very lengthy shots; an eschewal of close-ups that frame significant expressions, objects, movements; and a tendency to keep the camera relatively steady rather than moving it to again frame significant plot elements—allows space for the quotidian to unfold in its own temporality. This respect for duration serves, rhetorically, to frame the bodily quotidian. In other words, a repertoire of camera techniques is used in conjunction with a repertoire of bodily techniques to produce a charged gestural discourse.[39]

Second, on emptiness: critics (and Hou himself) have written at great length on the empty space. Much of this writing has attributed the phenomenon in Hou to a specifically Chinese sensibility, but much of the preoccupation with the empty signifier is simply a trope of reverential art cinema appreciation. What is significant in Hou's oeuvre is that the empty shot is generally an evacuated shot: it bears the trace of the figures and the gestural dispositions of those who have left the frame. In other words, it is a way of framing energy. Hou himself talks of his empty spaces as a way to "create, or to expand emotions."[40] The viewer becomes the locus of this memory, of the ghosting made material.[41]

If the first scene in our rhyming pair is characterized by restraint, the emptiness on which it ends is echoed in the second scene, which appears cinematographically more stylized or rhetorical (and more reminiscent of Mizoguchi in elegiac mode than of Ozu). This second scene is part of a sequence that begins with an extreme low angle looking up from the floor to a balcony where light streams in, creating a chiaroscuro effect. There are no human figures in the frame. Chiang Bi-yu's nephew enters on the upper floor, bringing her the news of her husband's death. There is a transition to the lower floor, and the camera then frames Chiang Bi-yu in medium close-up as she begins to climb the stairs. There is a refram-ing and tilting of the camera to accommodate her figure as she climbs, walks along the top corridor, and exits the frame, leaving the camera on an empty frame.

Does the camera gesture in these scenes? We have seen how the apparent restraint of the camera is actually a way of framing quotidian gesture. In a sense, the camera mimics the gestural modality of the actors. Rather than asserting unequivocally that the camera gestures, I suggest that we can identify here a charged gestural discourse, a discourse of passionate gesticulation that is produced through the deployment of a restrictive repertoire of camera techniques in conjunction with a repertoire of quotidian bodily techniques.

There are, however, some camera movements and cinematographic articulations that are far more ostensive, less dedicated to the "everyday," more deictic (where "deictic" indicates a modality of address, a particular instantiation of the authorial voice that summons the viewer via a demonstrative inflection).[42] Such is the case of the second instance, the death scene.

The death scene is both discrete and intertwined with the scenes that come before and after. First, let us take it as a discrete scene, or in Metzian terms, an autonomous syntagm.[43] Liang Ching and Ah Wei are dancing in a night club. In medium close-up, the camera follows them, moving with and between them, moving in closer, moving to their bodily rhythms. The proximity and motion of the camera and the blurred background studded with dancing specks of light reflected off a spinning glitter ball evokes an atmosphere of erotic intimacy, a space of desire removed from any larger context. They are in a world of their own, and we, via cinematic magic, are part of that world. Suddenly a loud gun shot punctuates, simultaneously, the sound track and the image track. On the instant of the shot, a razor sharp pan swishes from the lovers dancing, across the immensity of the empty dance floor, to the same couple in long shot. The camera remains in one spot—close to the dancing couple—but shifts focus by panning, turning on an axis. Pans are more commonly slow, often aiming to duplicate a panoramic gaze, taking in the scenery revealed by an arcing motion. Here the fast movement blurs the background, functions like an arm thrust urgently out and away from the body, pointing deictically. Just as they come into view in a long shot, Ah Wei falls forward into Liang Ching's arms and slithers to the floor where he lies, spread-eagled and face down. There is a scream (from Liang Ching?), followed by shouts of panic and distress. The camera holds; nothing moves except the pattern of the glitter ball, which washes the scene in green, red and blue.

So there it is: Jack Kao does nothing but fall, and moreover, he falls in long shot; the camera is not concerned to capture through close attention the gestural expression of his dying. He does not twitch and grimace, he does not approach death in incremental spasms as is the wont of cinematic gangsters. And yet my immobile body is seized, in this scene, by a sensation of falling. I experience it as something like a lethally forceful whoosh as the breath—the life—goes out of a body. Although Jack Kao is gesturally restrained, far from histrionic, something gestural—if we hold to the notion of gesture as pertaining to bodily movement—occurs. It is a charged image, this image of his falling, an image charged with a certain quantity of energy. A cathected image. To become cathected means to demand attention, to produce affect, to transmit pathos. Something, something powerful but hard to grasp, is exchanged between the immobile viewer and the moving image. Somehow energy (negative energy, we might say) is transposed as the film induces me to somatically enact the shooting/dying.[44] Gestural mimesis occurs even though the body on screen is decidedly ungestural (at least in terms of the familiar repertoires of dying). So where to locate the gestural force? Clearly, the cathected image, though crystallized in the intensity of the body falling, encompasses more than just a falling body. The entire scene-shot is charged, but the center of intensity is the swish pan. It is this camera movement that connects, impossibly, the two couples. Two couples who are the same and yet, by virtue of the camera movement, different, divided. One couple is on the side of life, the other of death. So the camera movement that connects also severs, and it severs precisely because it contains an invisible but lethal cut. The swish pan commands a mimetic response. The question (my question to and of the film, not a question exactly posed by the film itself), to recast Warburg, is not What does this expression mean? nor even Where is it moving to? but rather What happens in the "between"? The camera moves toward annihilation; literally it moves and it pulls my gaze, pulls my breath. It is in the space between, in the gestural sweep from the living to the dying, this sweep through the immensity of space and time, then and now, past and present, that I experience the sensation of breath being sucked out of the body.[45]

It is not the bodily technique of the actor (gestural modality) that performs an affective gesture but the technique of the camera (the performance of a technological potential). If we are to ask, Can the camera gesture? this example suggests an affirmative response. The camera has the potential for motility, and it is agentive—it has the capacity to move literally and in that movement to also move the viewer emotionally. It is in the viewing body that a mimetic conversion occurs: screen motility is performed by the viewer as somatic pathos. In the paradox of a movement that both connects and severs, in the in-between space, an uncanny and ghostly presence emerges. Throughout the film, Ah Wei's ghost, like the ghosts of Taiwan's past, is animated by a series of haunting machines that mediate between the present and the past.

Yet surely it is not merely the camera that gestures here. Crucial to the affect produced cinematically is the invisible cut, the cinematic magic that joins two impossible spaces and that introduces a lacuna where ghosts rush in and come toward me, you, Liang Ching. Similarly, we could point to sound as a crucial structuring element, crucial for disengaging the death scene from its autonomous status, for linking it to before and after in a highly emotive manner. In the scene prior to the death scene, Liang Ching (having done the treacherous deal, though this is not clear at the time and becomes so only retrospectively) is working as a hostess in the disco club. She is sitting and tossing back drinks, rises, moves drunkenly toward the stage, stumbles and falls—anticipating gesturally Ah Wei's fall—picks herself up and gets onto the stage where she seizes the mike and sings: "All around I see gilded lives / But mine is tarnished / All around I hear words like jade / But mine are luckless / Why was I born under a bad star? / Others bask in life while I struggle." This song, her voice, continues uninterrupted into the next scene, over the cut from a static long shot of Liang Ching singing to a mobile medium close-up of Liang Ching and Ah Wei dancing. After he is shot, the irruption of voices—shouting, sobbing, declaiming—continues into the next scene, over a cut from a long shot of Liang Ching standing, Ah Wei at her feet, to a medium close-up of Liang Ching crouching outside her bathroom. This is the scene discussed earlier. Her heavy breathing and moaning as she tries to pull her body up by clutching the door frame is overlaid by the sounds of death.

I began by asking whether the camera can gesture. In the process of attending closely to *Good Men, Good Women*, other aspects of the technological repertoire of cinema, sound and editing in particular, began to apply pressure on the analysis. Tony MacGregor, who works with the materiality of sound and with sound ideas, puts it thus:

> I wonder to what extent your idea of gestural camera might be expanded sonically? . . . Two things occurred to me while watching (and listening to) the scene. First, the sound is a seamless continuation of the shooting scene—it is not presented as "sound in the head," or as the "key" for a flashback. It is not treated in any way to suggest it comes from another time or place. And because of what sound is—simultaneously physically present (her howls animate the air, the vibration reaching our ears, producing, if you like, a direct mimetic response on our eardrums)—there is a sense in which the actress's grieving, keening self is actually occupying the same real-time space as her contemplating, sickening self—it's as if her visible self is silent simply to allow the invisible self to just as fully occupy the same space—and time. Perhaps there is a kind of sonic iteration of the camera gesture which immediately follows the SHOT—the camera whipping around, throwing the eye around the empty space, just as, a few moments later, the weeping is hurled through time, to fill the actress's bedroom? My second observation—which is really just an extension of the first—is that the only sounds from the "present tense" actress in the scene are those associated with her physical presence—highly amplified touching, scrapings, and then retching—but no breathing as I recall (compared, say, to much of Godard's soundtracks, where we are hyper-aware of the breathing body in similar moments of "silent" emptiness). As I say, this is just to extend the observation above—my sense that in the "present" (visible) scene, the woman is silent in order to allow her "past" self to be fully in the present, spatially and temporally: the wailing is as foregrounded as the physical scrapings of her hand on the door and so on—a kind of sign, perhaps, that the keening is just as real, as physical, as NOW as the movement and emotion we are registering with our eyes.[46]

The camera, then, cannot be thought of in isolation, just as a gesturing arm cannot be detached from the body of which it is a part. I need to reframe the question so that "the camera" in this context is understood to function metonymically, to stand for the whole, the whole cinematographic apparatus and technological potentiality (of course, it also retains a certain specificity). What also becomes apparent, through examining the gestural regimes of *Good Men, Good Women*, is the impossibility of thinking in terms of syntagmatic units, of dividing the apparatus, or the narrative, or the body, or memory itself into discrete units. If gestures elicit gestures, then they do so in part because memory traces attract energy and trigger a process of mimeticism and conversion, initiate a circuit of exchange. If the gesture of ascending, pulling the body up resonates across two scenes, so this gestural inflection is inversely mirrored in the falling gesture. Air whooshing out of a body is replayed in a body or bodies made heavy by memory. This burden of memory is transferred from screen bodies to viewing bodies and in the process transformed. Clearly, the film structures resonances between the personal story and the story of the nation, between various pasts and the present and the future, but although Liang Ching is haunted by Ah Wei and ghosted gesturally by Chiang Bi-yu, this is not a morality tale about the reformation of a bar hostess and the education of an actress. We can think of the film as a kind of atlas of moving images, akin to Warburg's Mnemosyne, in which the conceptual linking of gesture, memory, and movement is made manifest in the viewer. It is in the viewer that the possibility for movement, for historical change, is realized. A film is not like a body, and it does not behave like a human body. Yet the camera has the capacity to perform in such a way as to move and to mark: to move and mark bodies within the diegesis and to move and mark—kinetically, aesthetically, emotionally—viewing bodies.

Good Men, Good Women begins with a border crossing: from Taiwan into China. This crossing unleashes a series of bloody events, gives birth to ghosts who haunt the film and circulate beyond its borders. It reminds us of a very particular and largely suppressed history, but it also reminds us that every film-viewing experience involves a border crossing.

Notes

1. Hou has said that he feels the film (which pleases him least of all his films) ultimately fails to deal with time and to integrate the different viewpoints. See Emmanuel Burdeau, "Rencontre avec Hou Hsiao-Hsien," in *Hou Hsiao-Hsien*, ed. Jean-Michel Fredon (Paris: Cahiers du Cinema, 1999), 82.

2. Jerome Silbergeld has the most intricate breakdown of the film's temporality, attentive both to the historical/political dimension and the cinematic rhythms.

See Jerome Silbergeld, *Hitchcock with a Chinese Face: Cinematic Doubles, Oedipal Triangles, and China's Moral Voice* (Seattle: University of Washington Press, 2004), 75–116.

3. June Yip, "Constructing a Nation: Taiwanese History and the Films of Hou Hsiao-Hsien," in *Transnational Chinese Cinemas: Identity, Nationhood, Gender*, ed. Sheldon Hsiao-peng Lu (Honolulu: University of Hawaii Press, 1997), 139.

4. Shiao-Ying Shen, "Permutations of the Foreign/er: A Study of the Works of Edward Yang, Stan Lai, Chang Yi, and Hou Hsiao-Hsien" (Ph.D. diss., Cornell University, 1995).

5. Jerome Silbergeld writes, "*Good Men, Good Women*, like *Suzhou River*, can legitimately be regarded as a Chinese ghost story, rolling forward on wheels of karma. . . . Taiwan is full of ghosts; some are political, some personal, and they are often hard to separate and sort out. But the ghost that haunts all Taiwan today is the 'one-China policy,' first articulated in the Shanghai Communique of 1972." Then embraced by all, now rejected, this is one of the ghosts that haunts *Good Men, Good Women*, "the ghost of its government's own hubris." Silbergeld, *Hitchcock With a Chinese Face*, 107.

6. Hou has said that he likes to make films like Chinese poems, composed of three elements: narrative, metaphor, metonymy. Michel Ciment, "Entretien avec Hou Hsiao-Hsien," *Positif*, no. 423 (May 1996): 50.

7. And hence it is often damned or elevated as "art cinema." Yingjin Zhang, in situating new Taiwanese cinema as comparable to the fifth-generation Chinese cinema, discusses some of these approaches to art cinema. See Yingjin Zhang, *Chinese National Cinema* (New York: Routledge, 2004), 248.

8. Hou himself has talked about the way "goodness" applies not only to those in the past but to anyone in facing up to whatever their own circumstances are. Emmanuel Burdeau, "Rencontre avec Hou Hsiao-Hsien," 82.

9. Hou sees it otherwise. He has said that Annie Shizuka Inoh, whose first major role this was, was able to play the modern role perfectly, in part because it resonated with aspects of her own personal life, but that she was less successful in inhabiting the period role. "Today, I would use a different actress for the past period, and the effect of contrast would be stronger and more significant." Burdeau, "Rencontre avec Hou Hsiao-Hsien," 93.

10. Echoing Imamura Shohei's 1970 film, *History of Postwar Japan as Told by a Bar Hostess (Nippon Sengoshi—Madamu onboro no Seikatsu).*

11. Georges Didi-Huberman, "Foreword," in *Aby Warburg and the Image in Motion*, Philippe-Alain Michaud (New York: Zone Books, 2004), 16.

12. Burdeau, "Rencontre avec Hou Hsiao-Hsien," 78.

13. Burdeau, "Rencontre avec Hou Hsiao-Hsien," 94.

14. Serge Daney, "From Movies to Moving," *Documenta Documents*, no. 2 (1996): 77.

15. Sir James George Frazer, *The Golden Bough: A Study in Magic and Religion* (New York: Macmillan, 1951).

16. Sir Edward B. Tylor, *Anthropology: An Introduction to the Study of Man and Civilization* (New York: D. Appleton, 1903); *Researches into the Early History of Mankind and the Development of Civilization* (Boston: Estes & Lauriat, 1878); *Primitive Culture: Researches into the Development of Mythology, Philosophy, Religion, Language, Art and Custom* (Boston: Estes & Lauriat, 1874). Aby Warburg, *The Renewal of Pagan Antiquity: Contributions to the Cultural History of the European Renaissance*, intro. Kurt W. Forster, trans. David Britt (Los Angeles: Getty Research Institute for the History of Art and the Humanities, 1999).

17. Theodor W. Adorno, *Aesthetic Theory*, trans. C. Lenhardt (London: Routledge & Kegan Paul, 1984); *Negative Dialectics*, trans. E. B. Ashton (New York: Seabury Press, 1973); Theodor Adorno and Max Horkheimer, *Dialectic of Enlightenment*, trans. John Cumming (London: Verso, 1994). See also Susan Buck-Morss, *The Origin of Negative Dialectics: Theodor W. Adorno, Walter Benjamin and the Frankfurt Institute* (New York: Free Press, 1977).

18. Michael Taussig, *Mimesis and Alterity* (New York: Routledge, 1993).

19. Walter Benjamin, "Doctrine of the Similar," in *Selected Writings Volume 2, 1927–34*, ed. Michael W. Jennings, Howard Eiland, and Gary Smith; trans. Rodney Livingstone and others (Cambridge, Mass.: Harvard University Press, 1999), 694–98; "On the Mimetic Faculty," *Selected Writings Volume 2*, 720–27.

20. Miriam Hansen has explicated and developed Benjamin's notion of "innervation" to probe the nature of cinematic engagement. See her "Benjamin and Cinema: Not a One-Way Street," *Critical Inquiry*, no. 25 (1999): 306–43, and "Of Mice and Ducks: Benjamin and Adorno on Disney," *South Atlantic Quarterly* 92, no. 1 (Winter 1993): 27–61. Jodi Brooks and Laleen Jayamanne have written in illuminating ways on Benjamin and filmic performance. See Jodi Brooks: "Crisis and the Everyday: Some Thoughts on Gesture and Crisis in Cassavetes and Benjamin," in *Falling for You: Essays on Cinema and Performance*, ed. Lesley Stern and George Kouvaros (Sydney: Power Publications, 1999), 73–104; Jodi Brooks, "Performing Aging/Performance Crisis (for Norma Desmond, Baby Jane, Margo Channing, Sister George—and Myrtle)," in *Figuring Age: Women, Bodies, Generations*, ed. Kathleen

Woodward (Bloomington: Indiana University Press, 1999), 232–47; and Laleen Jayamanne, *Toward Cinema and Its Double: Cross-Cultural Mimesis* (Bloomington: Indiana University Press, 2001).

21. Sigmund Freud, *The Interpretation of Dreams*, trans. James Strachey (New York: Avon Books, 1965), 586.

22. See Georges Didi-Huberman, *L'Image Survivante. Histoire de l'Art et Temps Des Fantômes Selon Aby Warburg* (Paris: Éd. de Minuit, coll. Paradoxe, 2002)

23. Freud, *The Interpretation of Dreams*, 635–36.

24. Freud, *The Interpretation of Dreams*, 586–87.

25. In his earliest published article, Foucault was concerned with the untranslatability of one system to another: "Psychoanalysis has never succeeded in making images speak." Michel Foucault, "Dream, Imagination and Existence," in *Dream and Existence: Michel Foucault and Ludwig Binswanger*, ed. Keith Hoeller (Atlantic Highlands, N.J.: Humanities Press, 1993), 38.

26. In her very interesting book, *Au Lieu Du Geste*, Catherine Cyssau goes further than I would; she charges psychoanalysis with inheriting the renaissance morphology of clinging to "the project of expressivity" so words and behaviors become "sign-bearers of human pathology." Catherine Cyssau, *Au Lieu Du Geste* (Paris: Presses Universitaires de France, 1995).

27. See my "Paths That Wind Through the Thicket of Things," *Critical Inquiry* 28, no. 1 (Fall 2001): 317–54.

28. Giorgio Agamben, "Aby Warburg and the Nameless Science," in *Potentialities: Collected Essays in Philosophy* (Stanford, Calif.: Stanford University Press, 1999), 89.

29. Philippe-Alain Michaud, *Aby Warburg and the Image in Motion*, trans. Sophie Hawkes (New York: Zone Books, 2004), 39.

30. Moshe Barash, "'Pathos Formulae': Some Reflections on the Structure of a Concept" in *Imago Hominis: Studies in the Language of Art* (Vienna: Irsa, 1991), 119.

31. Michaud, *Aby Warburg and the Image in Motion*, 82.

32. Barash, "Pathos Formulae," 127.

33. Didi-Huberman, "Foreword," 16.

34. Peggy Chiao, "Great Changes in a Vast Ocean: Neither Tragedy Nor Joy," *Performing Arts Journal* XV11, no. 2/3 (May/September 1995): 50.

35. In Olivier Assayas's film, *HHH: A Portrait of Hou Hsiao-Hsien* (France/Taiwan: Arc Light Films, 1997).

36. Hou has said, in relation to *Goodbye South, Goodbye*, that his intention is

to depict and preserve the "quotidian space" of Taiwan. Yueh-Yu Yeh, "Politics and Poetics of Hou Hsiao-Hsien's Films," *Post Script: Essays in Film and the Humanities* 20, no. 2–3 (Winter–Summer 2001): 71.

37. Emmanuel Burdeau, "Goodbye South, Goodbye," in *Hou Hsiao-Hsien*, ed. Jean-Michel Fredon, 169.

38. The camera moves are more varied in *Good Men, Good Women* than in most of the earlier films, and the subsequent *Flowers of Shanghai* and *Millenium Mambo* break with the middle-distance, fairly static camera. However, the camera has always had more mobility and variation in Hou's cinema than the critics have allowed.

39. Although it is not necessarily a harmonious complementarity devoid of tension. Berenice Reynaud observes that sometimes the human figures seem redundant: "[P]eople are floating over the composition of the shot like unnecessary ghosts. The shot does not need them. And they do not need the shot either." But then, she argues, another third meaning emerges: "There is an implicit *resistance* on the part of these bodies who exist, indulge in everyday, mundane activities, without paying attention to the organization of the shot. They are both ghost-like (and unnecessary) and mineral (and permanent)." Berenice Reynaud, *A City of Sadness* (London: British Film Institute, 2002), 74.

40. Reynaud, *A City of Sadness*, 81.

41. Youn-Jeong Chae speaks of this, when the viewer grasps more than the character, as a "poignant structure." Youn-Jeong Chae, *Film Space and the Chinese Visual Tradition*, Ph.D. dissertation (New York University, 1997), 132.

42. See my discussion of the opening shot of *After Hours* as deictic in *The Scorsese Connection* (Bloomington: Indiana University Press, 1995), 104–05.

43. Christian Metz, *Film Language: A Semiotics of the Cinema*, ed. Michael Taylor (New York: Oxford University Press, 1974).

44. I say "I" purposively, not to foreground my subjectivity, nor in the assumption that everyone will react in this way but rather to suggest how subjectivity might be shaped by these particular cinematographic procedures.

45. My thanks to J. P. Gorin for a good discussion about this notion of the "between."

46. Tony MacGregor, in response to a version of this paper presented at the Power Institute, University of Sydney, personal communication (2005).

CHAPTER 8

The Gestures of Bharata Natyam: Migrating into Diasporic Contemporary Indian Dance

Ketu H. Katrak

> What concerns me is not the essential meaning of cultural terms, but how meanings mutate and metabolize in the course of their transportation, translation, and specific uses in other cultures. . . . My critical and cultural affinities [are] to the tensions of the "inter"[cultural]—"the cutting edge of translation and negotiation, the in-between space."
>
> —Rustom Bharucha, *The Politics of Cultural Practice: Thinking through Theatre in an Age of Globalization*

As gestures in the Indian classical dance style of Bharata Natyam travel from their native space of India into diasporic locations, they find new homes and lead to creative cultural translations that are meaningful in different environments. As performance studies scholar Rustom Bharucha remarks, "meanings mutate and metabolize" as they are transported from one cultural locale into another.[1] In this essay, I analyze how Bharata Natyam's highly elaborate movement system of *nrtta* (footwork) and *abhinaya* (gesture language), rooted (as are other classical Indian dance and theater traditions) in the ancient Sanskrit text *The Natyasastra*, are used and transformed in the meaning of gestures and the value systems underlying them, from native to diasporic reality, by dancers in the contemporary South Asian diasporic community of Southern California. "The cultural consequences of migrations from the Indian subcontinent," as anthropologist Sandhya Shukla notes, are significant "for interdisciplinary inquiries into difference and belonging [and for] multiple formations of nationality [that] take place in diasporic culture."[2]

This essay originates in my personal journey of studying Bharata Natyam (for over twenty years) with my teacher Medha Yodh (a disciple of T. Balasaraswati), undergoing a traditional training in learning the repertoire of Bharata Natyam's *nrtta* and *abhinaya.* My body memory underlies this scholarly study in which I explore Indian aesthetics and the theory of *rasa* (aesthetic pleasure). I link the aesthetic to the bodily by drawing upon *The Natyasastra*, which extensively documents various aspects of theater, including dance. The goal of evoking *rasa*, experienced both sensorily and intellectually, is accomplished for the dancer and the audience via the performing body in physical movement as well as the expression of human emotions via *abhinaya*.

Gestures have complex and layered uses in Bharata Natyam. First, gestures render the *nrtta* vocabulary (without verbal text) of feet/arms/hand movement patterns called *adavus*, set to particular rhythmic time cycles of Carnatic music from South India. Second, gestures convey stories and legends (from the Indian epics and folktales). Third, gestures render the emotional states of the characters being represented. A solo female dancer (in the traditional form) communicates stories and emotions via a wide range of gestures: expressive, representative, and emblematic. For instance, the moon's rays falling on the dancer's limbs represent desire and longing; a bee caught in a lotus flower is like the pining heart caught in the web of longing and desire for lover and deity. The light of the full moon is described in a *padam* (lyric poem rendered in gesture) in order to ask satirically why the womanizer-lover has lost his way. Hand gestures combine with facial expressions, movement of the limbs, and particular gaits to embody sadness, or grief, or love; all work syncretically to convey *bhakti* (inner spiritual devotion).

I analyze adaptations to the style by second-generation Indo-American dancers trained in Bharata Natyam in Southern California and the gains and losses in these contemporary expressions. Positive developments include creative experimentation with movement, even a collage of various dance traditions—Bharata Natyam, modern, ballet, jazz, yoga, as well as new content that draws upon ethnic and feminist concerns of diasporic life. The losses to the traditional form are mainly in conveying *bhakti*, which is dissipated or erased by the changes. *Bhakti* inheres in certain gestures, such as *shikharam* (thumb raised and hand in a fist), which conveys the god Shiva. However, the external manifestation via the gesture is only one conventionally accepted way of conveying *bhakti*. What is much more subtle and difficult to communicate is the inner feeling of devotion.

My study situates Bharata Natyam as practiced in Southern California by linking local and global styles in terms of the cultural politics of how a classical style is transformed for students and audiences here. There are positive, nurturing aspects of practicing traditional expressive arts; there are also disturbing resonances of nationalist deployments of the dance for Hindu fundamentalist ideologies. Specifically, Bharata Natyam, translated as "dance of India," is given exclusionary connotations as though other forms do not exist apart from those practiced by the Hindu majority. Recently, classical Indian dance styles are somewhat under siege by the huge popularity of Bollywood (commercial Indian cinema) style dance.

I explore the gains of creative experimentation with movement, a sort of collage of different dance traditions, often represented side by side and rendered via the dancers' bodies. I also recognize the importance of new choreography that draws upon content about diasporic life in the United States, including feminist concerns. The losses to the traditional form are mainly in conveying *bhakti* that is dissipated or erased by the changes.

The Natyasastra provides useful material for situating and contextualizing the contemporary adaptations of classical Bharata Natyam into contemporary Indian dance. The text includes detailed codification of body movements (the basis for traditional training regimes) and gestures (that convey narratives and emotions).[3] This training is passed down from teacher to student, and over the past century in India exceptional teachers such as T. Balasaraswati and Rukmini Devi have choreographed *varnams* and *padams* that are part of the Bharata Natyam repertoire.[4] The status of classical dance during and after British colonialism in India, along with Orientalist attitudes and anticolonial movements, played critical roles in the cultural revival of classical arts.[5] Indian reformers in the nineteenth century wanted to demonstrate both the distinctiveness of Indian classical arts and, at times, their superiority to western culture. In postcolonial times, and now within diasporic spaces, we find a paradoxical revival of traditionalism and religiosity in the representation of classical dance.[6]

In the late twentieth century, especially in the post-1965 wave of new immigrants from South and Southeast Asia who entered the United States, exceptional Bharata Natyam teachers such as Viji Prakash, Ramaa Bharadvaj, and Ramya Harishankar made Southern California their home.[7] These dancing bodies, as they migrated into new locales, established dance schools where they impart Bharata Natyam's rigorous physical training, enabling the second-generation youth to acquire cultural knowledge (albeit partial knowledge) via dance. This second generation of Indian or part-Indian ancestry has now come of age, and they experiment with their traditional training by creating new choreography termed *contemporary Indian dance.* They deploy the gesture language of *abhinaya*, much of which comes from *The Natyasastra*, and ascribe contemporary meanings to them. Innovations of Bharata Natyam into contemporary Indian dance, while they retain a feel, even an aura, of the classical style, also deploy other dance traditions such as modern, ballet, jazz, and yoga as inspired by these dancers' locations within diasporic communities where ethnic arts are reinterpreted and where the influence of new geographies and interculturalism assume increasing significance in the circulation of the expressive arts of dance and music from "native" into transnational spaces.

Contemporary Indian dance, delineating a new field, is pioneered by dance practitioners and scholars such as Uttara Coorlawala and Ananya Chatterjea.[8] They have played landmark roles as mentors of a younger generation of dance choreographers and performers. A 1993 essay by Coorlawala, "The Toronto Conference on 'New Directions in Indian Dance,'" notes many important factors—aesthetic parameters, financial constraints, communal realities for immigrant populations—that lie behind the practice, innovation, and patronage of classical Indian dance among South Asian diasporic groups.[9] Coorlawala remarks that "traditional and nontraditional Indian dance forms have been constantly evolving within India since Independence, and also beyond India, as immigrants [have tried to] make this art form an accepted part" (391) of their immigrant locales, whether in Canada or elsewhere. Coorlawala also reaffirms Ananya Chatterjea's remarks at the Toronto Conference calling "for the need to restructure dance policy-making and of the contemporary Indian artists' need to reinterpret creativity in terms not simply of traditional techniques being updated but also in terms of restructuring the basic approach to choreography" (394).

In the Southern California Indo-American community (that I have observed), classical Bharata Natyam is practiced and performed so widely that it is part of South Asian popular culture. First-generation teachers and second-generation students make concerted efforts to make the style accessible to a broad audience that may not be knowledgeable about Indian myths and legends portrayed in the dance. For immigrants, especially first-generation parents, the dance is a repository of cultural knowledge to be imparted to their children growing up in the United States where there exist many assimilative imperatives especially enticing for youth. Dance, as inscribed on the body through Bharata Natyam gestures, embodies Indian culture, which is a complex and diverse arena more intangible than cultural artifacts that can be transported into relocated homes. Bharata Natyam's *mudras* (hand gestures) represent cultural codes of an Indian socio-cultural framework. For instance, a lyric's meaning is conveyed through *abhinaya*, in which both the literal meaning as well as cultural connotations of proper behavior (especially for women) are subtly portrayed. A common Bharata Natyam *padam* depicts Radha scolding Krishna, her lover, for his flirtatious behavior with the *gopis* (milk-maids). The gestures, as codified, are both precise and evocative in their representation and depiction of cultural context. The *mudra mrigashirsha* renders a deer iconically, though it can also be used metaphorically in a poetic line, as in "the deer is like my friend to whom I confide my feelings of love for or separation from my beloved." Similarly, the *mudra suchimukha* is used literally to point to something in the everyday gesture of using the index finger, and when the same gesture is depicted as the index finger and rotating wrist at the heart center, it conveys love and desire.

In his essay "The Dance in India," Narayana Menon remarks, "The gestures, or *mudras*, as they are called, are the essence of Indian dancing. They are a very comprehensive language, and any story or incident or any shades of emotion can be satisfactorily expressed through them. . . . Their eloquence is the eloquence of poetry. . . . *They suggest but never imitate.* They evoke a mood, but never state it. . . . The traditional language of Indian dance is so rich, so complete, in fact, that it helps the creative artist and does not hamper him. This is the highest form in which any tradition should operate. It is the severest test of any tradition" (emphasis added).[10]

A significant text, considered a standard in the field, is Ananda Coomaraswamy's *The Mirror of Gesture;* Coomaraswamy states that *abhinaya*, with the root *ni* and the prefix *abhi*, "implies exposition . . . *abhinaya* is so called because it evokes flavour *(rasa)* in the audience."[11] This description conveys a sensory connotation, suggesting that *flavor*, or *taste*, is part of *rasa*. Coomaraswamy delineates three types of gestures: "bodily, vocal, and ornamental *(angika, vachika, aharya)*" (12). These gestures are further broken down into nine movements of the head, twenty-four hand gestures, eight glances, six movements of the brows, and four movements of the neck; hand gestures are classified according to those made with a single hand and those made with both hands.

In a *varnum* or *padam*, a verbal line is repeated three to four times and is rendered via varied gestures that include metaphoric renditions of the words. For instance, text such as "Oh, my friend, my heart is overflowing with love" can be conveyed via *suchimukha* (rotating wrist, hand in a fist with index finger pointed) then moving the hands outward to trace a semicircle indicating the emotion enveloping the physical body. Shivers or waves of emotion are indicated via the *patakam* gesture (palms flat) moving in a wavelike motion along the arms. The same poetic line ends with the question, "Why or how can I to cope with this overpowering feeling of love?" The same line is repeated three to four times, and if the dancer has live musicians rather than recorded music, she can gesture to the musicians to repeat the line or to move on. The repetitions pick up the emotional idea and convey it through poetic renditions such as "my feelings of love are like the waves of the ocean" or "desire and feelings of arousal are 'crawling' over my skin like the moon's rays." In conveying these emotions, the dancer emphasizes the bodily, even the erotic. Neither one is escaped or transcended. Rather, the bodily feelings of passion move the dancer into that same feeling for the deity to whom the dance is dedicated. It is almost a seamless movement—from human lover to love of the deity.

The Natyasastra is believed to be the earliest treatise on all aspects of drama, including dance and gesture. The date is highly debated among scholars, and the text is placed anywhere between the second and fifth centuries BCE. Menon explains that the text "deals with Stage, Dancing, Drama, Music, Elocution, Aesthetics, Rhetoric, Grammar; details of the techniques and movements and gestures of the dancer; the attributes of dancers; descriptions of the stage; principles of elocution; and everything connected with the theatre. It is in thirty-six chapters of which seven chapters—the Fourth and the Eighth to the Thirteenth—are the most relevant to dancing" ("The Dance in India," 42). *The Natyasastra* is ascribed to Bharata, a legendary figure to whom the text was "revealed by Lord Brahma," although the text is also historically located, since it demonstrates knowledge of existing traditions of that historical time and other texts and authorities of that period.

As Kapila Vatsyayan, a prominent scholar of Indian dance and aesthetics, remarks, "Whether or not *The Natyasastra* was composed or written in a particular year is not as important a question as the fact that, like the Vedas, *The Natyasastra* lays down the foundations of a theory and practice of the Indian arts which was adhered to by theoreticians and practicing artists for a period of approximately 2000 years (until the nineteenth century or the modern period) consistently throughout the subcontinent. It had validity and applicability outside the country, especially in Asia, and continues to have relevance today for articulating a theory of art which can be clearly distinguished from Aristotelian or subsequent theories of aesthetic and art in the post-Renaissance West."[12]

Vatsyayan explores the need for such a text. Usually in Indian tradition, authorship is rooted in the Vedas and ascribed to God or a sage. Chapter I of *The Natyasastra* narrates what Indra says to Brahma: that the common man does not have access to the four Vedas, and therefore a fifth, called Natya Veda, should be created to be available to all. This new Veda will contain, remarks Vatsyayan, "the teachings of all the Shastras and will depict all the Arts. And so the Lord Brahma created the Natya Veda (the Dance) with its four limbs from the four Vedas. That which should be read, the intellectual content, he took from the Rig Veda; that which should be sung, the music, he took from the Sama Veda; the Abhinaya, the expression, from the Yajur Veda; and the Rasas, the emotional content, from the Atharva Veda" (20). Then Brahma entrusted Bharata to popularize the new Veda, the Dance, among the common people. Apparently, there was resistance to this effort, and Indra himself had to intervene and explain the true significance of the new Art of dance: "This (play) is not exclusively for presenting you or the Devas (Gods), but exhibits the Bhava (mood, emotion) of all the three worlds. I devised this play as the representation of the world . . . sometimes, it depicts virtue, sometimes play, profit, peace, laughter, battle, love, or slaughter; yielding the fruit of righteousness to those who follow the moral law, pleasure to those who follow it . . . a representation of the deeds of mankind; dealing with the acts of men—the best, the middling, and the low—this drama shall afford benevolent counsel. This drama shall be the source of all counsel, in all its rasas (sentiments), bhavas (moods), and actions" (25–26).

Even as the *Natya Veda* advocates aesthetic pleasure as democratically available to all human beings, it also emphasizes its moral purpose of uplifting the spirit toward a divine world. How this morality and aesthetic joy are to be attained is described both through detailed physical movements and the inner feelings of devotion. *The Natyasastra*'s detailed movement descriptions fragment the physical body—the face, including eyes, eyebrows, lips, and cheeks, and the thirty-two *angharas,* which derive from the 108 *karanas* that include positions of the hands and feet as in dance, in walking, or in fights. A three-volume study of *Karanas* (including text and elaborate photographs) by Dr. Padma Subramanyam, a scholar and performing artist of Bharata Natyam (that she renames Bharata Nrityam), makes a significant contribution to the field.[13] Perfecting the movements of the separate parts of the body and then integrating the whole produces the desired effect of aesthetic pleasure for dancer and audience.

Vatsyayan provides a somewhat different way of interpreting the physical bodily movements as described in *The Natyasastra.* Vatsyayan advocates placing "movement" within the larger context of Indian philosophy and worldview that she describes as "the conceptual ideational background of Indian culture in general and the laws of 'movement' in particular." She usefully analyzes the human body in relation to the space around and above it and connects its expression, whether in dance, speech, or other dramatic movement, as rooted in *prana*, the breath. "The mere fact of my physicality" she remarks, "determines certain possibilities of relationship with space outside and the relationship with the self within."[14] Vatsyayan emphasizes "the interdependence and interconnectedness" of the human body with natural elements of fire, water, air, sky, and wind, as well as with the plant and animal kingdom and the realm of the gods and demons. Such "an organic worldview," according to Vatsyayan, provided to Bharata "a grammar of artistic expression. He brings together into one fold the essentials of this speculative thought, particularly the complex system of establishing correspondences between the limbs and organs of the human body, the senses and aspects of the cosmos, as also the methodology (the *vidhi*) of the Brahmanas where earth, space, time are consecrated to suggest a cosmic order and the repetitive rhythm of cosmic time" (30).

Vatsyayan discusses how *The Natyasastra* uses such an organic methodology to create "a language of artistic form." The square and the circle, important architectural demarcations, play a role in the enunciation of space, "enclosed by lines of opposites (i.e., the square) [as] basic to the physical ground plan and the conceptual structure of the *Natyasastra*. In ritual the celestial fire was a square and the terrestrial fire a circle: in the arts the motifs provide the beginning of an elaborate grammar of form" (42).

Although *The Natyasastra* describes exact positions of body and gestures, it is significant to note that the mind–body–spirit connection, integral to Indian philosophy and yoga, is crucial in Indian aesthetics. The body is a vehicle that is trained rigorously through physical practice and yogic breath. The route to a higher spiritual realm is via the body, not by its denial. The integration of the mind and body with the spirit, rather than their separation; in contrast, the Cartesian western philosophy upholds the tenet of "I think; therefore I am." In classical Bharata Natyam, the goal of aesthetic pleasure or *rasa* is attained by the very correctness of the use of the body, particularly the positioning of elbows, wrists, hands, and fingers to depict *mudras* (gestures), and the dancer's felicity in dancing to the rhythmic time cycles.

The mind–body connection is essential to the paradoxical separation of "body parts" designated by the strict placement of feet; the type of gait; the separation of the upper and lower body as the foot rhythms follow the time cycle and the upper body twists at the waist; and the use of the hands, arms, and face to convey narrative and emotion. So, as the face and upper body convey the story and feelings, the feet stamp a rhythmic pattern and the body and mind work together to attain *rasa*. As Vatsyayan remarks, "Within the *Natyasastra* system, this Man-Body is broken up into its smallest constituents . . . and then [brought] together . . . to suggest or evoke a psychic state" (49). An integral connection exists between the "anatomical and the psychic" that is further related by Vatsyayan to how "the unit of measurement . . . a head, or the stretched hand, [works] on a principle . . . in the context of sculpture" (49). She relates *The Natyasastra*'s engagement with the anatomical structure, especially the bones and joints, as "points of articulation" to "Ayurvedic texts and others followed by the Hathayoga systems" (49).Vatsyayan's emphasis on the interconnectedness and "multidimensional totality" of the body, mind, and spirit is useful. She comments on how, in hatha yoga, the control of the mind is achieved via the control of the body, and "in the *Natyasastra*, the possibility of the physical body to manifest and evoke psychic states is thoroughly investigated" (51). As the body moves, it creates geometrical shapes in space, such as triangles and curves that "have their own logic and meaning in the Natyasastra. . . . *Bharatanatyam* is a series of triangles in space" (56). The body works within the circle created by the space around it in extended arms to the side and above the head. The feet are grounded to the earth, and the downward thrust of stamping and deriving energy from the earth is distinct from dance forms such as ballet with its emphasis on leaping and stretching beyond the spatial limits of the body. Vatsyayan notes that Bharata predates by two millennia the notation system used in western form as evolved by Laban and that the "relationship of the parts to the whole, the unit and its multiples in varying proportions, provide the key to the structural frame and have a validity both on the plane of physical existence and kinetics as well as in the sphere of symbolic design" (57).

Vatsyayan is a key scholar who "investigates the nature and extent of the part played by other arts, especially literature, sculpture, and music, in the development of Indian dance and in determining the role of dance in these arts."[15] In particular, she studies how dance movements are represented in sculpture on Indian temples such as the Chidambaram temple.

In Indian aesthetics, the expression of the nine primary emotions (love, laughter, fear, sorrow, grief, disgust, heroism, wonder, peace) is discussed extensively in *The Natyasastra* both in terms of the emotions' physical embodiment and representation on stage as well as their goal of kindling *rasa*. "A meaning which touches the heart creates *Rasa*," notes a traditional verse, and "the entire body feels the *Rasa* like fire consuming a stick."

In conveying *rasa*, an accomplished Bharata Natyam dancer also leans on acting skills. In fact, as Adya Rangacharya's translation and critical notes on *The Natyasastra* indicate, "Natya implies both *acting and dancing*. The line of demarcation between the two is a very thin one. We find stage directions that say, 'He (the actor) should register contemplation.' The word register here stands for dancing. He should dance contemplation. At least there is no English word which can describe the action meant in the direction as it implies dancing and acting. . . . Acting and dancing and music are treated as one indivisible activity. And in this the audience also has an active role to play."[16] Indeed, as Vatsyayan also remarks, "The *abhinaya* portion of dance was indeed conceived originally by Bharata as an integral part of *natya* (drama). In the *Natyasastra*, he discusses it as an aspect of *natya* which constitutes dancing also: the human form is analyzed from the head to the toe to show, on the one hand, the various possibilities of movement of every part of the human figure, and, on the other, the use of these movements to express certain states *(bhava)* and emotions" (*Classical Indian Dance*, 19). Dance is "a limb of the drama proper," notes Vatsyayan, and as in drama, there is an emphasis on stylization of presentation through gesture of all situations and emotions" (20). Vatsyayan's work is truly significant in her analysis of "the valuable role played by Indian dance in the history of Indian sculpture."

In Vatsyayan's discussion, she connects dance to all the Indian arts and situates its goals within the general rubric of Indian aesthetics and the goal of evoking aesthetic pleasure or *rasa*—an art-related experience that is in a realm totally different from other forms of pleasure and that touches the higher realms of the spiritual. In the representation of dance, she notes that "novelty of theme or context is an irrelevant consideration" (25). This comment is important in the following analysis of how the innovations of Bharata Natyam, along with other dance vocabularies, have metamorphosed in the diaspora into contemporary Indian dance and how this form relies on "novelty of theme and content."

Contemporary Indian Dance

One of the most talented of the second-generation dancers whose work I have followed in Southern California, Shyamala Moorty, in her piece entitled "Rise" (which I have seen twice since its opening in Fall 2003), presents a fascinating combination of dance and theater, effectively recreating the tradition of *natya* that translates as a blending without strict boundaries of acting and dancing. *Natya* embodies different characters out of the single body of the solo female dancer as in traditional Bharata Natyam, using *nrtta* and *abhinaya* in the representation of the nine primary emotions delineated in *The Natyasastra*. Shyamala's spoken script and her animated face and body movements (rooted in her Bharata Natyam training) also work within the Brechtian tradition of political theater that both educates and entertains the audience. In "Rise," Shyamala probes the arena of communal violence and the genocide of Muslims in the state of Gujarat in India in 2002. She embodies, very effectively, both Hindu and Muslim fundamentalist voices, much as in the tradition of a Bharata Natyam female solo in which different characters are embodied and depicted by a dancer's single body.

The female protagonist played by Shyamala evocatively represents six of *The Natyasastra*'s nine primary human emotions: (1) love (the female narrator in the United States talking to her lover, who is in India); (2) fear (a young girl, terrified of being left alone, looking for her father, whose mutilated body she discovers); (3) grief, sorrow, and (4) disgust (at the senseless carnage the young girl witnesses); (5) anger (in the fundamentalist voices of Hindus and Muslims); and (6) peace (invoked through the image of a flowing river). Shyamala is adept at using *abhinaya* via facial expression and body language to evoke these emotions.

A central icon on stage—a toilet bowl overflowing with waste—represents the hopeless carnage. Shyamala communicates the emotions of disgust and devastation via her face, especially her eyes, as she physically pulls from the toilet bowl wet pieces of dirty cloth, along with a doll that triggers a story of a young girl, terrified of being left alone. As she talks to her doll, symbolically named Ganga after the river Ganges, sacred to Hindus, she eventually discovers the brutalized dead body of her father and is struck with terror, conveyed by the body cringing in fear and disbelief.

Shyamala's artistic re-creation of the violent situation in India evokes parallel histories of violence in other parts of the world as well as events in the United States such as the recent Patriot Act, which takes away with impunity the basic civil rights of American citizens under the guise of protecting them from terrorism. After one of the performances of "Rise" in Los Angeles, I assisted Shyamala in leading a question-and-answer session with the audience and heard the viewers drawing local–global connections. Such responses were a heartening testimony to the power of artistic work that can touch and transform an audience and challenge them to be involved responsibly in our increasingly shrinking world. Contemporary Indian dances such as "Rise" demonstrate how global events in faraway Gujarat have eerie echoes for local and regional communities here. In the local–global dynamic, courageous citizens play a significant part in speaking out for justice and fairness.[17] If the Gujarat horrors were rooted in religious fundamentalism, so were the many religious and racially motivated killings of innocent South Asians during the period of fear and hatred immediately after 9/11.[18]

Another of Shyamala's contemporary Indian dance pieces is entitled "Balance of Being." My discussion emulates what Deirdre Sklar, in the context of her research on the religious fiesta of Tortugas in New Mexico, calls "an integration of description and analysis." The description is itself analytical, or 'thick,' to use Clifford Geertz's sense of the word. Embedded in the descriptions are analytical processes of determining recurrent movement motifs, the selection of relevant contextual data."[19] Sklar also combines observation with "empathic kinesthetic perception" that enables a researcher to analyze "the whole complex of concepts, values, affects, and action" (7). Shyamala's choreography relies on the abstract movements of Bharata Natyam *nrtta* as rooted in *The Natyasastra.* The content about identity is conveyed via *abhinaya*'s gesture vocabulary, mainly relying on facial expression.

"Balance of Being" represents a striking bodily conflict, a struggle between Shyamala's practice of ballet and of Bharata Natyam, depicted graphically with tights and a ballet slipper worn on the right leg and foot, and on the left, tights up to the ankle and a bare foot, as in Bharata Natyam. Shyamala wears a black, knee-length dress with a red scarf draped over her left shoulder. On the stage, there is a dividing vertical line of red and white flowers, reflecting the red scarf, and the dancer stands astride the line, separating the two sides of the body doing ballet and Bharata Natyam.

The piece composed by Jonathan Marmor begins with the sound of a drone-type instrument—like a tambura—common in Indian musical performance, followed by a slow *alap*-type sound of the sitar. The left hand depicts a *shikharam* (a gesture with the thumb upright and the hand in a fist—usually represents male energy and the phallus embodied in the god Shiva) and is placed in the open palm of the right (evoking a female body), moving into joining the palms of the hands at heart center in prayer *mudra*, then flowing upwards. The joined hands stop between the eyes, and the eyes look from right to left with the neck movement so distinctive in Bharata Natyam. The two hands then open with the palms, one facing up and the other down, and the head looking from left to right, registering a kind of anxiety and confusion. Now, a gentle piano strain picks up. The dancer remains rooted to the spot, and this static stillness on stage is very powerful. It makes the viewer concentrate on the small movements, such as the foot flexing and resting the heel on the ground (as in Bharata Natyam) or pointing the toes (as in ballet). Still rooted to the same spot, the dancer stamps her foot as in Bharata Natyam. She makes a tentative move back and forth, finally breaking the line of flowers and moving outside the line, then returns to the line with ballet movement. Once again the dancer is still; only her hands move between showing a standing Shiva with the right palm facing the audience in a gesture of blessing, comforting the devotee, and the left hand placed diagonally across the body with palm pointing to the ground (indicating the correct path according to Shiva). This is a common iconographic representation of Shiva as Nataraj (the God of Dance). The dancer then floats with her arms in ballet's fourth position and then back to Shiva. The body then moves into pirouettes, with one foot flexed, as though leaving behind the Bharata Natyam for a moment. The movements become more integrative between the two styles with pointed toes as in ballet and hand gestures as in Bharata Natyam. Going from arabesque to the *patakam* hand gesture (palm flat, facing up or down), the dancer briefly establishes a flow, moving around the stage and keeping both vocabularies in view for the audience. As she returns to the middle line, Shyamala picks up some flowers and bathes her face with them. Then the two "conflicting sides" become more frenetic as the piece develops, and it concludes with a series of pirouettes, as if she is circling around rather than integrating, bodily, the two different dance traditions.

The overall effect is that of the body moving between ballet and Bharata Natyam. Points, arabesques, and pirouettes contrast and yet synchronize with Bharata Natyam, which is grounded to the earth with stamps and incorporates the hand *mudras alapadma* (fingers stretched out and the hands open like a flower), *shikharam*, and *hamsasya* (index and third fingers touching the thumb; fourth and fifth fingers extended upward). The contrast between the leaping body in ballet and the grounded feeling of Bharata Natyam that connects with the earth is choreographed intricately, even the feet going from heel to pointing the toe and then to heel again. Shyamala executes each style with incredible grace (an especially beautiful hallmark of all her movements), intensity, and passion. This piece, using the solo body through gesture, movement, and music rather than words, conveys two different dance styles, evoking two cultures and two different dance traditions. For the dancer, part-Indian and part-Caucasian, who grew up in the United States, these varying dance vocabularies of ballet and Bharata Natyam also embody the conflicts and confluences about belonging.

Multiple, hyphenated, migrating identities may be commonplace as facts; however, reconciling the different, at times warring, cultures and identities remains challenging. This is particularly so in a racialized society such as the United States, where race and ethnicity continue to mark individual identities.

"Balance of Being" emphasizes the abstract rather than the devotional aspect at the heart of traditional Bharata Natyam. Bharata Natyam comes across in its bare-bones usage of *nrtta*, *mudras* without traditional text or music. However, the word *balance*, part of the piece's title, symbolizes the search for a way to keep both traditions of ballet and Bharata Natyam in balance in the dancer's body. The piece vividly embodies the two different movement philosophies at the heart of each classical style. Shyamala's use of *nrtta* evokes what Vatsyayan describes as key to *nrtta* technique: "a series of poses, sculpturesque in quality, almost static impression. . . . Indian dancing seeks to depict the perfect point or the moment of balance" (*Classical Indian Dance*, 30). Ballet's emphasis on leaps and covering space contrasts with the Indian dancer's "preoccupation with time . . . trying to achieve the perfect pose which will convey a sense of timelessness" (30).

Shyamala's piece also contains other kinds of "texts." An analytic interpretation is evoked as the viewer responds to the dancer's body standing astride the vertical line in the middle of the stage and viewing two different dance traditions at play in the same body. The piece also evokes questions of emotional allegiance to particular dance traditions, and most personally and intimately, in the bi-ethnic identity (Indian father and American mother) of the dancer herself.

For some performances, Shyamala includes text that is read as voice-over: "My father migrated to the United States with only twenty-six dollars. My mother hitchhiked all the way from Colorado to California, where they met. She used to dream that they were paving the path to peace between East and West." This text has elicited interpretation of how the male and female energies come together, also depicted in Indian mythology and iconography as *ardhanareshwari*, or Shiva's embodiment as half-male and half-female, both principles needed for life. Shyamala described her choreographic thought process as trying to bring together the male and female, half-him and half-her, half-Nataraj and half-ballet. An interesting reversal in her intelligent and engaging choreography also occurs: the usual identification of the East as feminine—often interpreted as instinct, emotion and weakness—and the West as masculine—embodying reason, intellect, and strength—is reversed. In this piece, the East is depicted as male via the Shiva and the symbol of the *lingam* (icon of the phallus), and the West is depicted as female via the balletic movements. Although Shyamala does not use *abhinaya* as in classical Bharata Natyam to convey stories from Indian epics, she does use *abhinaya*'s gesture language to convey her own themes of ethnic identity and femininity. She also uses the distinctive neck movements of Bharata Natyam, and her training in *abhinaya* is evident in her highly expressive face. Certainly, the individual and subjective are at play, whereas in traditional classical dance, the dancer's individual body is only a vehicle for the expression of the stories of gods and goddesses. In diasporic locations, gesture and ethnicity interrelate and create meaning. Connections are made among gestures used in a formal, stylized sense and gestures of everyday life, especially ethnic uses of body language for communication. If Bharata Natyam "narrates" epic stories, or conveys lyric poems via gestures, it also draws upon, as does contemporary Indian dance, the movements of everyday life—dressing, putting on make-up, plucking flowers and making a garland, cooking, feeding a child. Some of these movements, such as making a garland, may not be as familiar to dancers and audiences in the diaspora as to those in India. A dance piece entitled "Sakhi" (in two parts danced by Shyamala and by Sandra Chatterjee) portrays the contemporary reality of being stuck in traffic on Southern California freeways and relying on cell phones, along with the challenge of moving the body when strapped in a seatbelt.

Shyamala grew up in Monterey, California. Her evolution as a dancer is based in her biracial ancestry. She fits into an Indian community because she looks Indian, although at times, she feels that she is "playing a part" and faking it. She wants to use her "privilege of in-betweenness rather than be restrained by [her] Indian appearance like the second-generation caught into a type of narrow nationalism because of prescribing to Indianness, though for quite some time [she] felt like [she] did have to because [she] felt like an outsider." However, she has "made a choice recently to identify as Indian." Even embracing "Indianness" for someone of Shyamala's aesthetic and choreographic talent is certainly not narrowly nationalist. Rather, it is a sense of belonging within one part of her ancestry that happens to be Indian while remaining receptive to the polyglot cultures from all over the world that make up a city like Los Angeles, where she lives. Los Angeles is a sort of miscrocosmic global city with an ongoing flow of new and old immigrants, along with third- and fourth-generation peoples of color.

Shyamala and other talented second-generation choreographers, such as Sandra Chatterjee, Parijat Desai, and Anjali Tata, have performed in venues that welcome their contemporary Indian dance: the Diasporadics Festival in New York City, Carve Something Straight at UCLA, and International conferences such as "Indian Dance in the Diaspora: Traditions and Innovations" held in Houston, Texas (September 2001). These dancers are interested in including contemporary themes in their choreography. For instance, they plan to use *abhinaya* to create a piece about the environment. Shyamala Moorty, Sandra Chatterjee, and Anjali Tata are the founders of the Post-Natyam Dance Collective. They plan to work together and make new work using processes of creating movement via writing, discussion, making frameworks, and exploring intentions. This contemporary work has much thought and intellectual probing behind the movement, just as there is remarkable logic and thought behind the choreography in traditional classical styles that have been passed down through the generations from teacher to student. Members of the Dance Collective face an additional spatial challenge in that they live in three different parts of the world—Shyamala is in Southern California, Anjali is in Kansas, and Sandra is in India. They hope to create a piece about how they relate their ethnicities as represented in their dance to their locations and to notions of femininity.

These dancers are interested in "intercultural choreography" and in exploring "new ways of approaching interculturalism." The *inter-*, notes Shyamala, "can include negotiations and translations between cultures that is inherent to our work."[20] However, Shyamala also agrees with Rustom

Bharucha's critique of interculturalism, namely, that it ends up appropriating nonwestern forms of dance and theater without adequate knowledge of the philosophies and aesthetic principles that underlie several traditions.[21]

Bharucha argues convincingly for "a critique (or at least a cognizance) of global capital . . . for the democratization of intercultural practice and discourse" (7). Cultural discourses on rights and ownership of dance forms have become significant in a global cultural scenario in which performances take place regularly across national borders. Who is entitled to perform, to innovate, and which forms are considered classical? The government plays a role in the aesthetic production and experimentation of dance forms; for example, the Indian government provides funds to particular artists to travel abroad. Ramaa Bharadvaj presents a useful critique of the Indian government's ageist criterion allowing dancers only up to a certain age to be funded for travel abroad.[22] Bharadvaj rightly points out that audiences outside India would rather experience the work of mature, older dancers than the work of younger dancers who may have mastered the technique but have a long way to go in communicating the kinds of *bhava* and *rasa* that usually come with age and life experience.

Such government policies encourage a disturbing deployment of *The Natyasastra*, one that gives legitimacy, even "classical" status, to dance styles clamoring for such a stamp. It is a recent and troubling strategy ot evoke *The Natyasastra* as the originary text in order to gain classical status for dance styles. The underlying reason for such a strategy is clearly economic: the Indian government funds opportunities for artists to travel abroad *only* if they belong to one of the recognized classical traditions.

It is important to recognize the slippage among the concepts of the national, international, and increasingly, the transnational in analyzing cultural forms particularly for diasporic communities. I agree with Bharucha that "intercultural interactions" are hardly "free from the mediations of the nation-state. . . . There should be no false euphoria about the celebration of autonomy in interculturalism" (5). Bharucha remains skeptical of Richard Schechner's "rather cavalier distinction between 'nations' (which are 'official') and 'cultures' (which are 'free')." And Bharucha's holding on to the national in discussions of culture is appropriate not in a narrow sense of cultural nationalism but in an even more necessary sense of "uneven globalization," as Samir Amin has put it. In other words, the concept of the "nation," with all its positive and negative baggage, must be dealt with and not elided into notions of *inter*national, *trans*national, global, or cosmopolitan. The problems in the concept of "nation," whether economic or cultural, must be faced squarely, and critiques of both the national and global are important in analyses of cultural production and dissemination. I agree with Bharucha's warning that "the 'global' is in a position to hijack the assumedly democratic interactions within the 'autonomous' agendas of interculturalism."

The local and the global interact in discussions of the intercultural. For dancers like Shyamala and others of her generation who live in the United States and connect with a local community of Indo-Americans and the mainstream, their creativity resonates in this context. Simultaneously, since the dance styles of Bharata Natyam and contemporary Indian dance are global phenomena today, these dancers respond to that climate as well. For instance, the Post-Natyam Collective was invited to perform in Chennai, India, at the ninth contiguous event of The Other Festival in December 2006. This festival showcases provocative and cutting-edge work in dance, theater, music, and art. Chennai is regarded as a fairly orthodox space for the performance of Bharata Natyam, and traditionalist voices are prominent, as I experienced firsthand during a recent Fulbright research residency in Chennai. At the same time, there are many variations on "tradition." For example, prominent dancer and choreographer Anita Ratnam, who is a major presence on the Chennai scene along with theater director and art critic Ranvir Shah, conceived The Other Festival as a statement that contemporary Indian dance itself, even as it may remain rooted in the Indian aesthetic, is enriched by creative choreography that brings in multiple movement vocabularies. Ratnam created the space for contemporary Indian and other international dancers, as well as for experimental theater work, spoken word, fusion music, and other forms of cultural expression; the conference has been held each year since 1998 during the first week of December. The timing is significant because Chennai is well known for "the December season" when several *sabhas* (auditoriums) across the city are alive with Carnatic classical music and dance programs that take place throughout the day from seven o'clock in the morning until nine o'clock at night. The Other Festival makes its own statement and has good audiences who follow this contemporary work every year.

In conclusion, the migration of gestures from one space into another and from the ancient times of *The Natyasastra* to the contemporary innovative choreography by second-generation and biracial Indo-Americans provides fascinating cultural material for understanding the role of artistic forms in diasporic communities. Contemporary Indian dance draws upon the rich *nrtta* and *abhinaya* traditions of Bharata Natyam, as rooted in *The Natyasastra*, as well as upon other movement traditions such as modern dance, jazz, ballet, and yoga.[23] The dancing body itself is the site from which productive dialogue is initiated among movement traditions enabling cultural translations of new and old dance forms in diasporic locations.

Notes

1. Rustom Bharucha, Introduction, *The Politics of Cultural Practice: Thinking through Theatre in an Age of Globalization* (Hanover, N.H.: Wesleyan University Press, 2000), 1.

2. Sandhya Shukla, "Locations for South Asian Diasporas," *Annual Review of Anthropology* 30 (2001): 551–72.

3. Many translations and critical commentaries on *The Natyasastra* are available. A reliable and standard translation is *The Natyasastra of Bharata Muni* by Manmohan Ghosh (Calcutta: Granthalaya Private Ltd., 1967). Volume I includes an extensive and useful introduction.

4. A *varnum* is the most complex central item in a traditional Bharata Natyam recital in which the solo female dancer displays intricate *nrtta* training (foot patterns set to the Carnatic musical time cycles) and *abhinaya* (gesture language) in conveying narrative as well as emotions. The *varnum* is usually thirty to forty minutes long. A *padam* is a lyric poem set to music. The piece uses only *abhinaya*, and the dancer takes on a loving or an angry or a satiric *nayika* (heroine) conveying a complexity of emotions connected to human love.

5. I do not develop this history here. See Avanthi Meduri's essay, "Bharata Natyam: Where Are You?" *Asian Theatre Journal* 5, no. 1 (Spring 1988): 1–23. See

also Priya Srinivasan's doctoral dissertation "Performing Indian Dance in America: Interrogating Modernity, Tradition, and the Myth of Cultural Purity" (Northwestern University, 2003), which adds usefully to scholarly engagement with the historical and contemporary renditions of Indian dance.

6. See a useful volume of essays edited by Kumkum Sangari and Sudesh Vaid, *Recasting Women: Essays in Colonial History* (New Delhi: Kali for Women, 1989; republished by Rutgers University Press, 1990, 1997). See especially Uma Chakravarti's "Whatever Happened to the Vedic *Dasi?* Orientalism, Nationalism, and a Script for the Past," 27–87.

7. See Lisa Lowe's *Immigrant Acts: On Asian American Cultural Politics* (Durham, N.C.: Duke University Press, 1996) for an excellent discussion of the history of U.S. exclusion laws that have controlled the entry and family formations of different Asian subgroups such as Chinese, Japanese, and South Asian during the late nineteenth century and throughout the twentieth century.

8. See Uttara Coorlawala's many useful and scholarly engagements with the history of Bharata Natyam in its traditional and contemporary forms. A particularly informative essay is "Ruth St. Denis and India's Dance Renaissance," *Dance Chronicle* 15, no. 2 (1992): 123–52. See also her significant contributions over the years to *Dance Research Journal*, a key publication in dance studies.

Ananya Chatterjea's essays have also made important contributions to the study of dance, as has her book *Butting Out! Reading Resistive Choreographies: The Works of Jawole Willa Jo Zollar and Chandralekha* (Middletown, Conn.: Wesleyan University Press, 2004). See also Priya Srinivasan, "Performing Indian Dance in America."

9. Uttara Asha Coorlawala, "The Toronto Conference on 'New Directions in Indian Dance,'" *Dance Chronicle* 16, no. 3 (1993): 391–96.

10. Narayana Menon, "The Dance in India," in *Balasaraswati*, ed. Narayana Menon (New Delhi: International Cultural Centre, 1963), 42–60.

11. Nandikeśvara, Ananda Kentish Coomaraswamy, and Duggirāla Gōpālakrsna. *The Mirror of Gesture, Being the Abhinaya Darpana of Nandikesśvara* (New Delhi: Munshiram Manoharlal, 1970), 12.

12. Kapila Vatsyayan, *Bharata: The Natyasastra* (New Delhi: Sahitya Academi, 1996), 26. See also Padma Subramanyam, *Natya Shastra and National Unity* (Tripunithura, Kerala: Sri Ramavarma Government Sanskrit, 1996).

13. Padma Subramanyam, *Karanas: Common Dance Codes of India and Indonesia, Volumes I & II. Volume III: A Visual Elucidation* (Chennai, India: Nrithyodaya, 2003).

14. Kapila Vatsyayan, *The Square and the Circle of the Indian Arts* (Atlantic Highlands, N.J.: Humanities Press, 1968), 4.

15. Kapila Vatsyayan, *Classical Indian Dance in Literature and the Arts* (New Delhi: Sangeet Natak Academi, 1968), 1.

16. Adya Rangacharya, *Natyasastra: English Translation with Critical Notes* (Bangalore: IBH Prakashana, 1986).

17. Another striking example of local–global progressive action was the recent legal harassment of prominent dancer Mallika Sarabhai in Gujarat, India, for her open criticism of a corrupt Gujarat state government. Her passport was impounded, and a global protest at such illegal action on the part of the Indian government finally made them back down. Another such instance in India was the legal harassment of Booker prize–winning writer and activist Arundhati Roy when the Court attempted to silence her from speaking out against the atrocities of the Narmada Dam that made hundreds of thousands of the poorest tribal populations homeless. A recent documentary entitled *Dam/Age* movingly recreates this history.

18. Shyamala was invited to perform "Rise" most recently (July 2007) at the South Asian Arts Festival entitled Masala! Mehndi! Masti! in Toronto, Canada. Shyamala has also performed a 60-minute version of "Rise" for the South Asia Conference at the University of Wisconsin, Madison (October 2005).

As political commentators such as Noam Chomsky and Arundhati Roy have indicated, 9-11 is also a fateful date in world history—Pinochet came to power in Chile, backed by the United States, and Steve Biko was murdered by the fascist apartheid regime in South Africa.

19. Deirdre Sklar, "On Dance Ethnology," *Dance Research Journal* 23, no.1 (Spring 1991): 6–10. See also Sklar, "Dance Ethnology: Where Do We Go from Here?" *Dance Research Journal* 33, no. 1 (Summer 2001): 90–92.

20. Personal e-mail correspondence.

21. Rustom Bharucha, "Somebody's Other: Disorientations in the Cultural Politics of Our Times," *Third Text* 26 (Spring 1994): 3–10. See also Rustom Bharucha, *The Politics of Cultural Practice: Thinking through Theatre in an Age of Globalization* (New Delhi: Oxford University Press, 2001). I am grateful to Sohini Ray for sharing her personal copy of this text with me. Of further interest are Bharucha's *Theatre and the World: Essays on Performance and Politics of Culture* (New Delhi: Manohar, 1990); and Richard Schechner's "Intercultural Performance," *The Drama Review* 26, no. 2 (1982), and *The End of Humanism: Writings on Performance* (New York: Performing Arts Journal Publications, 1982).

22. Ramaa Bharadraj, "Past Your Prime: Ageism in Dance?" *India Currents* (June 2003): 23–24.

23. In my larger project, I explore contemporary Indian dance in India, as I did in 2005–06 on a Fulbright Research Award to Chennai in Southern India. I also plan to study the innovations in Bharata Natyam as presented in other parts of the United States, such as New York, Minneapolis, and Houston. The creative linking of Indian dancers based in India and Indo-American dancers who have migrated to and settled in the United States is part of my project of enriching cultural knowledges and sharing them in an increasingly global context.

CHAPTER 9

Mimique

Mark Franko

Mimique Revisited

My interest in writing "Mimique" in the early 1990s was to come to terms with what deconstruction had "let loose" in its influential constructs, such as the trace, spacing, and play. (Of the two traditions of twentieth-century critical theory outlined by Blake Stimson in this volume, my account is decidedly French rather than German). Should moving bodies recognize themselves in these ideas? Have they already done so prior to their articulation? Was the unrelenting philosophical focus on writing that characterized much poststructuralist thought an unconsciously rear-guard action for having missed the embodied subject of movement? Writing "Mimique" was a way both to acknowledge the importance of deconstruction for any self-aware critical treatment of dance and choreography and to signal the inherent drawbacks of deconstruction for dance theory. I wish to stress that these drawbacks have absolutely nothing to do with the unsettling of the canon. Rather, deconstruction's claim for an embodied writing still suffered egregiously from disembodiment. (A radical expression of this complaint is found in Deidre Sklar's call for "qualities of vitality" in any description of symbolic action.) Writing both with and against Derrida, I engaged with a *miming* of his theory, where out of what was "wrong" with it we could reconstitute what was "right." Out of writing we could get to dance. But in order to get dance "out of" writing, it was necessary to shift subjects, as it were, to exit from the necessity of writing. Or, to define where dance wrote, where dance redefined writing. Clearly, we are here in the domain of migrations.

The essays in this volume pick up on this theme: the outlines of an invisible history emerge that probably begins with the *alphabeto figurato* of

Bracelli and late-Renaissance geometrical dances and continues through moving pictures (Lippitt), graffiti (Phillips), and gestural signing (Noland).[1] Taken as a whole, one might say they constitute what Susan A. Phillips calls "strategies of mimesis in dance," but they also include strategies of dance in writing and other visual media. It is as if the history of dance and writing are caught up in mutually co-opting mimetic strategies, or what Phillips names "reverse mimicry."

I am pleased that the editors of this collection consider "Mimique" relevant to the vanguard inquiries presently gathered under the rubric of gesture's migrations. When Sally Ann Ness pushes the notion of movement as inscription as far as it can possibly go while conserving its cogency, she pursues a parallel poststructuralist conceit. My analysis focused on the trace as the inverted figure of writing: writing's disappearance in the very moment of its inscription. It seemed to me that this was the basis of consanguinity from which Derrida elaborated his notion of the mime within *mimesis*. Faithful to Mallarmé's "unwritten body writing," Derrida pointed to the impossibility of inscribing meaning in stone, as it were, and the importance of writing's performativity. The lack of stability and fixity characterized all written language for him, and this was what brought writing into the dancing fold. Yet the principles of this mime's motions were of such a purely indexical order that they could hardly have engaged in a struggle for power. I wanted to show what revisions were necessary for this power struggle occurring across corporeality and inscription to materialize.

One could reframe the question another way. What does it mean for dance to function in the entire absence of writing? In what sort of mimesis can dance engage when it eschews scriptural representation? My framework in "Mimique" boils down to the following: there is, first of all, a primary mimesis to which I wanted to lay claim. Primary mimesis, or mimesis-play, was for Mihai Spariosu one of the most important play concepts in prerational thought. He explains that before Plato, mimesis designated a performative act in which "miming" for the purposes of "invoking, calling something forth" predominated.[2] There was then secondary mimesis, or representation, which the trace put into question with its sliding lateral movement between signifiers. But both secondary mimesis and its antidote—the trace—left the dancing body in a bloodless state. So, I wanted to ask after a "tertiary mimesis," one in which what was called forth without leaving a representation could be re-called. It was for me less about interrogating the presence of movement in writing through a valorization of the *act* of inscription over the *fact* of inscription, as Carrie Noland does so penetratingly with respect to Henri Michaux's gestural alphabets, but more about how gesture "writes" itself into existence (primary mimesis) and inscribes itself in memory ("tertiary" mimesis). The writing metaphor becomes something more than a metaphor in the third case.

I ended with the idea of a reverse architecture. Just as Mark Wigley had clarified the debts of deconstruction to architecture, so did I aspire to clarify deconstruction's debts to movement. Derrida wrote several texts on architecture, but there is virtually nothing to my knowledge about dance, with the exception of the interview "Choreographies."[3] So, I concluded by reinterpreting the Derridean trace not as disappearance but as a reverse architecture: that which institutes the *habitus* for an as-yet nonexistent environment. There is resonance here with Carrie Noland's conclusion that Michaux's performance of inscription "offers phenomenological existence (a movement-form) to a kinetic energy that has no single, ontological shape or movement pattern of its own." In this particular migration of dance out of its mimetic rapport with writing into one with a proleptic architecture, one wonders whether dance is a generating trope of modernity or the only one capable of turning the deconstructive screw. What is mimed in this case is space as a container within which all mimesis eventually takes place. Perhaps such an idea of space is appropriate to deconstruction's energy, but it is equally necessary in recognizing the political force of dance in and beyond mimicry.

Mimique

> We would have to choose then, between writing and dance.
>
> —Jacques Derrida, "Force and Signification"

Must we choose between writing and dance? Has deconstruction set us at liberty to believe dance and writing are identical forms of inscription? And is the mirror-opposite belief—that dance is writing's absolute other—not just a comparable assertion of their "sameness-in-difference"? Under the sign of play, dance has become a new identity of writing within Jacques Derrida's deconstruction of the transcendental ego as "presence." Yet, when Derrida treats the play of dance or the subject of performance, distinctions between presence and difference become uncharacteristically slippery. In an essay on Antonin Artaud, for example, Derrida concludes that Artaud is after "pure presence as pure difference."[1] This statement hints that Artaud's project locates dance neither in writing nor in writing's other.[2] Instead, dance becomes located *outside* a "closure" that bounds the play of differences itself, outside a "closure of representation" from which Derrida declares Artaud, in fact, unable to escape. Whereas in other of Derrida's writings from the sixties, play is boundless precisely because it exceeds the closure of (structuralism's) structure against which he wrote, in his second essay on Artaud, play becomes uncharacteristically bound within an enclosure. Meanwhile, the play of dance (of cruel theater) occupies an impossible outside. Its impossibility, however, is significantly situated in a possible space, "outside" the possible. As Mark Wigley has written: "whatever philosophy places outside is still inside precisely because it is 'placed.'"[3] Such ambivalence is the price of Derrida's opening gambit in "La parole soufflée" where he refuses to allow Artaud's madness to become an exemplary case for literature.[4] Let us follow suit by refusing to consider dance a "case" (even an exemplary one) for literature. It is to Stéphane Mallarmé, however, that I turn as a literary locus of the danced as writing, the written as dancing, and too, as a rendezvous of deconstructive thought.

Mallarmé's dancer at the inception of modernism—an unwritten body writing—represents a strong moment of conjuncture between dance and literature. The poet as danseuse has pointed literary critics from literature to performance theory and back, introducing a mimetic relation between dance and writing. Recent studies of Mallarmé's performance theories by Evlyn Gould and Mary Lewis Shaw position dance relative to literature in suggestive ways.[5] Since both critics have contended with Derrida's influential reading of Mallarmé's "Mimique" in "The Double Session," I move from Gould and Shaw toward a consideration of Derrida's concept of trace and its import for performance theory.[6] I argue that the disappearing presence of the trace—unrepeatable but not for that reason culturally irrecuperable—is the "being" of performance, its "once" as memorable, its inscription as "enduringly" worldly. This is to write with but also against Derrida because my argument rehabilitates "primary mimesis," a concept purely of operative value for Derrida's reading of Mallarmé.

It is apparently ironic that a poet associated with the autonomous work of words should have reemerged in poststructuralist theory of the late 1960s as a champion of the body's claims vis-à-vis literature. Mallarmé's proposal that the work of art does not *exist*, that its presence denotes an absence, has decided resonance for dance studies.[7] In rethinking Mallarmé's poetics, the old trope of dance's ephemerality becomes rejuvenated and essentially transformed into that of the "disappearing body." Whereas "ephemerality" had glorified but also trivialized and marginalized dance as that profoundly apolitical activity (its deepest nature unplanned, its most essential sense irrecuperable), the "disappearance" trope recasts the body's provisional interventions in space or theory as a textuality of its own making. Dance's change of cast has deconstruction to thank. Furthermore, ephemerality-as-disappearance is a synonym of the Derridian trace: "The very thing that has no meaning, is ceaselessly re-marking itself—that is, disappearing" ("Double Session," 250). Yet parity with the trace can prove problematic, for it removes another sort of presence from dancing: the presence of dancing subjects themselves in their gendered, cultural, and political distinctiveness. Having thankfully graduated from the "elegant gratuitousness of the dance," as a critic once phrased it apropos of Paul Valéry, we still abide—at least as long as we read Mallarmé—with the essential conditions of meaning in modernism/postmodernism: mobility, indeterminacy, multiplicity, reflexivity.[8] The palpability and concreteness of differences get lost in Derrida's trace. Hence the question that dance raises: How can difference itself display difference?

Evlyn Gould focuses on the relation between virtuality and actuality in Mallarmé's thought on performance. She argues he was the first to develop a performative writing enabled by his notion of virtuality: "Mallarmé's reconciliation of a virtual with an actual theatricality creates an important link between the metaphor of the theater to describe the functioning of a psychical apparatus and the relationship of this apparatus to actual performing arts" (142). Dance, in other terms, is virtual writing, and writing virtual dance. For Gould, theatrical virtuality resides in a mobility of subject positions engaged in an experience of staging. But Gould focuses on Mallarmé's performance theory through the lens of his "virtual plays." Here literature can appropriate dance as a way of rendering performance imaginary. In a more recent article, Gould addresses Mallarmé's writings on ballet.[9] This essay clarifies how the reading of a literary text *about* performance leads to a theory *of* performance. The "difficulty" of Mallarmé's prose (his ballet reviews), made up of "potential associations among words" and "a constant confusion of subjects of discussion and their interlocutors," is said by Gould to "approximate the imaginary representations or, what I also call 'virtual theater,' that accompany any attendance at a theatrical performance" (98). Here, dance becomes truly virtual, and thus paradigmatic for literature. The link between dance and poetry, Gould claims, is that both offer an experience of reading/spectatorship in which there is a confusion of subject and object, where no meaning is fixed, but all are projected onto a psychic stage in a play of memory and forgetfulness. "The stage is transformed into an ephemeral two-way mirror making it unclear if the reviewer [Mallarmé] translates the ballet performance in his writing or if the ballerina translates the reviewer's mental (virtual) performance in hers" (104). The virtuality of performance can be turned inside out to reveal poetry's performativity. Dance and writing become mirrored in one another, but their ensuing mimetic rapport only renders further exploration of performance illusory: the two-way mirror is "ephemeral." In this second version of virtual theater, a notion of performative writing as the only possible response to dance—and of dance as a "writing" whose imaginary suspends interpretation—gains focus but still appears quite limited as an explanation of anyone's save Mallarmé's spectatorship. It does not account for what may be lost in Mallarmé's translation. Gould's remarks speak above all to the lack of a unified "point of view" which makes performance a difficult object of study, actually not an object at all. But, there she stops. To organize that multiplicity, to confront its intersubjective complexity in historically grounded instances of cultural practice, remains the task of dance studies and not literary studies. "The corps-graphy or body writing on stage" is for Gould "that part of the spectacle one cannot quite remember" (101). I return later to why it is important and also revealing that memory be omitted from poststructuralist theories of bodily writing.

Mary Lewis Shaw's treatment of dance's place in Mallarmé's poetic is more exhaustive than Gould's, but also surprisingly restrictive. Shaw insists on a Cartesian rhetoric wherein dance expresses "the inherently corporeal and contingent" (9).[10] In the chiasmus she sets up between dance and literature, "literature and the performing arts reflect each other as identical contraries" (27). This chiasmus is designed to show dance as "a negative poetic sign." Performance indicates the poetry it is not (thus, its status as "unwritten poem"). Poetry, for its part, although also tangible because "writing or print on paper," actually "directly (i.e. verbally) transcribes thought" (59, 58).[11] Shaw's analysis of the place of dance in Mallarmé's poetic neglects the preponderance of signifier over signified, the productive web of connotations. Moreover, the sheerly negative apprehension of performance as missing literature (with all its damning weight of the accusation of illiteracy) undermines the very ramifications of dance as a model for this productivity: "Whereas he [Mallarmé] considers literature . . . as a means of access to the *intangible* presence of the idea through acts of language that abolish nature, he sees the performing arts as a means of access to the *tangible* presence of the idea through nonverbal, corporeal acts that conversely nullify *la parole*" (16). To abolish nature is obviously to foster the Idea; to "nullify *la parole*" is to be "a negative form of writing" (17). This analysis is unsatisfying for the way it undervalues the productivity uniting performance and literature in modernism. Without that union, there would be little attraction to Mallarmé as performance theorist.

Although both Gould and Shaw are influenced by and also reacting against Derrida, his formulations seem to engage performance more directly. Perhaps this is because French poststructuralist thought of the 1960s employed the terms "stage" *(scène)* and "gesturality" as models of deconstructed philosophy, as if performance were that "outside" always denied an ontological dimension in thought. Poststructuralist critical theory self-consciously constituted itself as a performative enterprise, indeed, as the project of a theater through its emphasis on the gestural.[12] Even if this critical language designated no existing performance, it suggested the possibility of one: the performance of "inexpressive" gesture. Deconstruction indirectly undermined the foundations of expressive performance by destabilizing the ontological dimension of the term "expression" itself.[13] More particularly, it constructed gesture as a polemical weapon against phenomenology (although Merleau-Ponty was significantly left out of this polemic). Opposing the privilege of the voice, gesture was equated with writing (the trace). In "The Double Session," the gesture of Mallarmé's mime becomes Derrida's model for the trace. And in Derrida's analysis, Mallarmé's texts on dance are never far in the background.

Like the cogito, Mallarmé's mime engages in a mute soliloquy and thus raises issues of mimesis (both as self-presence and as imitation) and of mimicry (as simulation) to which Derrida devotes considerable attention. He establishes a primary sense of mimesis as *eidos*, the presentation of the thing itself which occurs in the cogito in the form of an image: "*Logos*," remarks Derrida, "must indeed be shaped according to the model of the *eidos*" ("Double Session," 188).[14] "Even before it can be translated as imitation, *mimesis* signifies the presentation of the thing itself, of nature, of the phusis that produces itself. . . . In this sense, *mneme* and *mimesis* are on a par since *mneme* too is an unveiling (an un-forgetting), *aletheia*" (193).[15] Appearing form is material provided by sense perception for the "idea." The return of appearing form as an image in the wake of sense perception is a function of memory. Thus "*mneme* and *mimesis* are on a par." This "movement of the *phusis*" is actually "the ideality *for* a subject—of what is" (193, 194). Thus the ambivalent relationship of Cartesian metaphysics to imagination and memory. On the one hand, Descartes conceptualizes ideas as images: "ideas exist in me as pictures or images."[16] On the other: "this power of imagination which I possess, in as far as it differs from the power of conceiving, is in no way necessary to my [nature or] essence, that is, to the essence of my mind" (112). In traditional metaphysics from Descartes to Husserl, memory as repeatable experience yields only probable or inferential knowledge. Production/reproduction cannot compete with the cogito as presence of the self-same, empirical certainty, truth. The image and memory are evicted from the cogito, along with the body, as figures of space. Conversely, primary mimesis does not imply reproduction of the self-same; it is the taking of bodily form by bodies, the material occasion for the presentation and transmission of behavior. Mihai Spariosu has identified primary mimesis as a pre-rational form of play, which he calls "mimesis-play" as distinguished from "mimesis-imitation."[17] Prior to Plato, as Spariosu explains,

> The *mimesis* semantic group was employed in a ritualistic-dramatic context, designating a performative function that we moderns associate with play. Consequently, this semantic group, at least before Plato, should not be understood as conveying the idea of imitation in the sense of "representation or reproduction of an original or a model," but rather the idea of "miming," "simulating," or even "presencing" (invoking, calling something forth). (*Dionysus Reborn*, 17)

Given the frequency with which Derrida has linked the trace to play, primary mimesis would seem to describe how or what performance traces, how dance is a particular form of "spacing."[18]

Nevertheless, primary mimesis quickly disappears from Derrida's reading of "Mimique." He understands Mallarmé's mime at first to be non-imitative: "there is no imitation. The mime imitates nothing. . . . There is nothing prior to the writing of his gestures" ("Double Session," 194).[19] But Derrida does not focus on performance theory in deference to "Mimique" as written text: "Before we investigate this proposition, let us consider what Mallarmé is *doing* in *Mimique*. We read *Mimique*" (198). Reading writing about the unwritten body's trace, Derrida nets the performing body thematically but only mimics its theory. In this sense, performance itself appears in "The Double Session" in the very guise of primary mimesis: it both appears without naming its source and withdraws back into the work of performance, leaving its status as theory ambiguous.

Mallarmé's own proposition regarding performance is nevertheless entertained. Derrida writes: "Since the mime imitates nothing, reproduces nothing, opens up in its origin the very thing he is tracing out, presenting, or producing *he must be the very movement of truth*" (205; my emphasis). The movement of truth, stresses Derrida, would not be any form of superior mimesis involving an imitator and an imitated but rather "truth as the present unveiling of the present: monstration, manifestation, production, *aletheia*" (206). Derrida discounts this approach, however, as "one of the most typical and tempting metaphysical reappropriations of writing" (206). "One could indeed push Mallarmé back into the most 'originary' metaphysics of truth if all mimicry *[mimique]* had indeed disappeared, if it had effaced itself in the scriptural production of truth" (206). But this is not the case because "*There is* mimicry. . . . We are faced then with mimicry imitating nothing . . . a reference without a referent" (206).

The contradiction Derrida locates in "Mimique" is between the copresence of "mimesis-play" and "mimesis-imitation." No-thing is being imitated. Yet, as Spariosu shows, the pre-rational tradition of primary mimesis goes beyond a visual unveiling. It *does* have to do with an imitator and an imitated. Historically associated with dance and music, primary mimesis is a doing, a physical participation. A certain performance logic seems required to explain that no-thing (substantively) be imitated. As Merleau-Ponty has pointed out: "The cultivation of habit as a rearrangement and renewal of the body image presents great difficulties to traditional philosophies, which are always inclined to conceive synthesis as intellectual synthesis."[20] It is possible that memory itself and its physical manifestations in habit imitate no-thing. The issue becomes how to understand the projection of the habitual past into a future governed neither by conscious representation nor irrational (empty) reflex. Only "praxis" avoids these two extremes, and I wish to theorize dance as "praxis."[21] Although Mallarmé's text on mime may unfailingly posit mimicry, as Derrida claims it does, such mimicry does not inevitably undo the movement wherein the *eidos* is formed, the movement of the *phusis* as *mneme*.

Primary mimesis does not entail an originary metaphysics so much as a project of becoming. If one conceives the danced trace as primary mimesis, dance need not be identified with an originary metaphysics on one hand, nor with referenceless reference on the other. As Carol Barko has remarked, the dancer Loie Fuller "illustrates his [Mallarmé's] principle of the expansion of the book from the letter."[22] Barko's example is of the dancer inside her enveloping fabrics, whose undulating and metamorphosing shapes danced, thereby suggesting different natural forms to Mallarmé and finally, in their entirety, a poem. According to Barko, this occurred through a "tension between its [the body's] center (self) and its expanding periphery (its production as emanation)" (179). Derrida leaves out of his discussion a productive aspect of appearances in which "utterance means production" ("énoncer signifie produire").[23]

Derrida only considers primary mimesis in a rational perspective as being rather than as becoming. "The Double Session" appropriates mime, and dance as well, to the logic of the trace as "hymen"—that which disappears in the course of its own inscription.[24] When deconstruction brings about the convergence of dance and writing, one surmises an unwitting replay of metaphysics's reservations with respect to memory.

Frances A. Yates has shown that classical arts of memory operate by situating bodies mentally in architectural spaces. Yates refers to these spaces as "inner writing": "A *locus* is a place easily grasped by the memory, such as a house, an intercolumnar space, a corner, an arch, or the like. Images are forms, marks or simulacra *(formae, notae, simulacra)* of what we wish to remember. . . . The art of memory is like an inner writing."[25] By the same token, Mallarmé's dancer as unwritten body writing suggests through its very engagement with space the recuperability of its own passage. What the movements (spacings) of dance establish is a *space* charged with absent presence, a space that intends to become. Mallarmé identifies the movement of Loie Fuller's voluminous costumes with a becoming of place ("the withdrawal of skirt or wing instituting a place"—"les retraits de jupe ou d'aile instituant un lieu" [308–9]). Movement through space leaves the trace of place that would have made movement possible, architecturally inevitable. In other terms, dance is reverse architecture, taking down what was not there. This is its monumentality. The architectural fantasm of dance is impermanent but not unstable, under erasure but not as "non-sense."[26] Movement both evokes and shapes a surviving social response as a physical environment. Dance, in other terms, calls social space into being. In

"Choreographies," Derrida asserts, "The dance changes place and above all changes *places.* In its wake they can no longer be recognized" (69). I differ. Its places are noted and retained. Dance is about the enactment of future place through the memory of "spacing." The places of dance always *will be* recognized. They are habitually absent.

Derrida's framing of mime as "reference without a referent" denies or significantly underplays the inscriptive *force* of gesture necessary to the claims I make for dancing bodies.[27] For Derrida, corporeal inscription is nothing more than an "*index sui,*" "the same as not being a sign . . . present to itself without indicative detour" (*Speech and Phenomena*, 61). By becoming "reflective," the performed trace becomes "unproductive." The trace, as presented in "The Double Session," is too formalist an entity to encompass what performance re-presents, what its persistence re-marks. It is entirely reliant on the negative residue of deconstructed metaphysics. Derrida's trace is what movement leaves behind, sense as fade, vector becoming shapeless. "For difference," writes Derrida, "is the necessary interval, the suspense between two outcomes, the 'lapse of time' between two shots, two roles, two chances" ("Double Session," 277). Yet between self-referential mimicry and trace lies performance as what can materialize, and therefore "retain" what is not, re-call it. I invoke memory not as reproduction (copy) but as the capacity to perform anew, although always differently, to reproduce by repetitive otherness. In other words, time in performance is not only given as a "spacing out" passing toward itself as nothing, but also as a "spacing in," an introjection of uncertainty about something to be readdressed (redressed). Through the memory implied by such repetition, the unrepeatable avoids being irrecuperable.

"What takes place," in "The Double Session," "is only the *entre*, the place, the spacing, which is nothing, the ideality (as nothingness) of the idea" (214). Having exposed the metaphorical ideality of "full presence," Derrida develops a conceivable notion of time as non-self-presence (gesture rather than voice) with only a virtual body to inhabit that time. His prodigious gesture reaches out from nobody. It is an abstraction of difference as the nonessential. For dance studies, the ideality of movement as trace begs reformulation. Instead of emptied space "between" two virtualities,

I propose the following rewriting: the indicative function of the trace is forceful action taken on behalf of what is not. Let us imagine "spacing" itself as subject to a black or red spot, like the eyes of Paul Margueritte's mime in the libretto Mallarmé read prior to writing "Mimique." To be faithful to that libretto, the mime is not, as Derrida claims, white on white (the blank), a symbol of mimicry as referenceless reference. "His [the mime's] head is marked, eyes and lips, as black and red" ("la tête, yeux et lèvres, s'y marquent, qui de noir, qui de rouge").[28] Theatrical presence emerges as memory hastening melancholy deferral toward fully artificial presence, "fictive or momentaneous" ("fictif ou momentané" [Mallarmé, 296]). Having given up "the most 'originary' of metaphysics of truth," we can welcome nevertheless the uniqueness of each re-marked moment, dancing as the "flesh of *différance*."[29] The uniqueness of difference (the plurality of differences) needs to be understood as performances. Dance performs still nonexistent social spaces constructed from the memory of what is not, and never was, "under a false appearance of a present."[30] Taken in this sense, dance presents itself as a project, which is also to say, "a direction of action that is not free from dangers and uncontrollable ambiguities."[31] The very fact that its dance occupies no present enables the memory its presence incurs to be a memory for some politics. A setting, perhaps, rather than a *scène:* what remains is the place, repeatable through the impossibility of its inhabitation.[32]

Notes

I thank Sam Gillespie, Christian Herold, Randy Martin, and Theresa Senft for their helpful comments during the preparation of this chapter.

Notes to "Mimique Revisited"

1. On the first two phenomena, see Mark Franko, *Dance as Text: Ideologies of the Baroque Body* (Cambridge: Cambridge University Press, 1993); *La danse comme texte: idéologies du corps baroque* (Paris: éditions Kargo, 2005).

2. Mihai I. Spariosu, *Dionysus Reborn: Play and the Aesthetic Dimension in Modern Philosophical and Scientific Discourse* (Ithaca, N.Y.: Cornell University Press, 1989), 17.

3. Jacques Derrida and Christie V. McDonald, "Choreographies" in *Diacritics* 12 (1982), 66–76. The interview was republished in *Bodies of the Text.*

Notes to "Mimique"

1. Jacques Derrida, "The Theater of Cruelty and the Closure of Representation," in *Writing and Difference,* trans. Alan Bass (Chicago: University of Chicago Press, 1978), 247.

2. Artaud's radical vision of theater, as is well known, relied on rendering conventions of theater more like those of dance.

3. Mark Wigley, *The Architecture of Deconstruction: Derrida's Haunt* (Cambridge, Mass.: MIT Press, 1993), 158. The convolutedness of dance/play as a figure of deconstruction parallels Wigley's analysis of the architectural figure and "a thinking of architecture" in Derrida's writing.

4. See Jacques Derrida, "La parole soufflée," in *Writing and Difference,* 169–74.

5. Evlyn Gould, *Virtual Theater from Diderot to Mallarmé* (Baltimore: Johns Hopkins University Press, 1989); and Mary Lewis Shaw, *Performance in the Texts of Mallarmé: The Passage from Art to Ritual* (University Park: Pennsylvania State University Press, 1993).

6. Jacques Derrida, "The Double Session," in *Dissemination,* trans. Barbara Johnson (Chicago: University of Chicago Press, 1981), 174–285.

7. Maurice Blanchot describes Mallarmé's project with reference to precursor Joseph Joubert. Both are concerned with "The power to represent through absence and to manifest through remoteness, a power that lies at the center of art, that seems to move things away in order to say them, to keep them at a remove so that they may become clear, a power of transformation, of translation, in which it is this very removal (space) that transforms and translates, that makes invisible things visible, that makes visible things transparent, that thus makes itself visible in them and then discovers itself to be the luminous depth of invisibility and irreality from which everything comes and in which everything is concluded." Maurice Blanchot, "Joubert and Space," in *The Notebooks of Joseph Joubert: A Selection,* ed. and trans. Paul Auster (San Francisco: North Point Press, 1983), 170.

8. "Valéry's prose often attains the elegant gratuitousness of the dance," writes Victor Brombert. "This is why," the same critic concludes, "he rarely went to the far end of his own thought." Brombert, "Valéry: The Dance of Words," *Hudson Review* 21, no. 4 (Winter 1968–1969): 675, 686, respectively. In an interview with Christie V. McDonald, Derrida defines dance as "surprise." "It should happen

only once, neither grow heavy nor ever plunge too deep." See Derrida and McDonald, "Choreographies," *Diacritics* 12 (1982): 66. Derrida and Brombert seem almost to be in agreement, which is disturbing. For a useful comparison of Mallarmé and Valéry on dance, see Magalie D. Hanquier, "Je pense donc je danse?—Danse/Poésie, Mallarmé/Valéry," in *Bulletin des Etudes Valéryennes* 64 (November 1993): 111–27.

9. Evlyn Gould, "Penciling and Erasing Mallarmé's Ballets," *Performing Arts Journal* 15.1 (January 1993): 97–105.

10. Mallarmé is said to have "a deep-rooted awareness of the mind/body duality" (27) thanks to which "what dance signifies most keenly is the physical dimension of the human self" (62).

11. "Literature," Shaw notes, "is more closely associated [than is performance] with the signified, the immaterial concept" (57).

12. For a perceptive analysis of the transition between theater semiology and poststructuralist theatricality, see Maria Minich Brewer, "Performing Theory," *Theatre Journal* 37, no. 1 (March 1985), esp., 16–19. See also Michel Foucault, "Theatrum Philosophicum," in *Language, Counter-Memory, Practice*, trans. Donald F. Bouchard and Sherry Simon (Ithaca, N.Y.: Cornell University Press, 1977), 165–96; Jean-François Lyotard, "The Tooth, the Palm," *Substance* 15 (1976): 105–10. The process through which Derrida arrived at indexical (inexpressive) gesture was the deconstruction of Husserlian phenomenology, particularly in Derrida, *Speech and Phenomena and Other Essays on Husserl's Theory of Signs*, trans. David B. Allison (Evanston, Ill.: Northwestern University Press, 1973). To outline his itinerary is beyond the scope of this essay, but let us note that gesture displaces voice, which historically had subsumed it. On the historical background of this contest between gesture and voice, see Mark Franko, "Ut Vox Corpus," in *Dance as Text: Ideologies of the Baroque Body* (Cambridge: Cambridge University Press, 1993), 32–51.

13. If truly displaced into the domain of performance, deconstruction says that within every expressive gesture is an inexpressive gesture that renders expression possible.

14. *Eidos* could be thought of as the form something takes: "*Logos* . . . arises as a sort of primary painting, profound and invisible" (189). This "psychic painting" "gives us the image of the thing itself, what communicates to us the direct intuition, the immediate vision of the thing, freed from the discourse that accompanied it, or even encumbered it" (189–90).

15. This primary form of mimesis, which is actually an operation of memory as appearance, is important for my ensuing argument.

16. Rene Descartes, *Discourse on Method and Meditations*, trans. John Veitch (Buffalo, N.Y.: Prometheus Books, 1989), 91.

17. See Mihai I. Spariosu, "Introduction," in *Mimesis in Contemporary Theory: An Interdisciplinary Approach, vol. 1, The Literary and Philosophical Debate* (Philadelphia: John Benjamins Publishing, 1984), i–xxix. For a full discussion of the "*atopian* quality of play as the Other of Western Metaphysics" (3), see Spariosu, *Dionysus Reborn: Play and the Aesthetic Dimension in Modern Philosophical and Scientific Discourse* (Ithaca, N.Y.: Cornell University Press, 1989). Philippe Lacoue-Labarthe also deals interestingly with a parallel distinction between "restricted" and "general" mimesis in modernity, showing that theater itself is the model of "general" or primary mimesis. See Lacoue-Labarthe, *L'imitation des modernes: Typographies II* (Paris: Galilee, 1986).

18. "Spacing" *(espacement)* is a term Derrida adopted from Mallarmé. As Mark Wigley points out, "*Spacing*, as distinct from space, is first and foremost not a thing but a movement" (73).

19. This is Derrida's response to the following lines of Mallarmé: "The scene illustrates but the idea, not any actual action, in a hymen (out of which flows Dream), tainted with vice yet sacred, between desire and fulfillment, perpetration and remembrance: here, anticipating, there recalling, in the future, in the past, *under the false appearance of a present.* That is how the Mime operates, whose act is confined to a perpetual allusion without breaking the ice or the mirror: he thus sets up a medium, a pure medium, of fiction." I am following here the translation reproduced in "The Double Session" (175).

20. Maurice Merleau-Ponty, *The Phenomenology of Perception*, trans. Colin Smith (London: Routledge and Kegan Paul, 1962), 142.

21. In a parallel manner, Michael Taussig's retheorization of "contact" in the "copy" concept of mimesis is relevant to my argument. See Taussig, *Mimesis and Alterity: A Particular History of the Senses* (New York: Routledge, 1993).

22. Carol Barko, "The Dancer and the Becoming of Language," *Yale French Studies* 54 (1977):179.

23. Stéphane Mallarmé, "Crayonné au théâtre," in *Oeuvres complètes* (Paris: Gallimard, 1945), 295. This is a fundamental difference between Derrida and Heidegger. See Timothy Clark, "Being in Mime: Heidegger and Derrida on the Ontology of Literary Language," *Modern Language Notes* 101, no. 5 (December

1986): 1003–21. Julia Kristeva gets at this practice of productivity by plumbing beneath the surface of language toward the semiotic material (best exemplified in her terms by dance and music) that underlies and disrupts it. This amounts to another form of mirroring that ingeniously dodges metaphysical fixity because its "originary metaphysics" is motility itself without spatial coordinates. See Julia Kristeva, *Revolution in Poetic Language*, trans. Margaret Waller (New York: Columbia University Press, 1984). Derrida discusses the relationship of "production as mimesis" to Western aesthetic theory in his "Economimesis," *Diacritics* 11 (1981): 3–25.

24. The reading of "hymen" as both union and barrier should be understood as the inability of the signifier to wed its signified and unite with it. It is the very productivity of language that the notion of barrier introduces, rather than, as in Robert Greer Cohen's critique, a grotesque misreading. See Robert Greer Cohen, "Mallarmé on Derrida," *French Review* 61, no. 6 (May 1988):884–89.

25. Frances A. Yates, *The Art of Memory* (Chicago: University of Chicago Press, 1966), 6.

26. Derrida remarks that the trace "re-marks itself forever as disappearance, erasure, non-sense" ("Double Session," 253).

27. Derrida's early writings that incriminate structuralism, particularly "Force and Signification" (1963) and "Structure, Sign and Play in the Discourse of the Human Sciences" (1966), both reprinted in *Writing and Difference*, thematize play and theorize the trace as force. Later, notably in "The Double Session," he theorizes the trace as death (the introduction of alterity into presence as the selfsame). Yet this apprehension of spacing as death is only convincing inasmuch as it "performs" a critique of presence. The more Derrida broaches the subject of performance per se in which movement acquires its own consistency, the more there appears a nostalgia for presence in his texts.

28. See "Double Session," 195; and Paul Margueritte, *Pierrot assassin de sa femme* (Paris: Paul Schmidt, 1882), 1.

29. See Mark Yount, "Two Reversibilities: Merleau-Ponty and Derrida," *Philosophy Today* 34, no. 2 (Summer 1990):139.

30. Derrida's interpretation of mime hinges on the moment in "Mimique" when Mallarmé envisions performance as a union (hymen) of the past and the future "under the false appearance of a present" ("sous une apparence fausse de présent").

31. Remo Guidieri and Francesco Pellizzi, "Shadows: Nineteen Tableaux on the Cult of the Dead in Malekula, Eastern Melanesia," *Res 2* (Autumn 1981):67.

32. Here I concur with Spariosu's perspective according to which "art and play are not a subversion of or an alternative to power, but an older, more immediate form of it" (*Dionysus Reborn*, 96). For a more specific delineation of this view in dance modernism, see Mark Franko, "The Invention of Modern Dance," in *Dancing Modernism/Performing Politics* (Bloomington: Indiana University Press, 1995).

Conclusion

Sally Ann Ness

The introduction to this volume centers on a discussion of "gesture"—the concept that gave rise to this collection. Gesture is the idea that has been with us all from the beginning: gesture seeking recognition, as Mark Franko's "Mimique" illuminates it, within the contours of poststructuralist thought. In conclusion, I gravitate toward the other concept that shares the volume's title, "migration," a relatively late arrival in our creative process. Migration emerged as a theme at one of the group's final meetings at the University of California–Irvine Humanities Research Institute. In a sense, we started out with "gesture" and ended up with "migration." I close this text with some thoughts about how and why migration ultimately came to matter to our project and where it leaves us as we move ahead.

As the essays illustrate, the concept of migration can be set to work toward a variety of purposes, along a spectrum that ranges from the transcontinental, even global, on one extreme, to the microscopic, cellular, even molecular, on the other. In every case, however, the relation of migration to gesture characterizes a distinctive dynamic: a movement not of things but of other movements. The migration of gesture speaks about movement of one kind moving movements of quite another. It speaks about the transportation of actions through a constantly changing world, the mobilizing of smaller moves—each itself an affective force, a potential stimulant of yet more movement. The "migration of gesture" is an entirely movement-based conceptualization, not surprising in a world that virtually all culture theorists now seem to agree is characterized first and foremost by mobility. However, to think *foundationally* in terms of movement, to suggest, as the phrase does, that movement goes "all the way down," that things boil down, in the last analysis, to movement, takes contemporary discourses on mobility and culture a step further than they have generally gone. It moves them into a space that, as "Mimique" previously announced, may have been somewhat neglected by poststructuralism.

Migration, as opposed to gesture, denotes a kind of movement that necessarily covers ground. While a gesture may involve no change of the gesturer's *place* whatsoever, migrations, by definition, are movements that progress through territory, in and through realms that, regardless of their actual size, are relatively vast with respect to the entities doing the traveling. Migration is essentially areal or "placial" in orientation. Its motion is "loco"-motive in character, fundamentally transportational in design. It is generally defined, as Carrie Noland's comments in the introduction specify, as the shifting of place, often periodic in character—as an action of resettlement. Although place is not an element original to the concept's Latin root (*migrare*, "to remove, change, pass away; to transport, transgress"), it is difficult to imagine migration occurring except within a realm designated by some sort of locational terms. However, that realm can be highly variable in character. It can be virtual, as in Susan Phillips's discussion of the Internet, or in the filmic worlds described by Lesley Stern and Akira Lippit, or even the disciplinary and conceptual fields evoked by Blake Stimson. On the other hand, it also can be actual, as with the Pacific Rim in Ketu Katrak's essay or the transatlantic corridor Susan Phillips mentions in relation to African American migration.

Migration, however, does not have to be understood as derivative of the places it connects, any more than dance—as Franko's discussion of "reverse architecture" makes clear—has to be understood as derivative of the environment in which it is performed. As several of the essays in this volume argue, migrations can actually bring "realm-ness," "area-hood," and "placeness" into existence. The concept that migration creates place is another consequence of a movement-based perspective. Places, as well as things, can be understood to emerge out of movement, rather than the reverse.

From the standpoint of the human figure, migration is generally conceived, again in contrast to gesture, as a movement that shifts the location not only of an entire, individual person—a movement of the whole body—but as a collective movement involving many individuals. One thinks of the seasonal migrations of other species, of flocks of birds or herds of caribou, in the same collective regard. So conceived, migration normally functions on a scale of enactment vastly greater than gesture. Gesture can be enacted by, and tends to be associated with, relatively tiny, isolated parts of an individual body: the gang-walking fingers described by Susan Phillips, the balletically-arching feet analyzed by Sally Ness, the minute brush stroking of Henri Michaux, the *mudra*-sculpting hands defined by Ketu Katrak. Gesture is not about collective locomotive mobilizing per se. Rather, as Noland notes in the introduction, the concept denotes movement that bears an explicit connection to acting and to action, to the making of a statement or signification of some kind, be it conventional or idiosyncratic, organic or mechanical, natural or cultural. Gestures have the capacity to move others, to affect them—as Lesley Stern's essay illustrates so vividly. However, they typically do not manifest the capacity to transport the performing agent to a new place.

Migratory movements are particularly bound up with power and often in awesome proportions. They can be understood as a symptom of the fluctuations of global power structures. They are fueled and motivated by power relations, and they often require great amounts of both fuel and motivation to occur. Migrations move within and through colossal fields of power, fields that exert pressures and influences, and that can create tensions, obstacles, diversions, and other resistant or facilitating features of their own. The attainment of a new place in the world, a far removed place—the main consequence of a migratory move—is always in some sense a power play. Migrations can themselves be sources of power, enabling their travelers as well as the places they move among in various ways. However, they can as well be disempowering, draining their constituents of energy, strength, and other resources, and leaving them in locations nowhere near those in which they previously cultivated and maintained power. Movement of any kind is never neutral with regard to power. However, migration tends to engage, reflect, reveal, and transform power relations in a particularly dynamic way and on a grand scale. The movement-space of migration, like the space of Franko's tertiary mimesis, produces a politics of a very different kind from power structures in which order is defined by stability, control by fixity, and power by the bodies, or other *material*, in which it has been vested.

It is important for the purposes of this collection to note that gesture is the more inclusive term. It is not limited in reference to the movements of body parts or to the actions of a single individual. An entire migratory event, in and of itself, might even be understood as making a gesture of a certain kind. Migrations can serve as colossal gestures under the right circumstances. But what can it mean to assert the reverse? What can it mean to say that a gesture can be a migration? One expects to look into the sky and see a huge cloud of waving hands flying northward. Here, we arrive at the question that has brought the essays in this volume into alignment with one another. It is the question of gesture's migration, the migration of gesture.

For gestures to migrate—for a gesture to become a migration—the action performed, the agency embodied, the subject constituted, the power entailed, the territory traversed, the *life* presented in the movement of the movement, must be understood as distinguishable, although *not* dissociable, from the bodies that are nonetheless, as Noland notes in the volume's introduction and as Franko underscores in his introduction to "Mimique," essential for their performance. This is why the idea of migration has come to matter in this collaboration. It provides a means of teasing even further apart the connections between the bodies on which gestures *must* depend, be they live bodies or mechanical apparatuses, the movements by which they are defined, and the places in which gestures gain their meaning, be they virtual or actual. By putting movement first, and by focusing on situations in which gestural moves are *placed into movement* through the specifically locomotive figure of migration, the approach opens somewhat further than would otherwise be conceivable a conceptual play between agency, subjectivity, and corporeality, on the one hand, and power, signification, and territory, on the other.

In conclusion, then, I want to ask of each essay written for the volume (as opposed to Franko's, which was persuaded to migrate into it) what it teaches us about two fundamental aspects of the movement of migration, seen through the guise of gesture. First, what does each teach us about power in a locomotive movement-space? Second, what does each teach us about migration's impact on intentional meaning-making—gesture's communicative specialty? The two questions are not unrelated and in fact become one and the same as the discussion progresses. Together, they throw into high relief the novel perspective a movement-based approach produces on the study of embodiment and culture.

Ketu Katrak's essay deals with the migration of gesture on an immense, transcontinental scale. The gestural moves, the *mudras*, on which Katrak's essay focuses, are archetypically gestural in that they are relatively miniscule movements of isolated body parts that *act* semantically as they dance through long-established conventions of interpretation. The essay presents a classic case of both gesture and migration.

With regard to power, Katrak argues that the postcolonial diasporic migration of Indian *mudras* can best be characterized in terms of a gain and loss of performative influence—a tradeoff that moves between individual and collective levels of action and experience. The tradeoff does not appear to be equal in proportion. The gain is one of an expansion in authorial reference that introduces novel content into *mudras* in diasporic contexts of performance. In the diaspora, the capability increases for making statements about a larger number of places and events, some of them familiar but now far out of range, and some of them relatively strange but now in close proximity. It is the power of new knowledge and new forms of relevance being associated by individual choreographers with the practice and its agents. The loss, on the other hand, is the disappearance of *rasa*, the aesthetic pleasure that was influential in the traditional places of the dance's traditional culture. New freedoms of expression and new opportunities to be influential are gained in the shift of place of individual artists. At the same time, the loss of the homeland also registers in Katrak's view as a diminishing of a more general aesthetic power in the migrant's gestures, one that carries with it the capacity to move audiences on a cultural depth and scale. Individual liberty in the creative process is expanded, referential capability is enlarged, but at the price of a collective aesthetic experience that generally compelled a profound affective response. This postcolonial tradeoff crystallizes a particular patterning of power: an individualizing of agency correlated with a shift from a relatively abstract affective *modus operandi* to a referential sociopolitical one.

Katrak's essay demonstrates an important general theme on meaning-making that reappears throughout the volume: how gestures appear destined to mutate as they migrate from one place into another. There seems to be absolutely no way around it. Transportation necessitates a transformation of meaning. We see through the lens of *mudra* migration how all gestures are semantically place-specific. They can never arrive in a new homeland unchanged. They cannot *be* at the end of the migration what they were at its origin, even though the bodies they depend on apparently can. The illusion that a performer can pull "her" *mudras* out of one place and deliver them into another with their meaning intact, simply because her body may be able to perform them in the same manner, is seriously challenged if not dispelled entirely. The attempt to reproduce the original signifying character, as the examples of each artist discussed demonstrate, bears the consequence of placing the gesturing subject in "in-between-ness," a no-place. In this regard, Katrak's essay shows how the migratory move can integrate gesture into its own process, and do so independently of the bodies involved. Gestures belong to places and vice versa.

Susan Phillips's description of gang walking moves further into the investigation of migration, gesture, and power, revealing the power that can be cultivated in a movement that is simultaneously gestural and migratory. The walking of gang walking, its baseline locomotive pattern, enacts on a microcosmic scale another historical experience of migration, one staged originally on a transcontinental scale similar to that of Katrak's *mudras* but motivated by colonization and embodied by the colonized. The walk *carries* the dancer, who gives the appearance of being transported by it and therefore subject to its inherent agency. Rather than directing it actively, the dancer appears to be getting himself or herself *delivered* into a new place of performance. Gang walking is movement that simultaneously travels as it writes, that uses the same moves to cover ground as it does to make letters. It is only through their fusion, in fact, and the disguise that each provides the other as a consequence, that migration and gesture together achieve in gang walking a symbolic, embodied triumph over the colonial legacy that continues to produce its inspiration. In their integration, the migration of gestures is shown to succeed, in Phillips's study, in dancing a victory of expression over oppression, of self-authorship over subalternity, and of liberation over domination.

Built into this retaliatory dance of "counterliteracy," however, is the brutality of the African American migratory history and the price it continues to exact from the bodies representing it. Phillips describes how the gang walkers' hands in performance are robbed of their inherent linguistic capacity (as the agents of writing), either silenced altogether or made to pantomime the encrypted actions of the legs. The walking of the legs—their gift to the human figure—is "erased" from view as well. Erasure, as the essay documents, is the ultimate act of violence in gang culture. Gang walking is choreographed so that walking becomes virtually impossible to witness as locomotion. Perception is apparently its greatest enemy, to such an extent that the dance will do the harshest form of symbolic violence unto itself—erase its own locomotive action—in order to achieve its vanishing act.

In its presentation of erasure, gang walking reenacts with eerie specificity the violence done not only to slaves as individual bodies but to their collective history, a history largely unrecoverable and so also lost to view. The dance memorializes in miniature form migrations that brought people through and into fields of power so oppressive, so unjust, so marred by violence, that all movements of the colonized, and the agency present therein, became potentially dangerous and criminal. It commemorates as well the skills by which individual mobility was nonetheless achieved and sustained even in such a difficult place, the ways travel could be made to go underground, surviving in a racialized world designed to stifle it.

Again, in the case of gang walking, Phillips shows how migration appears to necessitate a transformation in gestural meaning, this time one linked to changes in gestural form. Here, we see change occurring gradually all the way along the micro-migrational route of the gang walk, not only upon its arrival in a new location. The integration of migration and gesture is processually transformative. The letters signed while walking are simultaneously formed *and* transformed as they are placed into locomotion. Consequently, only a "practiced eye" can decipher them. Migration encodes and, in this power field, protects inscription.

Each larger migration of the gang walking practice into a new place—new clubs, the Internet, new media—produces changes in meaning as well. Phillips uses the idea of "co-option" to characterize these contextual migrations. Co-option occurs as gestures are pulled not only out of places as they migrate but out of bodies as well, sometimes with their consent, more often involuntarily. The case of gang walking illustrates migratory processes that are illicit, unprincipled, and which sustain a postcolonial "white marketing" of gesture. Phillips is careful to point out that there are high costs as well as limits to these acts of co-option for their perpetrators. Ripping off the dancing, albeit from a relatively powerless underclass of practitioners, carries with it the threat of violent retaliation. Even if the illicit co-option is successful, the gestures are believed to have the capacity to "empty" themselves of meaning, rendering themselves valueless as symbolic capital in the new places and/or bodies of performance. Co-option, even in the most successful instances, generally occurs only in "partial" form, if it doesn't fail completely. It does not produce an exchange or trade-off of meaning from the gang members' point of view but results instead in the erasure of meaning altogether. In this regard, gang walking illustrates how the meaning-making of gestures can be not only place-specific but body-specific as well.

Lesley Stern's essay locates gesture within the world of a film, which opens up the movements of gesture and migration to dramatically different possibilities. Movement, and particularly the energy of movement, is attributed a greater degree of autonomous *will* in this essay than perhaps anywhere else in the volume. As a result, within the world of the film *Good Men, Good Women*, new kinds of migratory pathways are defined. Stern speaks of them as gestural circuits of energy exchange. One of these circuits—and it is of central significance in the film—is an actual migratory event, the journey depicted in the film that moves from Taiwan into China and back again. However, other circuits move on very different kinds of pathways, through a diverse array of both spatial and temporal realms.

Stern's essay illustrates most boldly one main consequence of a movement-based approach: the identification it produces of embodiment and inhabitation. As several essays in the volume also demonstrate, "ghosting" shows how movement, when it is granted increasing autonomy as an active presence, compels bodies to take on the character of places rather than things. As with Deidre Sklar's description of the bodies of New York City immigrant families, who let go of their "native" gestures and, within a single generation, come instead to play host to the gestures that live and circulate within the American site, Stern's filmic and physical bodies act as havens for gestures that have a life and a world of their own. Bodies, in this perspective, provide life support, but they do not necessarily delimit or contain the migration of gesture.

Power figures prominently in Stern's essay. Cinematic gestures, operating within the world of a film, have the power to move both locomotively and affectively. One can ask of them, as Stern does, both what they mean and where they are going. They are endowed with agency both to transport themselves into new places/bodies and to compel a transformation of those places/bodies through their performative force. The energy they configure has the capacity to transmit itself and to cause emotional change. Their energetic, independent acting creates a being, a bodiless agency that Stern identifies as resembling that of a ghost.

However, the ghostly power of the cinematic gesture is far from omnipotent. Its agency is limited, in Stern's description, to the inspiration of mimesis in the bodies it affects. Gestures' powers of conversion are confined to creating compulsions to do likewise in their receptive hosts, to force the feeling of what the gesture's energy has already configured as a feeling. The ghosts of *Good Men, Good Women* have the capacity to haunt through mimetic means, transforming new locations into echoes of themselves. They can migrate through time from the past into the present, but once they arrive, their impact is one of re-presenting themselves and the past with which they are identified.

While Stern's cinematic gestures have the power to shape energy and so create affect in their own likeness, they appear to have little control over meaning-making. They bend bodies, but not signification, to their will. Gestures command the reproduction of their affective characters, but they cannot, as Stern demonstrates through the essay's pair of graphically detailed gestural portraits, mean the same thing twice. The pair of cinematic gestures travels through the essay's text, appearing in three different places in the essay in identical written form. Yet, despite this fixity, the gestures are powerless to retain and fix a stable understanding. They are subject to the changing contingencies that occur with time's passing. Stern shows how their meaning must necessarily change with each reiteration.

In the cinematic case Stern depicts, then, the migration of gestures through space, into different bodies/places, enables them to force persistent likenesses. Yet the traveling of gestures through *time* subjects them to alterations of their meaning. Time exerts a power that the migration of gesture, even in the world of film, apparently cannot transcend.

While it also focuses on the world of film, Akira Lippit's project is altogether different from Lesley Stern's. Lippit's survey of "digestive" experimental filmmakers is oriented around negatives: losses, lacks, absences, endings, differences, and "counters-" of various kinds. Nonetheless, it works to show how fundamental the relation of migratory forms of movement is to gestural forms. However, it does so by showing what it takes to *halt* the migration of gesture in and through the cinematic world and by documenting what results from the removal of that movement. The breakdown of gestural migration produces a systemic collapse, in Lippit's analysis. It brings about the end of the cinematic world, in its conventional form, an absolute ending that is also the origin of an entirely new form of filmic movement.

Lippit's filmmakers share in common an interest in developing strategies for creating filmic animations that purposefully intervene, disrupt, and discontinue the migratory flow of gestural mimesis on which, as the analysis in Stern's essay demonstrates, the meaning-making capability of film depends. In these experimental projects, the film becomes not a world unto itself but a kind of workshop—a singular place into which filmed gestures are brought and out of which the mimetic migration of gesture is impeded and at least crippled, if not brought to a complete standstill. Inside the space of the film, as Lippit's descriptions portray, representations of organic gestures are absorbed and destroyed. They become the building blocks for new, inorganic animations that are grafted onto photographic images of human bodies. The mimetic circulation in which gestures normally participate and cultivate their meaning is thus halted. It is intentionally blocked by the experimental project, for it is only in that stoppage that the kind of movement the filmmakers seek to fabricate can be created and presented.

As Lippit describes it, gestures must be "digested" by the cinema in order to create a space in which to construct a filmic expression of an entirely original kind, one that is absolutely and purely filmic in character. Such an expression has its being as a filmic equivalent of gesture, a type of pseudo-gesture, a movement that is as genuinely and fundamentally a product of film apparatuses (cameras, projectors, etc.) as gesture is, in Lippit's view, a product of human bodies. Gesture has to be immobilized, eliminated, sacrificed, and most of all, dehumanized in the filmmaker's approach so that a more purely filmic form of expressive movement can be brought into play.

Lippit's analysis of experimental film is grounded in a theory of gestural movement quite different from Stern's, as well as Katrak's and Phillips's. In this perspective, gestures are a bodily *product.* The energy that configures them, the movement by which they are composed, is not their source, and it has no ultimate circulatory autonomy in the virtual world of film or anywhere else. Bodies originate gestures. Living bodies are the constant sources of gesture, not simply its hosts. It is this insight into gesture that motivates Lippit's initial question: Can gestures *take place* without an organic body producing them?

This insight underscores not the mimetic fluency that connects the physical world to the world of film, or the formal congruence that allows "the same" gestures to migrate through actual and virtual media, but the opposite: the *lack* of similarity between the photographic images that are a film's actual constituents and the living, moving bodies they index. The "real" bodies (and thus the "real" gestures) have been lost to the film.

What film viewers witness in a film are imaginary signifiers, signals of removed bodies. It is this difference between filmic and living bodies that the experimental filmmakers concentrate on exploiting, exaggerating, even perverting, using it as a constant reminder to viewers that what they are experiencing in film, and only in film, is "pure motion"—movies. It is only filmic digesture that is movement "all the way down." Real bodies and their gestures must be understood as something other than this if the filmic character of the experimental expression is to prevail. The migration of gesture is halted because the bodies that might otherwise produce it have to be put to the service of a different form of movement, one that must go no place beyond the filmic work space if it is to remain absolutely cinematic and motionally pure.

The topic of power comes closest to the surface of Lippit's text when he relates how the bodies represented in experimental films are used, how that which arrives from the physical world is treated once it has entered the space of the filmmakers' workshop. It becomes clear that what power there is in this experimental economy is concentrated in the hands of the filmmaker. The digesture project itself can be read as an effort by the filmmaker to gain absolute control over all aspects of a film's being and meaning. Filmmakers dominate, filmic bodies submit. The workshop space, while it may be seen as a marginalized space in relation to the larger world of filmmaking (and beyond), has a master, and the agency of that master, inside the workshop, is absolute.

Lippit identifies photography as the determinate source of difference between real bodies and those of film, as the connection that itself creates the unlikeness on which the experimental film movement depends. Blake Stimson, however, finds in photography an entirely different potential for continuity between the physical and the filmic, and one that does not, as is the case with Stern's approach, confine itself to the transparent resemblances of mimesis. Stimson proposes that the *abstraction* of "photography," the concept that represents photographic practices in general terms, can be embodied and expressed gesturally. An abstraction (and the example of photography is not considered to be unique in this regard) can be made by a gesture whose meaning is not affective but referential, and referential on a grand scale. Via photography, Stimson enables gesture to migrate into the realm of abstraction and therefore into the realm of philosophy.

Basic to Stimson's argument is the assumption of an inherent conventionality in gestural movement. The recognition of a gesture as such—as a movement that embodies *intent*—depends, in Stimson's theory, on its conforming to socially constructed expectations. Gestures can become comprehensible objects in a photographing subject's gaze only because they have the capacity to embody the conventional. It is in their conventionality that Stimson sees gestures demonstrating the ability, in Merleau-Ponty's terms, to "outline the structure of the world." It is because they can embody convention that they can embody the movement of abstraction.

The key move in Stimson's argument occurs not in his attribution of conventionality to gesture but in his turn away from French structuralism and its descendants to define how conventions inhere in gestures. This move leads to the argument that what the philosophical work of abstraction requires is not the capacity to "differentiate," as the structuralists would posit, but the ability to *accumulate* experience. The gesturing photographer becomes apparent to Stimson as a site for such accumulation. The gesturer becomes a body in which the work of abstraction can be undertaken about the world, not just indicated through always already singular actions. Gestures, like photographs, exist, Stimson observes, not as discrete "little movements" but as vast accumulations, as movements that extend themselves through a continuity of experience gained from a plurality of incidents, a potentially infinite series of experiences over time.

This theory of gesture as the embodiment of a movement that is temporally and experientially accumulative sets up a new migratory possibility. It sets up the conditions for migration internal to the movement of the gesture itself. It is possible, in Stimson's theory, to migrate into and through the accumulations of experience, to travel *inside* the gesture's continuity of convention. The movement of the gesture becomes itself a realm that can accommodate migration. With this possibility of internal locomotive movement comes the capability to make and to recognize a gesture within a gesture as well, to nest an intent within another and another. With this possibility comes the capability to originate and set into motion relationships of intention and to enact abstractions gesturally.

In its accumulative character, Stimson's theory of gesture is migratory in design. Its design enables gesture to embody expressions that are also journeys through multiple places and incidents of experience. In so doing, it illuminates a new field of power relations that are actually contained within the gesture's "interior" realm. One might think of these as conceptual power relations, manifesting in the gesture's accumulative performance. The kind of gestural power implied in Stimson's theory is akin to what mathematical analysis has defined in its evaluations of functions of the calculus as "exponential" (for example, "two raised to the fifth power" or 2^5). Accumulative gestural power also bears a family resemblance to what the rhetoric of logic has termed "explanatory power" in the evaluation of a scientific theory. It resonates more broadly as well with what psychological discourse loosely refers to as "powers of concentration," sometimes attributed to great thinkers. It is the power of intelligence that emerges from a vast, living body of knowledge, in this case a human figure.

Sally Ness pursues a similar form of interior gestural migration in her essay on classical dance. Ness follows the accumulations of gestural symbols "inward" through the conventions of technical practice as they inscribe themselves into their individual human hosts. As in Stimson's essay, the characterization of gesture as an embodiment of a continuous intelligence creates a very different understanding of gesture's meaning-making capacity in comparison to that posited by the expressively oriented discussions of Stern, Phillips, and Katrak. The latter show in their essays the place- and body-specific character of gesture and its inability to migrate with its full meaning intact. Stimson and Ness, in contrast, describe the capacity of gestures to stabilize, and in some cases even to *fix*, meaning both through time and within their own migrational realms. As the internal realm of the gesture accumulates both bodily and temporal depth, it develops a commemorative capability, a capacity to re-mind itself in its performing body(ies). The meaning of a gesture is thus not necessarily bound to change as it covers ground. If it is understood to have the potential to play host to a relatively stable realm of meaning, it has the agency to remember and re-place itself consistently—to continue to come to its own terms within its performing self(ves), as Ness puts it. In this regard, a gesture may establish, preserve, and otherwise insure a constancy of meaning, even if it is simultaneously traveling through a rapidly changing "outer" world.

Ness's and Stimson's arguments suggest a place-*making* capability of accumulative forms of gesture. This argument allows for the possibility that places could themselves be gesture-specific, rather than the reverse. A new ontological power of gesture begins to come into focus here, a power to bring into being and give original definition not only to significance but to place and to selves as well.

This power of gesture would seem to celebrate individual liberty—particularly if Lippit's insight into the essential joining of gestures and living bodies is brought back into play. The bodies performing such gestures appear to become capable of determining, perhaps even to a magical extent, their place and identity in the world. As Ness notes, however, such gestural power tends to become available to performers only at the price of their body's individuality. It generally emerges as the outgrowth of highly conventional forms of practice, the mastery of which typically requires extreme forms of self-sacrifice. One thinks, here, of Deidre Sklar's dance students, weeping over their technically "tamed" bodies when the profound loss of their subjectivity is brought to consciousness by Sklar's meditative exercise on "preconventional" experience.

The essays by Katrak and Ness in particular, in this volume, indicate that the place/self-control enabled by accumulative gestural practice is generally gained via disciplines that subordinate individual will to conventional technical wisdom. When the power of such gestures moves "inward," in Ness's terms, and the agency and command of a gestural symbol re-places and inscribes itself more and more deeply in the body of a performer, it may well endow that individual with the elevated status of an "expert," an "elite," and even a "master" from culturally conservative points of view. It may even grant to that bodily host the capability of bringing the home place of a certain traditional cultural figure into being, no matter where the body is on the planet. It may provide its individual human master with an authoritative understanding of a certain way of life and a form of the human condition that no "external" migratory episode, however traumatic, could ever undermine. However, such capabilities of command and control also may be understood to erase, to follow Phillips, unconventional aspects of personhood as well.

The most powerful gestures, in this regard, may also produce the most dominated, tyrannized forms of being in relation to their performers. In gaining mastery, one becomes a slave to the powers structured by tradition. However, as Katrak's choreographers, Lippit's experimental filmmakers, and Sklar's example of stepping on the brakes in a traffic jam (and the original train of thought that follows from it) remind us, the hold of a gesture, even a powerfully conventional, *habitus*-sedimented gesture, on a performer, even a dedicated master of a classical technique, is never absolute, just as the place and meaning of a gesture are never totally or perfectly fixed. Whenever the movement-space of migration is brought into play, this cannot be the case. One must always be careful, in this regard, not to underestimate the plasticity of the individual human figure in its capacity to dance spontaneously, on its own terms, and for its own purposes, in the making of its own places, with even the most conservative, dehumanizing, and imperialistic powers of gestural convention.

It is in this specific regard that Carrie Noland's essay on the mark-making artwork of Henri Michaux forms a central nexus for the volume. Noland's analysis of Michaux's *Mouvements* situates itself at the crux of the intersection between originating and commemorative migrations of gesture, the only place from which it can reveal how Michaux set his technically informed yet "de-skilled" gestures to work against the age-old conventions of written languages. Michaux's project bears witness to the tremendous challenge presented by the act of an individual body declaring war on some of the most deeply rooted, power-laden forms of human convention—the conventions of writing itself. It also exemplifies the degree to which an untaming of gesture, and a disengagement with the disciplining movements of culture, can be achieved and documented by the unfolding gestural practice of a single human being.

Michaux's struggles against the conditioning of linguistic symbolism in many ways parallel the projects of the experimental filmmakers Lippit describes. Like the filmmakers, Michaux intervened into the flow of conventional communication, intent on derailing its meaning-making capabilities for liberatory purposes. In his emphasis on the *de-*, in his desire to "de-skill" to the point of complete "de-signing," Michaux shared with these later artists a similar interest in the production of postconventional forms of "pure movement" and in celebrating the emergence of new bodies created entirely through radically spontaneous artistic processes. The resistance movement Michaux engineered resonates deeply with the politics of cinematic digesture.

At the same time, however, one does not find in Michaux's work an attempt to resist the migration of gesture as such—the main project of the cinematic movement. Gesture itself is not under attack. One can even characterize Michaux's attempts to "un-learn" various writing systems by continuously shifting his mark-making practice from one to another of them as gesturally migratory in strategy. Here, the difference in artistic medium makes all the difference in the world, for it is Michaux's living body, not an "unreal" filmic body image, that is being put to the service of resisting convention. Michaux's body is de-conventionalized, but it is not digested.

What Michaux's sketchings map out in their de-conventionalized traces is, on the microcosmic level of performance, a migration of gesture as well. Michaux's contained, self-disciplined brush strokings, their signifying aspect all but erased, become choreographic in character. They are not unlike the movements of gang walking, both in their fusion of the processes of traveling and mark-making (although in this case it is the hands that are miming the locomotive actions of the feet) and in their "countermimetic" intent. Michaux's sketchings are crafted so as to make apparent the distinctive embodied motility of their creator, the manner in which their maker moved across the ground of their pages. The codex itself becomes configured as a miniature migratory realm by the movements of Michaux's mark-making. The characters traced serve as the places that make it identifiable as such. Michaux's marks, as they de-sign writing, also design a movement-based "place-ness" within the field of the codex.

While sociocultural signification and the circulation of signs of any standard kind are halted in this creative process, Michaux's sketches nonetheless trace out a migration of an individually significant sort across the pages of the volume. They inscribe the journey of an individual coming into his own practice within a world of writing systems. In this regard, while the gestures represented in Michaux's *Mouvements* are de-conventionalized, they are not de-humanized. As Noland's analysis demonstrates, Michaux's marks bear the character of methodical, human habits even while they have transcended *habitus*. In their systematic seriality, they practice a lucid embodiment of abstraction, in this case the abstraction of "script-ness." They are not chaotic. They do not do violence to the general character of human intelligence, only to the conventions that delimit its collective meanings. In a sense, Michaux's *Mouvements* demonstrates how far the human being, through gesture, can go, thinking beyond the box or outside the envelop, of the most fixed conventions of human language.

In this regard, Michaux seems to have moved along the same trajectory Ness investigates with respect to danced gesturing, although in precisely the opposite direction. Michaux pushes the gestures of writing as far *away* from their signifying capability as they can conceivably go, to the very edge of the place where they would lose their conventional identity entirely and trace nothing other than a dance of "pure movement." In so doing, he sketches out one territory of the Symbolic that is also verging on linguistic in character. His gestural consciousness becomes "interior" as he invests more and more of himself in this approach. He experiences gesture as "never closed in by skin." He becomes more aware of the gesture as a technical movement he performs habitually and less aware of it as an act producing a character expressed outwardly on a page—exactly what Ness defines as the "inward" understanding of a dance gesture Symbol. He becomes a performative self, a product of his own movement practices, inscribing into himself his studiously unlearned, yet highly methodical, graphemic technique. Michaux's art can be considered the trace of an inward migration of idiosyncratic yet symbolic movement. It exemplifies as well Franko's concept of "tertiary mimesis," representing an as-yet-unconventionalized writing system.

The essays of Lippit and Noland illustrate how the powerful hold of convention upon performing bodies can be loosened by practices of what might be called "de-formance." Such movement-based interventions create resistance by pitting themselves against established flows of meaning-making. In Deidre Sklar's essay on embodied schemas, the interest in the *de-* is replaced by an interest in the *pre-* as it relates bodies to movements of power and signification. In this shift, a very different awareness of individual plasticity and agency come into view.

Sklar's essay goes, perhaps, the furthest in giving credence to the argument that no convention, however powerful, can ever come to dominate absolutely the life experience of an embodied human being. Her essay also illuminates, in so doing, the importance of migratory forms of movement to human thought and experience. Of all the essays in this volume, Sklar's is the one that explores in most graphic detail what it means to recognize that movement goes "all the way down" in human experience—and that migratory forms of movement go down the furthest of all. The understanding of self happens first through movement, as a unique bundling of cross-modal (migrating) sensory happenings. It precedes the identity of self as an entity or separate thing. The awareness and creative patterning of movement, of movements that migrate intersubjectively, precede the recognition of discrete bodies or objects. Common sensing, the migration of experience through the senses, develops recognition before individual senses become recognizable. The experience of migration that *is* cross-referencing precedes referential differentiation. All of these developmental sequences originate from migratory movements, from the migration of perceptual dynamics across sensory boundaries and the resulting globalizing, experimental work of the imagination that accompanies it. While gesture may be the more inclusive term, Sklar's essay shows how migration is the more basic one. Migration is *the* experiential given, pre-objective, pre-linguistic, pre-world, pre-self, and even pre-power in a movement-based perspective.

Abstraction, and the creative synthesizing, generalizing work it entails, plays a key role in Sklar's theory of embodiment, as it does in Stimson's and Ness's essays as well. Sklar aligns with Ness and Stimson in arguing that abstraction is a movement of meaning that can be embodied by the human figure as a whole. However, Sklar's understanding of the movement of abstraction is explicitly preconventional. It is conceived as being more basic to human intelligence than either Stimson or Ness suggest. The capability to embody, and through embodiment define, abstractions emerges before the capability to conform one's self to the established practices of some collective Other.

Abstraction forms a bridge—a structure allowing migration to continue where it might otherwise be halted or turned away—between sensation and what Sklar defines as embodied schema. Abstraction is the process that connects—not through passive reflection, mechanistic transparency, or some other relatively mindless operation—but via an active, transformative, *configurational* repatterning. It connects the vital and the emotional, the phenomenological and the semiotic, the somatic and the epistemological, the material and the formal, and the organismic and the cultural. Sklar's theory provides, in this regard, a developmental model that underpins the claims of Stimson and Ness regarding gesture's capability to embody a working out or working through of logical operations. By the same token, Stimson and Ness illustrate how embodied schema develop into gestural abductions and conceptual abstractions, substantiating Sklar's claim that embodied experience and the schema it generates are central to cultural organizations of thought.

Ultimately, the migration of gesture leaves us with a sense that if we are to understand the role of mobility in contemporary life, we must be prepared to move along with migrations as they cover ground and change meaning. Such a dance will leave us with a heightened appreciation of the (dis)integrating influence of migratory forms of movement as they articulate themselves culturally. It will allow us to conceive in sharper images how place-like bodies can be, and how gesture-specific places can be, how movements survive in and give definition to both virtual and actual places and bodies through time. It will leave us with a more subtle awareness of how gestures may come to possess the agency to migrate into new bodies, and how those bodies may also have the capability to dance with them, to host them, to conform to them, to experiment with them, even to digest them, or to express them, and ultimately to pass them on and even to unlearn them. It may lead us to an understanding of how freedom—even radical forms of it—may be gained *both* within and outside the constraints of culture and its conventions. Perhaps most vital, the migration of gesture leaves us with the understanding that there are experiences of movement more basic to human life than the experience of power, be it the power of resistance, dominance, agency, mastery, knowledge, or mobilization itself. In the conceptualization and embodiment of that experience, a new movement-space may open up, containing new possibilities for human thought, action, and existence.

Contributors

Mark Franko is professor and chair of theater arts at the University of California at Santa Cruz. He danced professionally before becoming a dance historian, theorist, and choreographer. He is the author of five books: *Excursion for Miracles: Paul Sanasardo, Donya Feuer, and Studio for Dance (1955–1964); The Work of Dance: Labor, Movement, and Identity in the 1930s; Dancing Modernism/Performing Politics; Dance as Text: Ideologies of the Baroque Body;* and *The Dancing Body in Renaissance Choreography.* He edited *Ritual and Event: Interdisciplinary Perspectives* and coedited (with musicologist Annette Richards) *Acting on the Past: Historical Performance across the Disciplines.*

Ketu H. Katrak, originally from Bombay, India, is professor of literature in the Department of Asian American Studies at the University of California, Irvine, where she specializes in Asian American and postcolonial literature, third world women writers, and feminist theory. She is author of *Politics of the Female Body: Postcolonial Women Writers of the Third World* and has published numerous essays on South Asian American writers and cultural expression in the diaspora.

Akira Mizuta Lippit is professor of cinema, literature, and Japanese culture at the University of Southern California. He is author of *Electric Animal: Toward a Rhetoric of Wildlife* (Minnesota, 2000) and *Atomic Light (Shadow Optics)* (Minnesota, 2005). He is preparing a manuscript on experimental film and video.

Sally Ann Ness is professor of anthropology at University of California, Riverside, and a certified movement analyst from the Laban/Bartenieff Institute of Movement Studies. She is author of *Body, Movement, and Culture: Kinesthetic and Visual Symbolism in a Philippine Community* and *Where Asia Smiles: An Ethnography of Philippine Tourism.* Her current research, funded in part by a Guggenheim Fellowship, focuses on touristic practice in Yosemite Valley, illuminating connections between place, embodiment, and authenticity.

Carrie Noland is author of *Poetry at Stake: Lyric Aesthetics and the Challenge of Technology*, as well as numerous essays on poetic experimentation with sound, graphics, and the Internet. She is coediting a collection of essays with Barrett Watten, *Diasporic Avant-Gardes: Experimental Poetics and Cultural Displacement*, and completing a manuscript that juxtaposes theories of gesture drawn from performance studies and new media theory. She teaches French literature and critical theory at the University of California, Irvine.

Susan A. Phillips is assistant professor of anthropology and urban studies at Pitzer College, where she directs the Center for California Cultural and Social Issues. She is author of *Wallbangin': Graffiti and Gangs in L.A.* and continues to conduct field research in Los Angeles gang neighborhoods; she received a Harry Frank Guggenheim research grant to study the relationship between gang violence and police suppression.

Deidre Sklar is an interdisciplinary scholar with a performance background in corporeal mime and ensemble movement theater. Her movement ethnography, *Dancing with the Virgin: Body and Faith in the Fiesta of Tortugas, New Mexico,* addresses identity, community, and the embodiment of belief in the language of sensation. Her articles on embodiment theory, dance ethnology, and fieldwork methods, as well as on specific ritual and stage dance genres, have been published in *Journal of American Folklore, The Drama Review, Dance Research Journal*, and *International Mime Journal.* She has taught at UCLA; University of California, Irvine; Texas Woman's University; and Oberlin College.

Lesley Stern is professor of visual arts at the University of California, San Diego. She is author of *The Scorsese Connection* and *The Smoking Book* and coeditor of *Falling for You: Essays on Cinema and Performance*. She has published widely in areas of film, performance, photography, and cultural studies, and she also writes fiction.

Blake Stimson is author of *The Pivot of the World: Photography and Its Nation* and coeditor of three volumes: *Conceptual Art: A Critical Anthology; Visual Worlds;* and *Collectivism after Modernism: The Art of Social Imagination after 1945* (Minnesota, 2007).

Index